Inflation and Unemployment

CONGRESSIONAL QUARTERLY
1414 22nd STREET, N.W., WASHINGTON, D.C. 20037

Congressional Quarterly Inc.

Congressional Quarterly Inc., an editorial research service and publishing company, serves clients in the fields of news, education, business and government. It combines specific coverage of Congress, government and politics by Congressional Quarterly with the more general subject range of an affiliated service, Editorial Research Reports.

Congressional Quarterly was founded in 1945 by Henrietta and Nelson Poynter. Its basic periodical publication was and still is the CQ *Weekly Report,* which is mailed to clients every Saturday. The *Weekly Report* is cross-referenced quarterly in a cumulative *Index.*

The CQ *Almanac,* a compendium of legislation for one session of Congress, is published every spring. *Congress and the Nation* is published every four years as a record of government for one presidential term.

Congressional Quarterly also publishes paperback books on public affairs. These include the twice-yearly *Guide to Current American Government* and such recent titles as *Dollar Politics, Vol. II* and *Continuing Energy Crisis in America.*

CQ Direct Research is a consulting service which performs contract research and maintains a reference library and query desk for the convenience of clients.

Editorial Research Reports covers subjects beyond the specialized scope of Congressional Quarterly. It publishes reference material on foreign affairs, business, education, cultural affairs, national security, science and other topics of news interest. Service to clients includes a 300-word report five times a week and a 6,000-word report four times a month. Editorial Research Reports also publishes paperback books in its fields of coverage. Founded in 1923, the service was merged with Congressional Quarterly in 1956.

Senior Editor: Peter A. Harkness

Contributors: Thomas J. Arrandale, David Boorstin, Elizabeth Bowman, Mary Cohn, Edna Frazier, Martha V. Gottron, John Hamer, Ian McNett, Mary Newmann, Helen Shaffer, Donald Smith, Elder Witt.
Editorial Assistant: Robert E. Healy.
Cover Design: Howard Chapman, Art Director.
Production Manager: Donald R. Buck.
Production Supervisor: Richard Butler.

Book Service Editor: Robert A. Diamond

Library of Congress Catalog No. 74-25414
International Standard Book No. 0-87187-066-5

TABLE OF CONTENTS

INFLATION AND UNEMPLOYMENT

CASE STUDIES

PUBLIC POLICY

APPENDIX

Introduction

The decade of the 1960s is not one Americans remember with great nostalgia. The civil rights and student protests, the assassinations, the crime explosion and, finally, the brutal war in Southeast Asia do not make for fond memories.

But at least, despite all those problems, it was a decade of steady economic growth. It began with the tail-end of a recession and ended with the beginnings of another, but everything in between was bullish. More Americans were employed in better jobs at higher salaries, business mushroomed and the government set lofty goals—eradicating poverty, providing good medical care for the elderly and insuring that each citizen had a fair and equal chance for an education, a job and economic security. America could do all that, it was thought, and still maintain the military strength to protect friendly foreign governments from either internal or external threats.

America grew richer and richer, its economy more sprawling and complex. Europeans fretted that the great American corporations would soon gobble up their industries and assets. Third-world nations pleaded that such great wealth be shared, and Communist leaders realized that ideological struggles more likely would be waged in the marketplace than on the battlefield.

Even the burgeoning student protests late in the decade—staged mostly by the sons and daughters of middle- and upper-class parents—were aimed at telling Americans the country had become too opulent to care about the needs of the poor and the unfolding tragedy in Vietnam.

Seeds of Trouble

The expanding U.S. military commitment in Indochina in the mid-1960s is seen by many economists as one of the seeds of economic problems that sprouted into full bloom a decade later.

Rapidly rising defense spending, high consumer demand and continued substantial capital expenditures for new plants and equipment brought increased pressure on the economy, inevitably leading to higher inflation rates. While consumer prices had risen at an annual average rate of only 1.3 per cent between 1961 and 1965, the annual average shot up to 4.2 per cent between 1967 and 1968.

President Johnson had decided the nation could afford both guns and butter, and while the administration launched a series of costly "Great Society" social programs at home, it also was fighting an increasingly expensive war in Vietnam.

With the economy booming on into 1967-68, Johnson attempted some restraint by cutting spending and increasing taxes (through a tax surcharge). But it proved to be too little too late, and by 1969 the economy was faltering. Rising costs continued to push up prices, and unemployment edged up to 6 per cent.

Flip-Flops

Richard Nixon promised he would make controlling inflation his top priority, but the cure proved elusive. Gradual restraint through fiscal and monetary policy only led to a mild recession. The inflation rate dropped just slightly; unemployment rose to 6.2 per cent by December 1970 and stock prices plunged. The strong demand helping to pull up prices slackened, only to be replaced by new pressures—rising costs that pushed at the wholesale and consumer price indexes from underneath.

By mid-1971, the administration had realized that traditional remedies were failing. While economists in the 1960s were confident they could "fine-tune" the economy through spending, taxing and monetary policies, this new strain of inflation left them perplexed.

With the months ticking away before the 1972 presidential election, Nixon decided to make a dramatic change in the government's economic program. On Aug. 15, 1971, he announced his New Economic Policy—the most comprehensive peacetime economic controls in the nation's history.

The idea had originated in the Democratic Congress, which a year earlier had authorized the President to impose controls. At the time Nixon had accepted the responsibility only because the authorization had been attached to a defense bill the administration badly wanted. But the President stressed that he had no intention to use the authority because such a radical move "does not fit the economic conditions which exist today."

Pressures

While controls slowed inflation considerably, the program did not succeed in venting the mounting pressures that caused it. As the administration disassembled its controls structure and began to stimulate the economy, demand soared. The economy roared ahead in a boom in late 1972 (during the election) and into 1973.

The result was an unprecedented peacetime rate of inflation, and the situation was exacerbated by the Arab oil embargo and subsequent quadrupling of oil prices by exporting nations. At the same time, supply shortages of food caused further damage.

The government shifted to a more restrictive policy in an attempt to curb demand, but by late 1973 and through the first half of 1974 the economy was almost completely ignored. Watergate had caught up with Richard Nixon and for months he was preoccupied with the inquiry into his behavior during the 1972 political campaign. He lost his struggle for political survival in August 1974, turning over a myriad of long-neglected problems to his successor.

WINning

Gerald R. Ford made it immediately clear that, like Nixon, his first priority would be an all-out campaign to, as he put it, "Whip Inflation Now." But his critics in Congress were quick to charge that the WIN program was misdirected and insufficient. The real danger, they insisted, was an oncoming recession of possible record proportions.

By the end of the year, the recession had hit hard. Unemployment jumped to 6.5 per cent in November. Disposable income for the year actually fell. The auto industry was in what Henry Ford called a "depression," and business had started to cut spending on new investments and expansion. Stocks were trading at price levels of 20 years before, yet there were few who wanted to snap up the bargains. Consumer confidence, in short, was gauged at its lowest point since World War II.

For every possible prognosis there was at least one economist to advocate it. Opinions ranged from those of administration advisers, who predicted a turnaround by mid-1975, to that of a well-publicized economist, who advised people to buy land in rural areas in order to escape the chaos and violence he felt soon would be ravaging the nation's cities.

But the central question concerned the nation's double-digit inflation, whether it was already beaten, as some argued, or whether it had become so ingrained in the American economy that only a long-term harsh prescription could possibly wring it out.

Chapter Summary

This book is divided into three major sections. The first provides detailed background on the twin problems of inflation and unemployment during the last decade. The second explores specific economic problems the nation faced during the early 1970s. The third reviews government economic policy during the Nixon and Ford administrations—in Congress and in the executive departments and agencies.

Many of the chapters in this book originally appeared in the CQ *Weekly Report* or *Editorial Research Reports* during late 1973 and 1974. Wherever necessary, the material has been updated.

The book examines the following case studies:

Banking Stability. The stability of the U.S. banking system has been taken for granted since the recovery from the collapse of the 1930s. But concern about the system has been building up behind the scenes, and now the assumption of stability is being questioned openly. *(p. 21)*

Retirement Security. Recession and inflation are stirring new fears among those whose working years are nearing an end. Their prospect for a reasonably comfortable income in retirement no longer seems quite so secure as in the immediate past. *(p. 29)*

Housing Industry. The housing industry served as the whipping boy for many of the nation's economic ills in 1974, caught by the "double whammy" effects of inflation, which forced up the cost of its products, and tight monetary policy used to fight inflation, which dried up credit for the purchase of homes. *(p. 35)*

Economics of Scarcity. The American cornucopia, that overflowing horn of plenty, had an ominously hollow air about it in the early 1970s. It still was undeniably bountiful, but there was the feeling this land of material abundance had come up short of some important items—including food, fuels, lumber, chemicals and textiles, to name just a few. *(p. 40)*

Energy and Inflation. As the government struggled to end inflation, about half of the rate of increase in the cost of living seemed out of reach of traditional economic restraints. That was the share of the increase caused by soaring energy prices, which accounted for about 50 per cent of the annual rise in the consumer and wholesale price indexes. *(p. 47)*

Oil Taxation. Oil and taxes—two subjects most Americans would prefer to forget—were uppermost in many people's minds as they prepared to pay their income taxes in the midst of the nation's gas shortage in early 1974. That coincidence may help bring about the first changes in oil taxation in five years, and perhaps the first substantial changes in nearly 50 years. Dominated by a huge Democratic majority in both houses, the new 94th Congress seemed likely to make some substantial changes in oil tax policy. *(p. 55)*

Foreign Investments in the U.S. During the 1960s, a flood tide of American investments abroad brought anguished cries from Europeans who feared their national economies would be engulfed in Yankee dollars and dominated by faraway home offices. These cries have since been muffled by grave new economic problems on both sides of the Atlantic, and by a reverse flow of investments from overseas into the United States. *(p. 62)*

Peter A. Harkness
Senior Editor
January 1975

INFLATION: RESISTING CONVENTIONAL REMEDIES

Inflation became a chronic and corrosive condition of American life during the decade 1965-75. Through war and peace, plenty and shortages, expansions and contractions, prices rose persistently and the dollar's value dwindled.

By the end of that decade, prices were skyrocketing at rates of 10 per cent or more a year, making "double-digit inflation" an increasingly troubling threat to economic stability as well as to the well-being of individual Americans.

By 1975, soaring inflation was resisting conventional remedies, and government policy-makers faced cruel choices between restraining prices and encouraging economic expansion.

After a decade of inflation, the trade-off between stable prices and unemployment was becoming increasingly uncomfortable. Inflationary pressures were built into the economy, and the process of venting them was expected to cost the nation dearly in lost jobs and economic output.

Like other nations, the United States had suffered from inflation before, usually during and after wars, but not with such virulence and persistence. Ill-advised and badly timed government decisions bore much of the blame, but unforeseen and uncontrollable economic forces compounded those mistakes.

The pressures of an overworked economy started pulling prices upward when the nation went to war in Vietnam. Those pressures pushed business costs up with them, leading to further price increases.

Once underway, inflationary pressures proved strong enough to survive a recession, yield only temporarily under wage and price controls and take on renewed vigor when released from those restraints. Fed by shortages of key economic goods, the pressures overwhelmed a second set of controls and showed no signs of abating when a second recession set in.

The inflationary process began in 1965. Opting for both guns and butter, the nation intervened in Vietnam at the same time it launched costly Great Society domestic innovations. Rising government spending pushed demand for goods and services to the limits of the economy's capacity to produce them. With supplies restricted, demand pulled prices upward. Between 1965 and 1968, the annual rate of inflation increased to 4 per cent from 1.8 per cent.

The economy faltered in 1969, with monetary growth restricted to reduce overwrought demand. Unemployment edged up to 6 per cent, but rising costs continued the upward spiral in prices. Inflation still averaged nearly 5.2 per cent a year in 1969-70.

With the "stagflation" combination of inflation in a stagnant economy no longer politically tolerable, demand was restimulated. Wages and prices were frozen three months, then placed under detailed controls that remained in effect until early 1973. In 1972 alone, inflation still was 3.2 per cent.

Controls nonetheless were abandoned, and prices jumped amid a building economic boom. The boom quickly peaked, but supply restrictions on food, petroleum and other key commodities compounded price pressures even though the economy once more slowed down. During 1973, inflation was 5.3 per cent, and the worst was yet to come.

The slowdown became a downturn, and the economy headed toward a potentially long and severe recession. Confounding common economic principles, inflation reached new levels, averaging nearly 10.6 per cent during the first nine months of 1974.

And no significant abatement was in sight. With the process far from completed, the dollar's real value since 1967 had depreciated by more than 25 per cent. And it cost consumers $15 to buy what $10 had purchased in 1967.

To be sure, the economy had expanded during the decade, with the value of the nation's total output of goods and services doubling between 1965 and 1974. But most of that increase was illusory, as inflation ate away the value of the dollars used to measure that production. Real output rose about one-third.

References

Troubles in housing industry, p. 35; materials shortages, p. 40; inflation in energy prices, p. 47; government actions: Nixon administration, p. 71; Ford administration, p. 76; congressional action, p. 86.

Post-War Decades

The surge of prices after 1965 threw the U.S. economy off a high-growth, low-inflation track that economists thought they had engineered during the early 1960s.

From 1945 through 1965, the economy of a triumphant and world-powerful nation achieved record growth that contrasted sharply with the pre-war depression. Emerging from the war with its gross national product more than doubled from $100-billion in 1940, the nation enjoyed a rapid expansion in its total output of goods and services.

That expansion was not always smooth, however, as bouts with severe inflation followed the return to a civilian economy in 1946-47 and accompanied the Korean involvement in 1950. Upward pressures on prices persisted through the 1950s, although restrictive policies by the Truman and Eisenhower administrations kept inflation at modest levels.

Committed to pro-business economic concerns, the Eisenhower administration stressed anti-inflationary policies, balancing its budgets and restraining monetary growth. The nation paid a price in muting inflationary pressures, keeping economic growth below potential, tolerating less than full employment and incurring recessions in 1953, 1957 and 1960.

Kennedy

The transfer of power in 1961 from Eisenhower to President Kennedy brought to positions of influence in government economists who were committed to use of federal fiscal and monetary policies to guide economic growth. So long as the gross national product fell short of its potential growth rate, they believed that federal budget

CONSUMER PRICE INDEX
Rate of Change by Month and Six-Month Averages
1947-1973

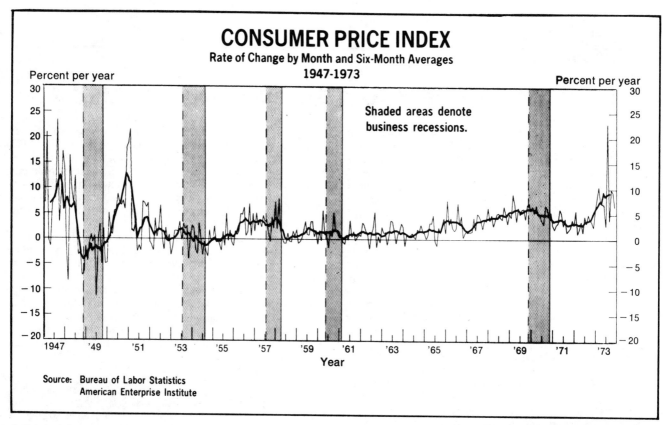

Percent per year

Percent per year

Shaded areas denote business recessions.

Year

Source: Bureau of Labor Statistics
American Enterprise Institute

deficits and monetary expansion could safely stimulate increased output without kindling unacceptable inflation.

Taking power as the recession bottomed out in early 1961, the Kennedy administration followed stimulative fiscal policies aimed at encouraging economic recovery toward the potential growth in output, defined by the Council of Economic Advisers as a 4 per cent unemployment rate.

The Federal Reserve Board helped fund the recovery by steadily enlarging the money supply to meet increasing credit demands, and Congress went along with stimulative budgetary policy by enacting a tax cut in 1964, even though the budget already was in deficit and the economy already expanding.

It worked, at least for several years. The expansion launched in 1961 lasted eight years, with gross national product rising to nearly $865-billion in 1968 from around $500-billion in early 1961. More than 10.5 million jobs were created, dropping the unemployment rate to 3.6 per cent in 1968 from nearly 7 per cent in 1961. Corporate profits doubled, and disposable after-tax income per person rose by a third. Until 1965, moreover, that steady growth was accomplished without uncomfortable inflation. From 1961 to 1965, consumer prices rose by an average of only 1.3 per cent a year.

There were some trouble signs. The nation's balance of payments showed a persistent deficit, and the Council of Economic Advisers felt it necessary to post wage-price guidelines to put public pressure against large increases by unions and industries that wielded great market power.

But with unemployment moving downward to 4.5 per cent, and price increases holding at less than 2 per cent, the nation seemed to be finding an acceptable trade-off between inflation and economic expansion.

Building Momentum

That balance was not enduring, however, as economic policy-making could not cope with the inflationa pressures mounted by U.S. intervention in Vietnam.

The period of steady and noninflationary growth came to an end in 1965 when the U.S. involvement in Vietnam escalated. At the heart of the problem was increasing pressure on the economy caused by rapidly rising government defense spending (which the Johnson administration repeatedly underestimated), by continued high consumer demand and by substantial capital expenditures for plant and equipment. The combination of all of these forces pushing on the economy inevitably led to inflation. Between 1965 and 1967, on the average, consumer prices rose 2.5 per cent annually. Between 1967 and 1968, they rose an average of 4.2 per cent annually. Average hourly compensation shot up dramatically as did unit labor costs. The rate of growth in the real GNP was more than 8 per cent between the second quarter of 1965 and the first quarter of 1966.

Efforts to restrain the economy during this period were inadequate at first and tardy when finally put into effect. When fiscal policy was not used effectively until near the end of President Johnson's term, monetary policy assumed a disproportionate share of the burden. The Johnson administration from time to time prior to 1967 mentioned the possibility of a general income tax increase but did not propose it.

The administration's public position in 1966 and 1967 was that the increasing costs of the Vietnam war could be financed by reducing nonessential expenditures and by speeding up tax payments and instituting graduated tax withholding. The latter two proposals, which were mild forms of fiscal restraint, were enacted by Congress in 1966.

Late in the year, Congress temporarily suspended the investment tax credit which was an incentive for business spending. (The credit was reinstated the following spring.) A reduction in federal expenditures, subject to many diverse influences, did not prove a very useful road to restraining the economy. Many observers doubted whether Johnson was serious about expenditure reduction in light of his administration's commitment to a far-reaching social program to alleviate a multitude of domestic problems.

A major part of the effort to restrain the economy during this period fell to monetary policy, although it too was applied unevenly by the monetary officials. In 1966, monetary policy resulted in the highest interest rates and the tightest credit conditions since the early 1920s. Money markets dissolved into near crisis in August 1966. Conditions eased after that but tightened again as Johnson's term came to a close. In 1966, the resulting scarcity of lendable funds and the accompanying high interest rates affected many persons and businesses but was most seriously felt by the housing industry and prospective homebuyers. The situation became so serious that Congress enacted legislation to control certain types of interest rates and to pump additional funds into the housing market.

Surcharge

The rapid economic advance of 1965-66 continued into 1967 and 1968, but by this time the Johnson administration had become convinced that increased restraint had to be placed on the economy. This view was shared by members of Congress and by many economists, businessmen and other individuals outside the government.

The first half of 1967 was sluggish as businesses consumed large inventory stocks accumulated previously. But the basic advance of the economy was still present, according to the government economists, and a strong second half was anticipated. President Johnson, in his budget message of January 1967, proposed a 6 per cent surcharge on individual and corporate income taxes. Because of the sluggish first half of the year, Johnson did not actually send a tax message to Congress until August, when the vigorous economic expansion resumed. Mr. Johnson then formally requested a tax surcharge, but at a higher rate of 10 per cent.

Congress failed to react quickly and the surcharge did not become law until the following summer, many months after the time when government economists believed it was essential. Congressional delay was due in part to lack of clear evidence that the economy was expanding at an excessive rate and in part to the preference of many members to exercise economic restraint by cutting federal expenditures rather than by—or in addition to—raising taxes. The battle over a tax increase was resolved by combining a tax hike (the 10 per cent surcharge) with a mandatory reduction in federal expenditures, but only after an international financial crisis developed in March 1968 and accelerating credit demands pushed interest rates to record levels.

As the battle continued, inflation marched on with no sign of relenting. When the year was over, figures showed that the consumer price index had risen 4.7 per cent from December 1967 to December 1968. The December to December increase for 1966-1967 was 3.1 per cent.

The tax increase and spending cut enacted in mid-1968 were widely thought to provide the major fiscal restraint which would slow and hopefully stop the inflationary spiral characteristic of 1965-68. However, many experts later concluded that the Federal Reserve Board had increased the nation's money supply so rapidly in 1968 that the restraining effect of the tax increase was neutralized. Delay in enactment also diluted the bill's effectiveness.

Defying Recession

However belated, the shift toward restraint on demand was made in 1969 when a Republican administration committed to more orthodox economics took office.

Making control of inflation a top priority—but mindful of the economic and political costs of unemployment—the Nixon administration attempted to wring inflation out of the economy gradually through fiscal and monetary restraint.

Accordingly, the Federal Reserve in 1969 cut monetary growth to half its 1968 rate, allowing the money supply to grow by 3.2 per cent in 1969 compared to 7.8 per cent in 1968.

And the administration, which had inherited from its Democratic predecessor a fiscal 1969 budget that wound up with a $3.2-billion surplus, revised the fiscal 1970 budget, cutting both defense and domestic spending to increase the expected surplus to $5.8-billion from the $3.4-billion planned by Johnson. (But with inflation increasing costs, business income lagging and Congress resisting spending cuts, the fiscal 1970 budget eventually ended up in the red by $2.8-billion.)

Gradualism failed. Its policies slowed economic activity, inducing a mild recession by 1970. But the payoff in reduced inflation was slow in coming and slight in impact.

From 1969 to 1970, the GNP increased by 5 per cent to $977.1-billion, but when inflation was discounted output actually fell by 0.4 per cent to $722.5-billion. With real output lagging in 1970, corporate profits fell by about $10-billion, industrial production dropped 3.7 per cent and private investment fell nearly $3-billion. Stock prices plunged.

Although the Federal Reserve allowed monetary growth to accelerate to 6 per cent during 1970, its 1969 restraint put a crunch on credit, causing interest rates to rise.

And unemployment, which had held nearly steady below 4 per cent in 1968 and 1969, crept steadily upward in 1970, averaging 4.9 per cent for the year and reaching 6.2 per cent by December.

Despite those dislocations of recession, inflation continued, with prices rising nearly as fast as before. At the end of 1969, consumer prices were 6.1 per cent above their level at the end of 1968, and by the end of 1970 they had risen another 5.5 per cent. For wholesale prices, the increases were 4.8 per cent in 1969 and another 2.2 per cent in 1970.

The slowdown during 1970 in consumer and wholesale price increases reflected slower rises in food prices. The index for consumer food prices rose only 2.2 per cent after a 7.2 per cent increase in 1969, and the wholesale price index for processed foods and farm products actually dropped by 1.4 per cent.

But the improved food-price performance was more than offset by rapid inflation in other sectors. The consumer price index rose 4.8 per cent for other commodities and 8.2 per cent for services. The wholesale price index for industrial commodities rose 3.6 per cent.

Pressures

At considerable cost to its economy in lost output and jobs, therefore, the nation was achieving only a slight tapering in the momentum of inflation. The Vietnam build-up pressures had eased, but inflation fed on other problems.

Those pressures were on costs, especially the costs of doing business that must be taken into account in setting prices. The cost pressures themselves were a hangover from the demand pressures of 1965-68.

With unemployment up and demand for labor lagging, under normal circumstances the pace of wage and salary increases should have slowed after rising sharply from 1965 to 1968. Instead, the rate of increase leveled off at about 7 per cent in 1969-70 but failed to fall as expected.

That wage spiral continued as workers and their unions demanded and received pay increases to offset the loss of real income to the previous cycle of inflation. In part, wage settlements reflected expectations that inflation would be with the nation for a long time. Thus, cost-of-living escalator clauses were negotiated into contracts.

Other business costs rose as well, again reflecting previous inflation that drove up prices that business itself paid for industrial materials. Like rising labor costs, those showed up in prices that business charged to consumers.

Another factor, one difficult to document, was the growing concentration of the U.S. economic structure. In some key industries such as steel and automobiles a few giant corporations and a few national unions dominated the market.

Immune from significant price competition, such industries were in a position to accept large wage and cost increases and pass them along in higher prices. Since their products were often staples for consumers and other in-

dustries, those "administered" price increases reinforced inflationary pressures on other prices.

Beyond Controls

Whatever the mix of demand-pull, cost-push and administered-price causes, inflation by 1971 had proved dismayingly resistant to traditional remedies applied by the federal government. By mid-summer 1971, inflation had outlasted the administration's patience with its own gradualism strategy.

The economy's performance actually had been encouraging during the first part of 1971. Output recovered and inflation diminished, but neither at rates that met the administration's goals for the year.

During the first nine months (three quarters) of 1971, for instance, GNP increased to a level 7.1 per cent above output in the third quarter of 1970. Of that increase, however, 4.6 per cent reflected inflation and 2.4 per cent the actual increase in volume. Some sectors were strong, with substantial increases in consumption, residential construction and state and local government purchases. But federal government purchases and business fixed investment lagged. Businesses cut their investment in inventories, and the trade deficit worsened.

As a result, unemployment hung around 6 per cent. At the same time, inflation moderated slightly but threatened to pick up again.

New Economic Policy

Those trends prompted a dramatic change in the government's economic policy. In a sudden presidential announcement on Aug. 15, 1971, the administration moved to

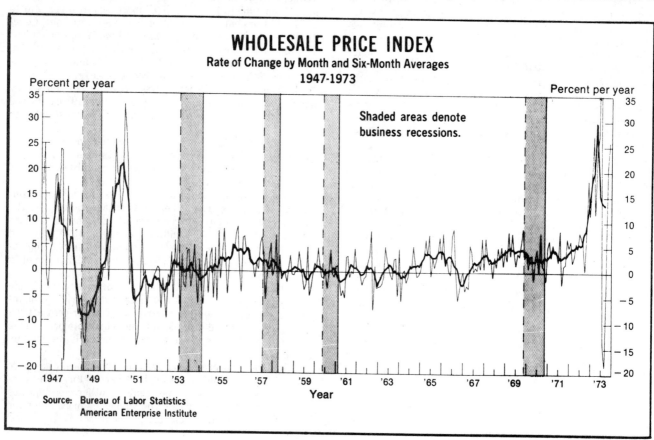

WHOLESALE PRICE INDEX
Rate of Change by Month and Six-Month Averages
1947-1973

Shaded areas denote business recessions.

Source: Bureau of Labor Statistics
American Enterprise Institute

speed economic recovery while intervening directly through wage and price controls to head off a resurgence of inflation.

Those efforts accompanied unilateral U.S. action to force revision of international monetary arrangements that had overvalued the dollar and forced the United States to take balance of payments deficits that were mushrooming in 1971.

For three months, the new economic program stopped inflation nearly in its tracks as the government imposed a 90-day across-the-board freeze on wages and prices. From August to November, the consumer price index rose at an annual rate of 1.7 per cent, that increase reflecting exemptions that were granted for raw agricultural products and imported goods on which costs were raised by the government's international monetary actions.

For the three-month period, moreover, the wholesale price index dropped at an annual rate of 1.3 per cent including reductions in most industrial commodity categories. The wage and salary freeze dropped the annual rate of increase in hourly earnings to about 1.75 per cent.

Phase II

When the freeze ended in November, it was followed by a detailed Phase II system of controls on both wages and prices. The lifting of the freeze produced an immediate bulge in price and wage increases as companies and unions were allowed justifiable increases that were deferred during the freeze. From November 1971 to February 1972, the consumer price index rose at an annual rate of 4.8 per cent, the wholesale price index at 6.9 per cent and the GNP price deflator at 6.1 per cent. Average hourly compensation jumped at an annual rate of 8.9 per cent.

For the rest of 1972, however, controls held further increases to annual rates of 3 per cent in the consumer price index, 6.5 per cent for the wholesale price index and 2.3 per cent in the GNP deflator. Compensation rose at a 5.7 per cent rate.

The 1971-72 controls brought inflation down to rates of less than 4 per cent a year, as measured by consumer prices and GNP. But wholesale prices still were rising by more than 6 per cent a year, and food price indexes showed especially disturbing increases during the controls period.

While controls restrained the rate at which inflation mounted, the program only temporarily bottled up the underlying pressures. Those pressures gained strength from the economic expansion encouraged by the government's stimulative actions.

Statistics

Fiscal and monetary policy was stimulative for both 1971 and 1972. The federal budget for fiscal 1972, from July 1971 to June 1972, incurred a $23.2-billion deficit that was deepened by $4.5-billion in tax cuts enacted as part of the 1971 new economic policy.

The fiscal 1973 budget followed with a more moderate $14.3-billion deficit.

In 1971, moreover, the money supply expanded by 7.1 per cent, although the Federal Reserve began to restrain growth in the last half of the year after monetary growth surged at a rate of more than 10 per cent in the first six months.

During 1972, the money supply expanded by 8.7 per cent, funding continued economic expansion that carried over into 1973. That expansion pushed the gross national product above the $1-trillion mark and brought unemployment down to 5.2 per cent by the end of the year.

Into Two Figures

The economy surged upward in the last few months of 1972 and into the first months of 1973. And the inflationary pressures that built up during that boom broke loose early in 1973 after the administration for the most part dismantled the controls program.

The result was an unprecedented peacetime rate of inflation that sent prices soaring more rapidly than at any time since the Korean War. Feeding off an extraordinary combination of forces, especially supply restrictions on food and petroleum, the inflation kept raging after the boom spent itself and the economy contracted into recession by the end of 1974.

From January 1973 through September 1974, the consumer price index had risen by 19 per cent, the wholesale price index by 34.3 per cent and the inflation component of GNP by about 16.5 per cent.

Prices rose that quickly regardless of government measures to slow inflation down. Fiscal and monetary policy turned restrictive—and controls once more were imposed and phased out—with little evident effect on the cost of living.

By the summer months of 1974, the measures of inflation continued to rise at "double-digit" annual rates of 14.2 per cent for consumer prices and 35.2 per cent for wholesale prices. Foreshadowing further consumer price increases, the wholesale price measure showed industrial commodity prices rising at a 28.3 per cent a year clip and farm product prices going up at 59.2 per cent a year.

Boom to Recession

The boom that carried over from 1972 pushed actual GNP up at an annual rate of 9 per cent in the first quarter of 1973. That rapid growth could not be sustained, the boom burned out and the rate of expansion dropped off dramatically for the rest of the year.

The boom conditions of early 1973 quickly reached their limit as output bumped up against the capacity for production in many industries. That experience was shared by other industrial nations, as a worldwide step-up in economic demand approached productive capacity and led to supply shortages.

In the first part of 1973, federal fiscal policy became less stimulative—most of the fiscal 1973 deficit had been incurred in July-December 1972—and the Federal Reserve Board shifted monetary policy toward a more restrictive stance. After growing 8.6 per cent in the second half of 1972, the narrowly defined money supply increased by 7.4 per cent in the first six months of 1973 and by less than 5 per cent in the last six months of the year.

The general downward trend in economic activity was accelerated late in 1973 by severe energy shortages brought on by petroleum supply restrictions and crude oil price increases dictated by oil-producing nations.

After rising at an annual rate of 9 per cent in the first three months of 1973, the growth in real output slowed to 2.5 per cent, 3.6 per cent and 1.3 per cent in the last three quarters of the year. By the fourth quarter, the energy crisis was being felt, housing was in a pronounced slump, automobile sales lagged, interest rates were high and unemployment was headed back up to 6 per cent.

The economic deceleration turned into a reduction in actual output in 1974, although inflation kept pushing the nominal total of GNP upward. The federal budget, which wound up with a $3.5-billion deficit for the fiscal 1974 year that ended on July 1, provided only a minimal stimulus to economic activity in the last half of 1973 and the first half of 1974.

The Federal Reserve Board, determined by now to discourage inflation-fueling monetary expansion even in the face of voracious demand for credit, adopted a sharply restrictive stance.

Interest rates once more soared as a result, the prime rate reaching a record 12 per cent, and the already beleaguered housing industry suffered as mortgage funds dried up. The stock market, which had recovered from its 1970 decline to reach new highs at the start of 1973, went into a prolonged decline.

Whatever the mix of causes, real output fell during the first nine months of 1974, meeting the rule of thumb definition of recession as a reduction of real GNP in two or more consecutive quarters. From $845.7-billion in the last quarter of 1973, real GNP fell to $830.5-billion in the January-March quarter of 1974, $827.1-billion in the year's April-June quarter and to an estimated $821.1-billion in the July-September quarter.

In those three quarters, real output fell by 5.8 per cent, 1.6 per cent and 2.9 per cent. But the inflation rates for those three quarters were 10.8 per cent, 9.4 per cent and 11.5 per cent.

Double Digits

That averaged out to nearly 10.6 per cent, and that kind of inflation while the economy was in recession made it clear that a number of forces were contributing to rising prices.

With demand lagging, and wage rates only starting to catch up with living cost increases, the 1973-74 inflation fit neither the conventional demand-pull nor cost-push causes blamed for earlier inflations.

The 1973-74 inflation found much of its strength in a combination of unexpected pressures that were beyond the control of the broad-scale fiscal and monetary tools of economic policy. Those pressures were created as much by international political strains and by natural misfortunes as by policy mismanagement.

The most telling inflationary pressures came from:

● A worldwide spiraling of basic commodity prices set off by the early 1973 boom. The declining foreign exchange value of the dollar, which was floating on world markets after devaluations in 1971 and 1973, raised the cost of imported raw materials and encouraged foreign demand for U.S. products.

● Continued increases in food prices reflecting bad weather that reduced crops, market inefficiencies stem-

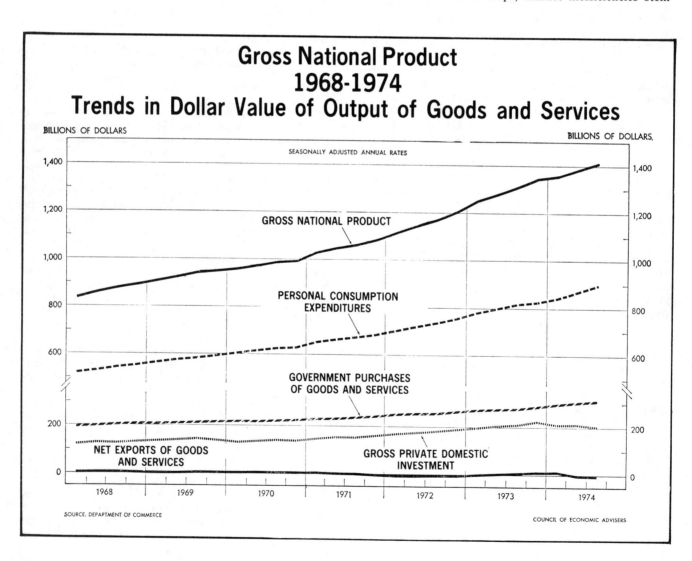

Gross National Product
1968-1974
Trends in Dollar Value of Output of Goods and Services

BILLIONS OF DOLLARS

BILLIONS OF DOLLARS

SEASONALLY ADJUSTED ANNUAL RATES

GROSS NATIONAL PRODUCT

PERSONAL CONSUMPTION EXPENDITURES

GOVERNMENT PURCHASES OF GOODS AND SERVICES

NET EXPORTS OF GOODS AND SERVICES

GROSS PRIVATE DOMESTIC INVESTMENT

1968 1969 1970 1971 1972 1973 1974

SOURCE: DEPARTMENT OF COMMERCE

COUNCIL OF ECONOMIC ADVISERS

Buying Power: Growing Affluence Still Beats Inflation

Economics don't work that neatly, but the average American worker theoretically came out ahead of inflation despite rapid price increases between 1965 and 1975.

For while the prices soared, so did wages. And a worker who made an average hourly wage in both 1965 and 1974 would have to work fewer hours in 1974 to buy most commonly purchased goods and services, a study of government statistics shows.

Being averages, those wage statistics of course ignore inequities in income distribution and pay increases, especially for persons with fixed incomes whose earnings may not have increased at all. And price statistics ignore variations in how much it cost to buy different brands in different areas at varying times of the year.

But disregarding those obvious conditions, government statistics show that a worker would have to work less time in 1974 than in 1965 to earn the money needed to buy most commonly needed purchases. That was because the average hourly wage—for production workers on non-agricultural payrolls—had risen to nearly $4.25 in 1974 from $2.45 in 1965.

Significantly, the purchases that cost more in work time in 1974 than 1965 included such necessities as hamburger, homeownership and hospital care.

But most other commodities and services included in the study were less costly. To buy a new refrigerator costing $160 in 1965, for instance, a worker who made the average hourly wage of $2.45 would have to work roughly 65 hours and 18 minutes.

By 1974, with the price rising to $181.99 (if it increased by the average for refrigerators), a worker who made the average hourly wage of about $4.25 would need to work only 42 hours and 48 minutes to earn the purchase price.

The following figures illustrate how increases in the average hourly wage could have offset price increases between 1965 and 1975. For each item, the computation was based on the average percentage increase in the Labor Department's consumer price index for that item and on an arbitrarily assigned base price in 1965. It assumed that the base price increased by the same percentage as the government's index.

	1965 ($2.45/hour)	1970 ($3.22/hour)	1974 ($4.25/hour)
1 lb. hamburger	13 min.	13 min.	14 min.
1 quart milk	6 min.	5 min.	5 min.
1 pair men's shoes	6 hr. 7 min.	6 hrs.	5 hr. 44 min.
single-family home	12,224 hr. 54 min.	12,909 hr. 19 min.	12,783 hr. 32 min.
refrigerator	65 hr. 18 min.	50 hr. 26 min.	42 hr. 48 min.
new automobile	816 hr. 20 min.	662 hr. 20 min.	552 hr.
1 gal. gasoline	8 min.	7 min.	8 min.
airline fare	40 hr. 49 min.	36 hr. 55 min.	34 hr. 59 min.
television set	122 hr. 27 min.	86 hr. 39 min.	65 hr. 35 min.
movie admission	37 min.	42 min.	39 min.
basketball	4 hr. 5 min.	3 hr. 44 min.	3 hr. 20 min.
magazine subscription	2 hr. 52 min.	2 hr. 43 min.	2 hr. 28 min.
hospital room (semi-private)	12 hr. 14 min.	17 hr. 50 min.	19 hr. 30 min.
tonsillectomy	61 hr. 22 min.	59 hr. 56 min.	57 hr. 59 min.
funeral	408 hr. 10 min.	366 hr. 49 min.	336 hr.
cigar	12 min.	13 min.	11 min.
6-pack beer	29 min.	26 min.	24 min.
short-form will	20 hr. 25 min.	20 hr. 58 min.	22 hr. 45 min.

ming from government policies and private practices, and growing worldwide demand for food.

● Mammoth increases in energy prices that largely were dictated by petroleum-producing nations and shortages created by an oil embargo against the United States prompted by the 1973 Arab-Israeli war.

Those pressures were unresponsive to government policy restraints, including a 60-day price freeze imposed during the summer of 1973 and a revived system of price controls that was phased out rapidly industry-by-industry and abolished four months into 1974.

Between the last quarter of 1972 and the last quarter of 1973, the food component of the consumer price index increased at a 19.4 per cent annual rate. For wholesale prices, the index for farm products and processed foods and feeds rose by 31 per cent.

During the same period, the increases in the energy components of the government price indexes were 12.8 per cent for consumer prices and 46 per cent for wholesale prices.

The pattern continued into 1974. For the first nine months of the year, the consumer price index for food rose through the first quarter at an annual rate of 19.4 per cent, at a more moderate second-quarter rate of 3.1 per cent and at an accelerated 12.3 per cent rate in the third quarter.

Food and energy inflation could be expected to moderate as production increases caught up with demand. But stepped-up production was subject to influences that were beyond the control of economic planning, notably bad weather for agriculture and petroleum price and supply actions by oil-producing nations.

And even if moderated, food and fuel price increases took disproportionate tolls on consumer pocketbooks, making demands for wage increases more urgent. Translated into higher costs pushing on prices, those demands could only contribute more strength to the inflationary process.■

JOBS: TRENDS AND FEDERAL POLICIES—1965-74

For millions of Americans, as AFL-CIO President George Meany has said, the "only hedge against inflation is their jobs." And with the unemployment rate standing at 6 per cent by the end of October 1974, and all but certain to go higher in succeeding months, the threat of a deepening recession was a more fearsome prospect to many Americans than rising prices.

Since Congress passed the historic Employment Act of 1946 declaring federal policy to be the promotion of maximum employment, production and purchasing power, federal economic policies have encouraged a fairly steady expansion of jobs and output. The labor force has grown from 60.9 million in 1946 to 92 million in 1974 and the number of employed has expanded commensurately. The real gross national product has climbed from $312.6-billion in 1946 to $839.2-billion in 1973.

But federal economic policy has not been able to prevent periodic upward surges in the unemployment rate. Indeed, during the 1948-49 recession, which the 1946 act was intended to at least minimize, the unemployment rate rose to 7.9 per cent in October 1949—the highest monthly rate in the post-war years to date.

A recession at the end of the Korean War in 1953-54 was followed in 1958-59 by the worst recession the country has experienced in the post-war years. Peak unemployment during that period registered 7.5 per cent in July 1958.

That recession was followed by the 1960-61 downturn, when unemployment reached 7.1 per cent in May of 1961. After registering a yearly average of 6.7 per cent in 1961, the unemployment rate fell throughout the decade to a low of 3.5 per cent in 1969. But it began to climb again with the recession of 1969-70, moving up to 5.9 per cent in 1971, then falling to 4.9 per cent in 1973 before it began its upward climb in mid-1974. *(Chart p. 13)*

Traditionally, the government had been able to help break recessions by stimulating the economy through expansion of government spending, tax cuts and a liberal monetary policy.

But by 1974 it was clear that the government could not rely on traditional solutions without risking continued damaging inflation. And the challenge to the federal government was double-edged: how to find a balance that would curb both inflation and recession without making one or the other worse.

Following is a brief examination of employment and unemployment trends over the past decade and a review of federal policies designed to hold unemployment during economic downturns to acceptable levels.

Who Is Employed

Despite periodic increases in the rate of unemployment, the actual number of people employed in the United States generally has increased from month to month over the last 10 years, as has the total number of people in the civilian labor force.

In 1965, 74,455,000 people were counted in the labor force, of which 71,088,000 held jobs and 3,366,000 were un-

employed. As of October 1974, 92 million people were counted in the labor force; 86.5 million held jobs and 5.5 million were out of work.

Growth in the labor force has been steady throughout the 20th century and consistent with the population increase. The percentage of people in the work force compared to all non-institutionalized people (those not in hospitals, prisons, etc.) has hovered around 60 per cent for more than two decades.

In addition to unemployment data, decreases and increases in the number of people actually employed also can signal spurts and declines in the economic picture, simply by indicating the availability of jobs. There was no significant change in the employment total between June and July, July and August or September and October. In the first three quarters of 1974, employment had risen by only 850,000, a quarter of the gain made in 1973.

Changes

But while the percentage of people working throughout the century had held fairly constant measured against the population growth, the people and the kinds of work they do has changed radically. Immigrants, who made up about one-third of the labor force in the first three decades of the century, have given way to women who now comprise about two-fifths of the labor force. The number of married men taking early retirement has begun to show a small but steady increase as has the number of teenagers entering the work force.

And as the number of farm workers declined from more than one third in 1900 to only about 3 per cent of the work force, the number of those classified as white collar workers has increased so that they now make up almost half of the labor force. Blue collar workers have held fairly constant, reaching a high of 41.1 per cent of the work force in 1950 and declining to 36 per cent in 1970.

White Collar Workers

The swell in the number of persons classified as white collar has come largely at the bottom rung in the lower prestige and lower paying clerical jobs—secretaries, telephone operators, office machine operators, mailmen and the like. The number of clerical workers has multiplied six times from 3 per cent of the work force in 1900 to 17.9 per cent in 1970.

Professional and technical white collar workers also showed significant growth, more than tripling in 70 years from 4.3 per cent in 1900 to 14.9 per cent of the work force in 1970. Teachers, nurses, health technicians and other health specialists and engineers were the professional careers showing the most growth in that time.

Blue Collar Workers

Among blue collar workers the shift has been away from the unskilled worker, with the number of non-farm laborers decreasing from 12.5 per cent of the work force in 1900 to 4.5 per cent in 1970. The number of

Job Categories

	1900	1930	1950	1970
White Collar	17.6%	29.4%	36.6%	48.1%
Blue Collar	35.8	39.6	41.1	36.0
Service	9.0	9.8	10.5	12.8
Farm	37.5	21.2	11.8	3.1

both skilled and semi-skilled laborers has increased. Craftsmen in 1970 accounted for 13.9 per cent of the work force compared to 10.5 per cent in 1900 while operatives (machine operators, assemblers, painters, packers, etc.) were 17.6 per cent compared to 12.8 per cent in 1900. However, the number of craftsmen has declined from a high of 14.2 per cent in 1960 and the number of operatives has fallen from a high of 20.4 per cent in 1950.

Among skilled workers, the largest increases have been registered among repairmen and foremen while big increases among operatives have occurred in the transportation field—an area which obviously registered few employees at the turn of the century.

Services

Paralleling the decline in the number of people who manufacture goods and the increase in the number who distribute and maintain those goods has been the growth in the non-professional services category—waiters, barbers, maids, hospital orderlies, janitors. While the percentage of those working in service jobs has increased only about 4 per cent since 1900, most of the service workers are no longer oriented to the private home but to providing services to the public at large. Food service, cleaning operation and health care jobs have all shown upward surges and are predicted to continue growing.

Government Employment

One area that has steadily provided new jobs is the government—federal, state and local. Contrary to what might be expected, the number of civilian employees of the federal government has increased the least, from 2.5 million in 1965 to 2.9 million in August 1974. Because of increased personnel needs during the Vietnam war, that figure stood at slightly more than 3 million in 1967-69 but did not reach the 3.4 million level attained during World War II.

The number of state government employees has increased at a greater pace—from 2 million in 1965 to 2.9 million in 1973—but the largest jump was posted in the local government sector, which rose from slightly less than 6 million in 1965 to 8.3 million in 1973.

While the rise in the number of state and local government employees was largely attributable to a parallel growth in the population and demands for expanded services, some increases in the early 1970s were accounted for by federal public service job programs operated at the state and local levels.

By far, teachers and other school employees made up the bulk of state and local government employees, totaling nearly 50 per cent. Hospitals employed the next greatest number of public workers, followed by highways and then police departments.

Working Women

Perhaps the most phenomenal change in the labor force has been the continuing increase in working women. In 1900, women comprised only 18 per cent of all workers; by 1973, they made up 40 per cent of the labor force.

Equally significant is the rising percentage of wives and mothers who work. The typical working woman in 1920 was single; if she married she quit work for good unless widowhood or desertion left her with no other means of support. The current pattern for a woman who marries is to remain employed, quitting only a few years for childbearing and child-rearing. More than two-fifths of all married women are in the labor force today compared with one-fourth in the mid 1950s. An acceleration of the working wife trend in recent years is attributable largely to younger women. The portion of wives under 35 in the labor market rose from 28 per cent to 40 per cent during the past decade. One-third of all women with children of pre-school age were working or seeking work in 1973, almost twice as many as nine years earlier. Among mothers whose children had reached school age, almost one-half were working.

Labor force participation does not tell the whole story of women's status in employment. Though most of the legal barriers to equality of opportunity in the labor force have fallen away, the over-all picture for the female worker has not changed very much in the half century since women got the vote. In 1900, 70 per cent of the working women were employed as operatives, farm laborers or servants, mostly in private homes. In 1972, 70 per cent of the working women were still in low prestige jobs—clerical, service and operative.

Clearly, women still have the poorest paying, least prestigious jobs. Among professionals, women have made some breakthroughs, especially in the financial, insurance and real estate fields, but most professional women are concentrated in the traditional professionals roles of teacher, nurse and social worker. And even among teachers, women come out second best: about 70 per cent of all college professors are men, while 70 per cent of all elementary and secondary school teachers are women.

Earnings in the female-intensive industries were still among some of the lowest. Average earnings in the service industry were $111 a week while weekly earnings among hospital workers average $108. Average weekly wages for retail merchandisers were $82.

Women's Occupations

The following chart shows the distribution of working women by occupation:

Occupation	1900	1930	1972
Clerical	4.0%	20.9%	34.7%
Service	35.4	27.5	22.0
Professional, Technical	8.2	13.8	14.5
Operatives	23.7	17.4	13.3
Sales	4.3	6.8	7.1
Managers, Officials	1.4	2.7	4.5
Farm Workers	18.9	8.4	1.7
Craftsmen	1.4	1.0	1.2
Laborers	2.6	1.5	0.9

Male-female pay differences run down the occupational scales from top to bottom, just as they did a half-century ago. On a percentage basis, women's pay has fallen further behind men's in recent years, as the following Department of Labor statistics illustrate.

Year	Women	Men	Income as % of Men's
1955	$2,719	$4,252	63.9
1960	3,293	5,417	60.8
1965	3,823	6,375	60.0
1970	5,323	8,966	59.4
1972	5,903	10,202	57.9

Black Employment

Black economic and occupational gains during and since World War II have narrowed, but far from wiped out, historic differences between the income status of the white and Negro population. In 1939, median earnings of nonwhite workers were scarcely more than one-third of the white median; today they are almost 60 per cent of the white median.

But within age and education brackets, the disparities are great. Earnings of black male workers between 25 and 54 are still substantially below white male earnings although the young black male with a college education showed signs of closing the gap. The only group equal with its white counterpart was the young black family in the North and West where both the husband and wife worked, a small proportion of the total number of black families.

The percentage of Negro families earning above $10,-000 a year has increased from 22 per cent in 1966 to 30 per cent in 1971, but that was still well under the 54 per cent registered for white families.

Black white collar workers also have increased, from 16 per cent in 1960 to 29 per cent in 1972, but few of those were holding high prestige, high paying jobs. Four per cent of the nonwhite workers held managerial and administrative jobs, compared to 11 per cent for whites. About 10 per cent of the nonwhite workers were classified as professional and technical employees compared to 15 per cent of the whites.

Among blue collar workers, blacks also were concentrated at the lower rungs, with almost double the white participation rate for unskilled nonfarm labor. The number has shown a decline, however, from 13.7 per cent in 1960 to 9.9 per cent in 1972. Black service workers were also double the rate of whites, with almost 7 per cent of all black service workers employed in private homes, compared to 1.2 per cent for whites. That gap, too, was narrowing; in 1960 14.2 per cent of the nonwhites were employed in private homes.

Concentration of employment in low-paying and insecure types of work accounts for the relatively low earnings and the frequency and long duration of unemployment among blacks. Despite some upward trends, nonwhites still register double the number of unemployed as whites do.

The following comparisons based on 1971 statistics collected by the Labor Department focus on the black unemployment problem:

• Three-fifths of all nonwhite men had year-round, full-time jobs, compared to two-thirds of all white men. Black and white women were equal at 42 per cent.

• Among nonwhite, 23 per cent experienced some joblessness during the year, compared with 16 per cent of all whites.

Unemployment Rate

	Total Work Force	Men	Women	16-19 Years
1967	3.8%	3.1%	5.2%	12.9%
1968	3.6	2.9	4.8	12.7
1969	3.5	2.8	4.7	12.2
1970	4.9	4.4	5.9	15.2
1971	5.9	5.3	6.9	16.9
1972	5.6	4.9	6.6	16.2
1973	4.9	4.1	6.0	14.5

• Among nonwhites, 42 per cent were unemployed for extended periods of time (15 or more weeks), compared to 36 per cent of the whites.

• Among males not in the labor force, more nonwhites are likely to think they cannot find a job, are disabled, have ill health or are in school; more whites are likely to be retired or think they are too old to work.

• Among females not in the labor force, more nonwhites are likely to think they cannot find a job, are disabled or are in school but more whites stay home because of family responsibilities.

Who Is Unemployed

Although the common definition of full employment in the United States accepts a 4 per cent unemployment rate, the yearly average has only been below that level in 11 of the 29 post-war years, and in all instances each unemployment low was followed by a recession with jumps in the number of jobless.

The increased number of women and teenagers in the work force has accounted for some of the relative increase in the level of unemployment. Both categories traditionally have had a harder time finding and holding jobs. *(Box, this page)*

According to computations made by the Labor Department, the changing character of the labor force has had an impact on the unemployment rate. In 1956, adult males made up 64 per cent of the labor force; by 1970 that ratio had dropped to 57 per cent. Department calculations found that if the labor force distribution had remained at its 1956 level while unemployment rates for age and sex categories changed as they actually did, the 1970 jobless rate would have been 4.4 per cent rather than 4.9 per cent.

Not only were women and blacks less well-paid than white men, but they also were less employed. In 1973, 8.9 per cent of the women were unemployed compared to 4.3 per cent of the men. Divided along racial lines, 5.3 per cent of all white women in the labor force were jobless, compared to 10.5 per cent of black women. Among males, the unemployment rate was 3.7 for whites, 7.6 per cent for blacks and other minorities.

White, Blue Collar Unemployment

The unemployment rate for blue collar and service workers generally was twice that of white collar workers. Among both white and blue collar workers, the rate increases at the lower levels of pay and skill, as the following chart illustrates:

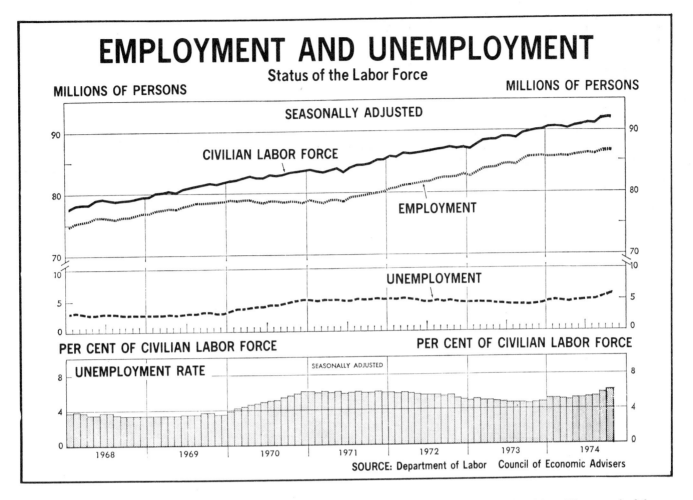

EMPLOYMENT AND UNEMPLOYMENT
Status of the Labor Force

	1970	1971	1972	1973
White Collar	2.8%	3.5%	3.4%	2.9%
Professional	2.0	2.9	2.4	2.2
Managers	1.3	1.6	1.8	1.4
Sales	3.9	4.3	4.3	3.6
Clerical	4.1	4.8	4.7	4.2
Blue Collar	6.2	7.4	6.5	5.3
Craftsmen	3.8	4.7	4.3	3.7
Operatives	7.1	8.3	6.9	5.7
Laborers	9.5	10.8	10.3	8.4
Service Workers	5.3	6.3	6.3	5.7

Youth and Veterans

A nagging problem for the federal government has been the persistently high unemployment rates for the 16-19 year-olds—the youngest category in the work force. Less trained and experienced and often less schooled, the worker in this category generally looks longer for a job, is among the first to be fired when hard economic times hit and is then among the longest unemployed.

The situation is particularly bleak for blacks and other minority group youth whose unemployment rate is more than double that of white youth. In 1973, 12.6 per cent of all white 16-19 year olds were jobless, compared to 30.3 per cent of all black and other minority youth. Among males, the rates were 12.3 per cent for whites; 26.9 per cent for minorities. Among women, the rates were 13.0 per cent for whites and 34.5 per cent for blacks and other minorities.

In 1972, 1973 and 1974, President Nixon pushed for a provision to the minimum wage bill that would allow 16 and 17 year-olds to be employed for six months at less than the minimum wage. Supporters argued that such a provision would aid unemployed youths and give them training which would make future employment more likely. But the provision was killed by opponents who argued that the provision would not create new jobs for youth and feared that youths would replace older workers.

Another embarassing problem for the government has been the high unemployment rate among Vietnam war veterans—despite several federal programs that give preference to veterans in both training and hiring.

Although unemployment rates for veterans decreased significantly in 1973, new returnees still had difficulties finding jobs and the rates for all veterans appeared to be on an upward trend during 1974.

In the 1970s, unemployment among 20-34 year-old vets reached a high annual average of 8.2 per cent in 1971, compared to 6.3 per cent for their nonveteran counterparts. The rate fell to 5 per cent in 1973, but by October 1974, had climbed back up to 5.6 per cent.

While the jobless rates in the 25-34 year age group closely paralleled those of their nonveteran counterparts, rates among the 20-24 year olds consistently have been higher. In 1974, those vets averaged an 8.9 per cent jobless rate, compared to 6.8 per cent for nonveterans.

As is true of nonveterans, the unemployment rate for black and other minority group veterans is almost double that for white veterans—8.4 per cent in 1973, compared to 4.3 per cent for whites. And, again, the biggest gap was among the youngest black vets who recorded a 13.5 per cent jobless rate in 1973.

Discouraged Workers

One technical component of any debate on full employment is the question of defining unemployment. The Bureau of Labor Statistics, which together with the Census Bureau collects unemployment data, defines a jobless person as anyone 16 or over who is unemployed but has been laid off his job and is waiting to be recalled or is waiting to begin a new job. Any other unemployed person is considered to be out of the work force. *(Details, box, p. 17)*

Over the years, it has been argued that certain categories of workers—largely teenagers still in school and housewives—should not be counted as unemployed because they either really did not need to work or were only in the labor force temporarily.

Others have argued that the unemployment statistics do not tell the full story. Part-time workers who want but cannot find full-time jobs and discouraged workers who have stopped looking for work are not counted among the unemployed.

Working from recommendations made in 1962 by the President's Commission to Appraise Employment and Unemployment, the Labor Department in 1967 began to collect data on discouraged workers. Of the 4.7 million unemployed persons in 1967 who said they wanted a job but could not work for various reasons, 732,000 said they had stopped looking for work because they did not think they could find a job. Of that number, fewer than 200,000 were adult males, the rest were teenagers, women and elderly persons.

A Department of Labor study in 1973 found that there were more discouraged workers when the unemployment rate was relatively high. But the correlation was not great. Between 1969 and 1971, when the jobless rate was increased by recession, the number of discouraged workers rose only by 200,000. The study also found that more discouraged workers gave the tight job market as the reason for their discouragement rather than personal factors such as job handicap or age.

The same study found that a disproportionately high number of discouraged workers were blacks who made up one-ninth of the persons outside the labor force but one-fourth of those who were not working because they did not think they could get a job.

Underemployment

To assess the true manpower picture in the United States, some experts claim that the number of persons who are underemployed must also be determined. While no one acceptable method of measurement has been devised, there have been varying estimates.

Counting the number of unemployed, discouraged workers, part-time workers seeking full-time jobs and workers who did not earn enough to support themselves or their families above the poverty line, the Senate Labor and Public Welfare Employment, Manpower and Poverty Subcommittee in May 1972 estimated that 31 per cent of the 13 million people living in the poverty areas of 51 cities were underemployed.

Using a more restrictive definition that excluded secondary workers in families, a report published in the October 1973 *Monthly Labor Review* estimated that 19 per cent of all workers in the 12 largest cities were underemployed. Of the total subemployed, 40 per cent were unemployed, 16 per cent were discouraged workers and 29 per cent were low-paid family heads. The report also estimated that the average family annual income of subemployed workers was $6,600—$3,200 less than the average annual income of families whose heads were not underemployed.

Using a formula that did not take into account inadequate earnings but only the unemployed, discouraged workers and part-time workers wanting full-time jobs, the Joint Economic Committee estimated that the national unemployment rate in 1971 should have been 8.1 per cent rather than the 5.9 per cent recorded. "Good statistical estimates of some of these aspects of underemployment are lacking," the committee wrote in its 1972 Joint Economic Report, "but there is no question of the enormity of the underutilization of human resources."

None of the three studies took into account the number of people who were employed at jobs that required less than their highest level of skill—a basic definition of underemployment and also a subjective evaluation that would be difficult to quantify with any degree of accuracy.

Federal Policy

Until the Great Depression of the 1930s, government concern with unemployment was directed toward problems of supplying employers with needed workers rather than assuring working men a sufficiency of jobs. Such measures as the establishment of land-grant colleges and provision of grants for vocational education reflected government interest in improving skills of the labor force to meet the demands of technologically advancing agriculture and industry. When workers lost their jobs due to economic setbacks, they were expected to fend for themselves somehow or to move on to some other place where job prospects were more favorable. The truly destitute might be sent to a "workhouse" where they could work off the cost of meager charity in low-grade employment.

The Depression

With the massive unemployment that followed the stock market crash of October 1929, the government's attention was forcibly turned to a national problem of what to do with an idled labor force of unprecedented dimensions. President Hoover was adamantly opposed to direct federal relief, whether in the form of a dole or a make-work job, though in 1931 he did create a National Committee on Employment Relief to encourage the growth of local citizens' groups concerned with the problem. Some 200 communities at that time were providing some kind of work relief, mainly manual labor jobs, for their unemployed. The Reconstruction Finance Corporation was created in 1932 to extend loans to forestall business failures and job losses.

These measures failed to restrain the economic toboggan. When President Roosevelt took office on March 4, 1933, nearly 13 million persons, one-fourth of the labor force, were out of work and looking for jobs. The national income was less than one-half what it had been when Hoover became President four years earlier. Unemployment relief was one of the first orders of business. The Federal Emergency Relief Administration (FERA), created by executive order under authority granted the President by Congress during the famous One Hundred Days (roughly March 4-June 16, 1933), began immediately to dispense both direct relief and work relief.

The Roosevelt administration was counting mainly on the Public Works Administration program to put masses of jobless workers on the payroll at various construction and reclamation projects around the country. Because PWA was slow getting started and the need was dire, an emergency program known as the Civil Works Administration was begun in November 1933 with the express purpose of getting the maximum number of jobless workers into paying employment as soon as possible. This was more feasible than under PWA because CWA operated its own work projects, the projects were on a smaller scale than those of PWA, and the emphasis was on jobs that did not demand much special training. One month from its beginning, more than 2½ million workers were on the CWA payroll and within another month the number had gone over four million.

The program put one-third of them at work building roads and highways. It also built or repaired 40,000 schools, hired 50,000 teachers, found jobs for 3,000 artists and writers and put others to work developing parks, clearing waterways, digging sewers and so on. The program lasted only 3½ months and cost nearly $1-billion. Unlike the continuing FERA work relief program, which paid subsistence wages, CWA paid the going wage.

To deal with the problem of idle youth, the Roosevelt administration devised two programs, the Civilian Conservation Corps and the National Youth Administration. The CCC, established in April 1933, took young men of ages 18 to 25 from relief families and housed them in army-run camps where they received some educational and job-training services and a small stipend. In return they engaged in conservation work, mainly for the National Park and Forest Services. Over the years some 2½ million youths spent from six months to a year in 1,300 of these camps. The value of the land improvements carried out by the CCC was estimated in 1959 at $1.75-billion. The National Youth Administration hired young people of both sexes who lived at home to perform various public service tasks, such as clearing land, helping out in schools or hospitals, for an average of 40 hours a month. They were paid up to $40 a month.

The WPA, 1935-1943

The best-known and most controversial of the job-making programs of this period was the Works Progress Administration, established as an independent agency in 1935. This was a massive hire-the-jobless program with the primary purpose of getting individuals and families off relief and putting them to work on socially useful jobs. WPA workers included the skilled and unskilled, professional and blue-collar. Over the eight years of its existence it spent nearly $11-billion and employed a total of 8.5 million persons, as many as 3.5 million at one time.

All of this helped, but unemployment persisted. By 1939 the federal government was spending around $3.5-billion for relief, nearly one-half of it for work relief, but 9½ million workers representing 17 per cent of the labor force were still without jobs. The situation changed rapidly after the outbreak of World War II in Europe in September 1939. A boom in defense spending at home began to draw men—and to an increasing extent, women—back to work. American entry into World War II in December 1941 brought an unprecedented utilization of the labor force. It became patriotic to work "for the war effort" in whatever

Federally Assisted Work Programs

Comprehensive Manpower Assistance. Funds assigned to "prime sponsors" (currently 403 state and local governments, singly or in groups) to carry on training, job placement and related activities under the Comprehensive Employment and Training Act.

JOBS (Job Opportunities in the Business Sector). Partially subsidized volunteer program sponsored by National Alliance of Business Men to encourage hiring of disadvantaged workers and upgrading their skills.

Operation SER (Service, Employment and Redevelopment). Nationally contracted program to aid employment of Spanish-speaking unemployed or underemployed persons.

NYC (Neighborhood Youth Corps).* A carryover from the Economic Opportunity (anti-poverty) program, mainly for inner-city youth, in three parts: (1) work and training for out-of-school teen-agers, (2) after-school work and (3) summer employment for students.

OIC (Opportunities Industrialization Centers). Community-based inner-city programs that are privately sponsored under national contract for training, job placement and job-upgrading.

PEP (Public Employment Program). Specifically authorized under the 1973 Manpower Act to put the unemployed in public service jobs during periods of job shortages.

Job Corps. A job training program, mainly for inner-city youth, that includes remedial education and bilingual instruction.

OJT (On-Job Training). A program to upgrade work skills, with government funds compensating employers for costs.

AOT and CO (Apprenticeship Outreach Training and Construction Outreach). Programs of cooperative effort by government, industry and labor to broaden the apprenticeship system, draw more minority youths into the trades and open the way for experienced minority workers to advance beyond journeyman status.

Operation Mainstream. A work-experience program for older workers.

Concentrated Employment Program. An outreach program, providing reception centers for urban and rural poor, leading to training or jobs.

WIN (Work Incentive Program). Job training and placement aimed at reducing the number of persons receiving welfare aid under the Aid to Families With Dependent Children program.

USES (U.S. Employment Service). A network of 2,400 state-run, federally financed employment agencies.

* NYC and other programs listed above may no longer be directly financed by the federal government but may be continued by state and local "prime sponsors" under revenue-sharing provisions of the Comprehensive Employment and Training Act of 1973.

capacity one could. Wives, teenagers, the elderly and the handicapped took jobs.

At the peak of war industry production, unemployment fell to a low of 1.2 per cent. But as the war neared its close, fear of a postwar recession arose and much public discussion was directed to the need for measures to forestall economic disaster when sharp cutbacks in war goods would coincide with the release of millions of men from military service. It was in this atmosphere that public interest turned to the question of government policy on unemployment.

This was an era when interest in economic planning was ascendant. The National Resources Planning Board, a New Deal agency that served as economic adviser to the government, had called in a 1943 report for a government policy to "underwrite full employment" and "promote...a high level of national production and consumption." Also influential was Britian's Sir William Beveridge, who argued for a similar position in his book, *Full Employment in a Free Society.*

Guarantee of Full Employment

President Roosevelt said in a message to Congress on Jan. 11, 1944, "the right to useful and remunerative jobs" was the first principle of an "economic bill of rights." President Truman on Sept. 6, 1945, called for "a national reassertion of the right to work for every American citizen able and willing to work" and "a declaration of the ultimate duty of government to use its own resources if all other methods should fail to prevent prolonged unemployment." By this time, Congress had been arguing for eight months over a pending bill to implement this principle. The bill ultimately became the historic Employment Act of 1946.

The final version of the Employment Act was different from the form in which it was originally offered by its liberal sponsors, and its main statement of principle has been subject to different interpretations. The lengthy debate that preceded the enactment of this law is worth reviewing because it reveals a basic difference of philosophy on governmental function that could surface again if unemployment should become more widespread.

The original bill would have established "full employment" as the declared policy of the government. This was defined in terms of employment opportunities for everyone able to work and seeking work. It would have put the government on record for the first time as "assuring" that a job would be available to anyone who was capable or desirous of holding one. The bill contained a "compensatory spending" provision. This meant that a "National Production and Employment" analysis would be prepared each year, with estimates of the amount of total spending by private and public agencies required to sustain "full employment" and the amount that would actually be spent without government intervention. If there was a gap between requirements and spending, the President would propose ways of closing the gap, providing whatever investment and expenditure might be needed "as a last resort to achieve full employment."

The bill passed the Senate in this form but was greatly modified by the more conservative House. The compromise bill that came out of a House-Senate conference was so far removed from the original that a leader of the opposition, Sen. Robert A. Taft (R Ohio), assured his fellow conservatives that they should have no qualms about voting for it. "There is now nothing in the bill to which any member...should take exception," Taft said when the compromise version reached the Senate floor, Feb. 8, 1946. "There is now no full employment bill." The word "full" had

been removed from the title and text of the bill as had the word "assurance" indicating a government guarantee of a job.

Supporters of the original bill reluctantly accepted the reduced version. While disappointed "that the basic concepts of the bill were not set forth in more clear-cut...language," its chief sponsor, Sen. James A. Murray (D Mont.), said he thought it did at least contain "all the essentials of a full employment...if properly and firmly administered." As if to make a case for later interpretations of congressional intent, Murray said he believed "the right to work is implicit in the language" even though the words themselves were not used.

The act stated: "The Congress hereby declares that it is the continuing policy and responsibility of the federal government to use all practicable means consistent with its needs and obligations and other essential considerations of national policy, with the assistance and cooperation of industry, agriculture, labor and state and local governments, to coordinate and utilize all its plans, functions and resources

"(1) For the purpose of creating and maintaining in a manner calculated to foster and promote free competitive enterprise and the general welfare, conditions under which there will be afforded useful employment opportunities, including self-employment, for those able, willing, and seeking to work, and

"(2) To promote maximum employment, production and purchasing power."

President Truman, on signing the bill on Feb. 20, 1947, said it was "a commitment to take any and all of the measures necessary for a healthy economy." A question remained, however, over the extent of a commitment to full employment. That the issue is by no means dead is indicated by the introduction in 1972 and again in 1974 of a bill to restore the original language and intent of the full employment bill of 1945.

Post-War Jobless Programs

The federal government instituted several programs during the post-World War II years to alleviate unemployment. The character of these programs has shifted with the changing concerns of public policy.

The G.I. Bill might be considered the first of the postwar measures that kept unemployment in check, first by diminishing a sudden swell in the size of the total labor force, and second, by upgrading the employability of the returnees to civilian life. Similar benefits accrued from the National Defense Education Act of 1958, enacted in response to the launching of the first earth-orbiting space vehicle (Sputnik) by the Soviet Union, to upgrade American education, especially in the sciences, and maintain U.S. technological ascendancy.

Beginning in the mid-1950s, interest centered on pockets of unemployment which persisted even in periods of relative prosperity elsewhere. Concern focused on those places where local industry had become obsolete or had moved on. Bills to help restore economic viability to these areas were twice vetoed by Eisenhower before Kennedy signed the Area Redevelopment Act on May 1, 1961. Among the criteria established for determining the eligibility of an area for assistance (including job training) under this act were the severity and the duration of its unemployment problem.

Unemployment Statistics

The monthly national unemployment data released on the first Friday of each month by the Labor Department are gathered as part of the Current Population Survey and are based on personal interviews in about 50,000 selected households across the country.

Respondents are queried about their work status in the week that contains the 12th of the month and are questioned in the following week.

The Bureau of the Census and the Bureau of Labor Statistics consider anyone to be employed if they have worked for at least one hour a week for pay or profit. Absent workers also are considered employed if they are ill, on vacation or on strike.

Unemployed workers are those who did not work at all during the reference week but took direct action to find a job within the last four weeks. Also considered unemployed are those workers who have been laid off and are waiting to be called back and those persons waiting to start a new job. Anyone else is not considered a part of the labor force.

The monthly figures also are adjusted for seasonal variations, including crop seasons, weather conditions (which affect the construction industry particularly), opening and closing of schools, holiday buying period and industry production schedules.

There followed the Manpower Development and Training Act of 1962, whose authors were mainly concerned with providing for unemployed individuals who had had a firm attachment to the labor force but whose jobs had disappeared because of technological or economic displacement. Retraining these persons for available jobs was considered a relatively simple task and the program had the advantage of a cost offset in savings from unemployment compensation and other transfer payments. The MDT program, which provided both enrollment in vocational classes and on-the-job training, was considered successful in that many of its participants found employment, but the program did not reach enough persons to make an appreciable dent on over-all unemployment rates.

Jobs for the Disadvantaged

During the 1960s, attention was turning toward another class of unemployed individuals, those who, because of social handicaps related to life-long poverty, racial discrimination or educational deficiencies, had never had a firm or rewarding place in the job market. This group included youths from big-city racial ghettos who had little prospect of making a successful entry into the job market. This area of concern stemmed not only from high levels of unemployment—which usually have a particularly devastating effect on the income of the poor—but also the rising social protest movement and urban disorders. All of this led to "acceptance of the principle that improving the competitive position of the disadvantaged was an appropriate goal for policy," two experts wrote. They added that, "Serving the undereducated, the undermotivated, and victims of discrimination demanded not only a reorientation in the values of existing manpower agencies, but also a whole set of closely interwoven new functions."

As the number of employment and anti-poverty work-relief programs grew under a variety of legislative and ad-

ministrative authorizations, it became apparent that the over-all structure of the government effort was unwieldy and not producing top results. After five years of debate on proposals for manpower program reform, Congress in December 1973 approved the Comprehensive Employment and Training Act to pull the existing programs under one agency, the Manpower Administration. The chief new feature was that the overall employment program now embodies the revenue-sharing principle: the federal government provides funds, but the choice of most of the projects and their operation lies with states and localities.

Public Service Jobs

Of the solutions put forward to solve the current inflation-unemployment dilemma, the one that receives the most widespread support would institute a flexible and potentially large-scale program of employment in public service jobs for persons thrown out of work as a result of anti-inflation measures.

The most recent experience with a public service jobs program began in 1971, when the national unemployment rate was around 6 per cent. Reminiscent of the WPA of 40 years ago, the Public Employment Program (PEP), established under the Emergency Employment Act of 1971, began as a temporary program to provide "transition employment" to the unemployed and the underemployed. Unlike other manpower programs, it was aimed at creating a job and putting a worker into it promptly, rather than preparing a worker for employment through training and work experience.

The major purpose of the 1971 act was to provide job opportunities in a period of relatively high cyclical unemployment. Funds were made available when national unemployment equaled or exceeded 4.5 per cent for three consecutive months, with extra funds going to areas with at least 6 per cent unemployment. The idea was to place workers in jobs that provided a needed public service in a field that was likely to expand when general economic conditions improved. Preference was given to Vietnam-era veterans, former enrollees in manpower programs, young and old workers, welfare recipients, migrants and others with disadvantaged backgrounds. Over its 23-month history—August 1971-June 1973—PEP employed some 404,000 persons, including 113,000 youths in summer programs. More than one-third were Vietnam-era veterans, three-fourths were men, one-fourth were black and 18 per cent represented other minorities, 18 per cent were poor and had at least one employment handicap, and 14 per cent were former welfare clients.

The Nixon administration sought to terminate the program after its two-year lease was to expire June 30, 1973. However, Title II of the Comprehensive Employment and Training Act (CETA), which Nixon signed Dec. 28, 1973, provided that at least $250-million of 1974 funds and $350-million of 1975 appropriations must be used for a PEP program in areas with at least a 6.5 per cent unemployment rate for three consecutive months. In addition, under Title I, "prime sponsors" (that is, a state, city, county or combination of local units designated to receive federal funds to operate a manpower program) may choose to use some of their funds for this purpose. The act provided no ceiling for an over-all appropriation.

Ford's Commitments

President Ford made his first commitment to an expanded public service jobs program Sept. 11 at a

White House meeting with the nation's top labor leaders. There Ford announced that he was asking the Labor Department to release additional funding for the CETA Title II program. In all, he said he expected that about $1-billion would be spent during the winter of 1974-1975 to provide 170,000 public service jobs.

Then on Oct. 8, Ford announced that he was proposing legislation to establish a new jobs program. Under the administration proposal, $500-million would be made available for public service jobs when the national unemployment rate averaged 6 per cent for three consecutive months. The funds would be channeled to labor market areas that had a 6.5 per cent rate or more for three consecutive months. An additional $750-million would be released if the national rate went to 6.5 per cent, and another $1-billion would be released if the rate hit 7 per cent for three months.

But bipartisan opposition developed almost immediately on Capitol Hill, with members of Congress contending that the proposal was too little too late. Some expressed fears that no funds would be given to urban centers and rural areas who were experiencing severely high unemployment rates.

Most legislative proposals would authorize up to $4-billion, with initial amounts triggered for release when the national unemployment rate averaged 4.5 per cent over three months and greater amounts released each time the rate climbed five-tenths of a point.

As the post election recess of the 93rd Congress began, it appeared likely that Congress would take no major action on an expanded public service jobs program until the 94th Congress convened, but would rather appropriate additional money for the existing program or approve interim legislation as a stopgap while more comprehensive measures were under consideration.

Outlook

Debate over the larger public service employment plans was likely to raise a number of issues, some practical and immediate, some basic and philosophic. On the practical side was the question of how far unemployment should be allowed to rise before the government intervenes by hiring jobless workers. Numerous questions then could arise over the level of wages and over who exactly among the jobless would be eligible for a government relief job. Would the participants include, for example, the wife and teenage offspring of an employed family head? Should there be tests for eligibility to hold a job under the program? How and when should the program unwind when general economic conditions changed? And almost immediately troublesome: how could the government reduce spending to curtail inflation while adding billions to its expenditures to support a new job-giving program? What could be cut from the budget to offset the new cost item?

Another question concerned the character of the work to be offered the unemployed. Some saw the program as a welcome opportunity to provide the population with more badly needed public services. Others approved of it as a means of providing more continuous and meaningful work to many individuals who otherwise might be consigned to dull, menial or casual labor. For this was an era when "job satisfaction" was receiving more attention as a valid social goal. "Leaf-raking"—that is, work of little value offered as a morally superior form of charity—tended to be deeply resented when offered to capable workers thrown off their jobs by the gyrations of an erratic economy. Nor did such jobs offer much of an opportunity for the chronically unemployed.

The root question, however, concerned the extent to which the government should be held responsible for assuring jobs for all who need and want them. A House subcommittee had promised to look into this question early in 1975.

Goals

Any renewed debate over a federal full employment policy that set as a goal an unemployment rate of 4 per cent or less was likely to run into opposition from the Ford administration. In its 1973 economic report, the Council of Economic Advisers said that the interim goal of 4 per cent aimed at in the Kennedy-Johnson years was "a less reliable guide to policy for the 1970s than for the 1960s" because of character changes in the labor force and prolonged inflation. "The policy goal is a condition in which persons who want work and seek it realistically on reasonable terms can find employment," the report said. "The government must make two kinds of contributions to the achievement of this goal. First, it must maintain reasonable stability in the over-all rate of economic growth so that the efforts of individuals to find work are not frustrated by erratic changes in the conditions on which work is available. Second, it must seek to eliminate obstacles that prevent willing workers and willing employers from getting together, insofar as these obstacles can be overcome without excessive cost."

Based on that definition, the council in its 1974 report said that "maximum employment" was approximately reached in 1973, even though the unemployment rate stood at 4.9 per cent.

Arguing that it was callous to think that women and teenagers (who accounted for the major character changes in the labor force) had less important employment problems than adult males, and pointing out that the number of unemployed adult males had increased more than unemployment for either women or teenagers, the Joint Economic Committee in its 1973 report disagreed with the administration's policy.

"Given the employment-inflation trade-off that exists today, employment programs and structural reforms will hasten the return to 4 per cent unemployment," the committee said, "and are absolutely essential if we are to achieve our long run goal of no more than 3 per cent unemployed."

CASE STUDIES

CQ

U.S. BANKING SYSTEM: WORRIES ABOUT STABILITY

The stability of the U.S. banking system has been taken for granted for decades, since the banks recovered from the collapse of the 1930s. But concern about the system has been building up behind the scenes, and now the assumption of stability is being questioned openly. Among bankers and their critics, concern has centered on three broad areas: aggressive expansion of the banking system, which has resulted in questionable practices; monetary and credit restraint imposed by the Federal Reserve Board in its fight on inflation, which can expose flaws in bank practices that might otherwise be obscured by easy bank credit; and international monetary and financial instability, aggravated by the oil crisis.

Potential weaknesses, previously seen mainly by the experts, were brought to public attention in May by the disclosure that Franklin National Bank in New York had suffered large losses—later estimated at $46-million—in foreign exchange trading. Franklin National's financial position promptly began to crumble. On Dec. 31, 1973, it had ranked as the nation's 20th largest bank, with deposits of $3.732-billion. By June 30, 1974, it had dropped to 47th place, with deposits of $2.085-billion—a 39 per cent decline in just six months. Despite $1.7-billion in loans from the Federal Reserve Board, Franklin National collapsed Oct. 8 in the largest bank failure in U.S. history.[1]

Although banking leaders insisted Franklin's problems were isolated, the bank's well-publicized troubles sent tremors through the financial community and shook the public confidence on which the banking system depends. Jittery money markets were swept by rumors that other banks and businesses were bordering on failure, reviving memories of widespread bank closings, financial collapse and economic depression in the 1930s.

Confidence in the financial system suffered another blow June 26 when one of West Germany's largest private banks, Bankhaus I. D. Herstatt, was forced into liquidation, also because of foreign exchange losses. Herstatt was the first big institution known to have collapsed because of foreign exchange trading since major currencies were set free to float in response to market conditions more than a year earlier. Its failure disrupted international markets and involved losses for other banks and businesses. Morgan Guaranty Trust Co. of New York said it might lose as much as $13-million because of dealings with Herstatt, while Seattle-First National Bank said its Zurich subsidiary stood to lose $22.5-million.

Although Karl Klasen, head of the West German central bank, said that "comparisons with the world monetary crisis of 1931 are completely false," Herstatt's failure heightened fears of domino-like bank failures. Richard F. Janssen wrote in *The Wall Street Journal,* June 17, "Investments and debts have become so successfully internationalized—and confidence is such a volatile international commodity—that sober and senior financial men can be heard worrying that the planet could be plunged into depression if any of the dominoes tilts too far."

Federal Reserve Chairman Arthur F. Burns defended the basic soundness of the American banking system in an Oct. 21 address before the annual convention of the American Bankers Association in Honolulu. Burns cited as major sources of banking strength the safeguards built into the financial system after the 1929 crash and the Fed's willingness to lend money to banks that are temporarily squeezed for funds. *(Banking reform, p. 25)*

While noting "several disturbing trends in modern banking"—including excessive foreign exchange trading by some banks—Burns insisted that "only a very small number of banks can be justly described as being in trouble. Despite all the strains recently experienced in credit markets, the banking system remains strong and sound." Burns cautioned, however, that faith in the banking system "now rests unduly on the fact that troubled banks can turn to a governmental lender of last resort," whereas "the basic strength of the banking system should rest on the resources of individual banks."

Tightening Money Supply

The Federal Reserve Board's tight money policy has imposed severe strains on the rapidly expanding American banking system. The Fed, the nation's money manager, has tried to restrain excessive expansion of money and credit, which it views as a major factor in the current "double-digit" inflation.[2] Fed action has raised interest rates and squeezed financial liquidity—the ability of banks and other businesses to raise short-term funds. But the Fed has assured that it will not permit a credit crunch or liquidity crisis to develop that would destroy the ability of sound banks and other institutions to raise money to meet their obligations. "We will always respect our obligation of being a lender of last resort," Burns said April 22. That commitment was underscored a month later when the Federal Reserve stepped in with huge loans to shore up Franklin National.

The Fed has resolved, however, that it will not allow high interest rates and financial jitters to deflect its tight money policy, merely to avoid some painful dislocations. While recognizing that severe, widespread distress would compel it to relent, the Fed feels it must take some risks to curb inflation. Burns warned on May 26 that "the future of our country is in jeopardy" because of inflation. "One essential ingredient in the fight against inflation is continued resistance to swift growth in money and credit," he said in a commencement address at Illinois College, Jacksonville, Ill. "The Federal Reserve System, I assure you, is firmly committed to this task. We intend to encourage sufficient growth in supplies of money and credit to finance orderly economic expansion. But we are not going to be a willing party to the accommodation of rampant inflation."

Burns conceded that the Fed policy would result in high interest rates, particularly on short-term loans. "Troublesome though this rise in interest rates may be, it must for a time be tolerated," he said. Since late in 1972, the Fed has attempted to limit monetary growth by tightening bank reserves and raising interest rates.[3] Open market operations—buying or selling government securities in the open market—are the Fed's most important policy tool. Selling government securities has the effect of decreasing reserves and lendable funds of commercial banks by several times the actual value of the securities sold, while buying securities causes a corresponding increase in reserves and over-all money and credit.

Through much of 1973, open market operations were directed at restraining the growth of bank reserves and the money supply. This policy eased slightly as the growth in money and credit slowed toward the end of 1973, then became more restrictive early in 1974 as business demands for credit grew faster than expected and the money supply surged. The impact of the Fed's open market operations has been reflected in the federal funds rate—the cost of excess reserves lent by one bank to another. After declining moderately since October 1973, the funds rate began to climb in February and by mid-June was hitting record highs.

Successive increases in the discount rate—the rate of interest commercial banks pay when they borrow from Federal Reserve Banks—have reinforced the open market operations. Changes in the discount rate frequently are used to signal the direction of monetary policy. Restrictive open market operations and discount rate increases, in the face of strong demand for credit, have raised interest rates across the board. The impact has been most direct on short-term credit, including the prime rate—the interest that commercial banks charge their best business customers. The discount rate was increased in stages from 4½ per cent at the end of 1972 to an unprecedented 8 per cent in April 1974; meanwhile the prime rate soared from 5¾ per cent to a record 12 per cent on July 3.

The Fed has supplemented the general pattern of tightening with several selective increases in bank reserve

Largest Banks in U.S.

Position	Deposits* (billions)
1. Bank of America, San Francisco	$41.844
2. First National City Bank, New York	34.950
3. Chase Manhattan Bank of New York	29.818
4. Manufacturers Hanover Trust Co., New York	16.977
5. Morgan Guaranty Trust Co., New York	15.367
6. Chemical Bank, New York	14.225
7. Bankers Trust Co., New York	14.022
8. Continental Illinois Co., Chicago	12.366
9. First National Bank, Chicago	12.083
10. Security Pacific National Bank, Los Angeles	11.403
11. Wells Fargo Bank, San Francisco	9.034
12. Crocker National Bank, San Francisco	8.016
13. Mellon Bank, Pittsburgh	7.350
14. Irving Trust Co., New York	6.970
15. United California Bank, Los Angeles	6.855
16. Marine Midland Bank, New York	6.655
17. First National Bank, Boston	6.103
18. National Bank of Detroit	5.523
19. First Pennsylvania Banking & Trust Co., Philadelphia	3.926
20. Franklin National Bank, New York	3.732

As of Dec. 31, 1973
SOURCE: American Banker

requirements—the ratio of cash reserves which member banks must keep in relation to deposits. Reserve requirements have the effect of making a portion of a bank's funds unavailable for loans. In addition to raising reserve requirements on most demand deposits (checking accounts), the Fed raised reserve requirements on increased amounts of large certificates of deposit (CDs). CDs are sold to corporations and other investors with excess cash to deposit for fixed periods of time. CD money has become a major source of bank funds for relending, especially to business borrowers.

Effect of High Interest Rates

By curtailing the availability of money and raising interest rates, Fed policies have made it difficult and costly for banks to obtain funds to meet loan demand. In recent years banks have relied increasingly on short-term borrowing as a supplement to conventional deposits to support their lending and investment, chiefly through borrowing in

> *"We will always respect our obligation of being a lender of last resort."*
> —Federal Reserve Chairman Arthur F. Burns

the federal funds market, through sales of short-term CDs in amounts of $100,000 or more and through borrowing of dollar-denominated deposits in banks abroad (Eurodollars). As these borrowings mature, they must be "rolled over"—extended or refinanced with new borrowing. Rising interest rates mean that banks must pay more to attract money and charge more on loans. In the week ending July 10, banks were paying an average of 13.34 per cent for federal funds and 13.80 per cent for 90-day Eurodollar borrowing. The secondary market rate for CDs was 12.30. By comparison, the Treasury was paying 7.58 per cent on its short-term bills, considered the safest haven for money. (Short-term interest rates declined from their mid-summer highs as the Fed eased monetary restraints slightly and credit demands slackened in the fall of 1974.)

Shaken confidence in the banking system has made it difficult for some banks to roll over their borrowings, even at high interest rates. Franklin National, for example, was forced to borrow at the Fed's "discount window" after its problems were made public because it could no longer raise short-term funds in the money market—even though the U.S. Comptroller of the Currency repeatedly assured that the bank was solvent, with assets sufficient to meet liabilities.

Large corporations with excess cash to invest appear to be doubtful about the CD market, especially in the wake of the Franklin National disclosures. One result, according to a June 8 report in *Business Week* magazine, has been the emergence of a two-tier market in commercial bank CDs. Corporation treasurers "seem perfectly willing to keep buying the CDs of the dozen or so very biggest banks," the magazine said. "But smaller banks—especially a couple of dozen regional institutions that have experienced super-fast growth in recent years—are finding they must pay a premium to sell their CDs."[4] Deteriorating confidence also has hurt the market for commercial paper—IOUs by which corporations borrow from each other as an alternative to borrowing from banks. Companies lacking prime credit ratings find it difficult to sell commercial paper, and so are compelled to increase bank borrowing. This increase in demand for bank loans intensifies the pressure on banks to raise funds through the sale of CDs.

Banking problems go beyond difficulties in borrowing. High interest rates have depressed the market value of bank investment portfolios. They also have caused an outflow of savings deposits from commercial banks and thrift institutions—savings and loan associations and mutual savings banks—as depositors transfer their savings into higher-yield market instruments. Banks and thrift institutions are "intermediaries" between savers and borrowers. The outflow of savings and their direct investment in the money market bypasses the intermediaries; savers lend directly to borrowers. This process, called "disintermediation," has hit thrift institutions particularly hard, and their loss of deposits has forced them to curtail home mortgage lending.[5] Financial experts warn that some institutions may go under unless competitive market interest rates come down; that could be a catastrophe for the depressed housing market.

Concern Over Lending Practices

The financial community is concerned that many banks, in their rush to expand, may have overreached themselves. One cause of uneasiness is the fear that lending practices have become too loose, leading banks to take on too many risky loans. Commercial bank loan losses increased sharply in 1973, according to a survey by Robert Morris Associates, the national association of bank loan officers. The survey, convering 473 banks that account for about 65 per cent of all U.S. commercial bank business loans, showed the banks wrote off as net losses an average of $26 for each $10,000 of business loans in their portfolios—a 24 per cent increase over 1972. Since recessionary tendencies in the economy make bank loans more vulnerable to default, there is little likelihood for improvement this year.

Increased reliance on short-term borrowing poses risks for the banks. When they lend short-term deposits to long-term borrowers, they must roll over the deposits. They can get into trouble if the short-term money is withdrawn or stops coming in—because of difficulties in selling CDs, for example—or if the rates they must pay to borrow money exceed the fixed yields on their long-term loans. Savings and loan associations, which have most of their money locked up in long-term mortgages, are more vulnerable to this problem than commercial banks.

Borrowing short and lending long also has international ramifications. Banks that form the vast "Eurocurrency" market—currencies circulating outside their native countries—were expected to serve as the principal mechanism for "recycling" Arab oil money to nations with large balance-of-payments deficits. But the tendency of Arab oil countries to deposit their money in European banks at very short term has strained the system. Secretary of the Treasury William E. Simon said in a Voice of America radio interview on June 19 that some banks in the international financial markets were refusing further short-term deposits from the oil-exporting countries and that others were paying interest rates on these deposits 2 or 3 percentage points below the prevailing rate for Eurodollar deposits. Simon called this "proper and prudent" banking practice, which he said would induce oil countries to invest at longer term.

The Euromarket is complex, and the Arabs are not the only investors who are apprehensive. The market has grown very fast in recent years, but its dimensions can only be estimated. The Bank for International Settlements has estimated that on a net basis the market's outstanding volume of foreign currency credit increased from about $105-billion at the end of 1972 to $155-billion at the end of 1973 and to about $170-billion at the end of the first quarter of 1974. The market operates largely beyond the control of regulatory authorities and central banks, and a major failure could trigger an international crisis. "Many of the fears about the Euromarket have been based on the fact that there is no international 'lender of last resort' to rescue a bank" that runs into trouble, Charles N. Stabler, banking editor of *The Wall Street Journal*, wrote June 28. "But such fears are probably overdone." He reasons that central banks would come to the rescue if disaster threatened.

Underlying the concern about bank lending practices is the question of capital adequacy. Brenton C. Leavitt, program director of the Fed's section on banking structure, said earlier this year that total assets of all commercial banks had almost trebled since 1960, increasing from about $253-billion to $888-billion in September 1973. "At the same time equity capital plus reserves for loan and security losses expanded only half as fast, resulting in a decline in the ratio of capital to total assets from 9.0 in 1960 to 7.1 in September of 1973, and a decline in capital to risk assets from 17 per cent to 8.6 per cent. For the largest banks the decline has been even more dramatic."[6] Loans and investments are the major assets of banks. Leavitt was questioning whether banks, aggressively building up their income-earning assets, have sufficient capital to cushion potential losses. The risks may be heightened by the growing reliance of banks on CDs and other relatively unstable sources of funds.

Signaling its determination to stop bank over-expansion and instill more caution in bankers, the Federal Reserve Board on June 19 rejected the bid of BankAmerica Corp.—parent holding company of Bank of America, the nation's largest bank—to join with Allstate Insurance Co. to establish a general insurance underwriting firm in Switzerland. The Fed said the capital position of the applicant was "somewhat lower" than what the board considered appropriate in view of recent growth in the holding company's assets.

Some bankers also urged caution. "I cannot recall a time when I have heard so much discussion of capital adequacy in relation to the volume of credit extended and the risks assumed," Guy E. Noyes, senior vice president and economist of Morgan Guaranty Trust, said June 6. Addressing the annual meeting of the D.C. Bankers Association, Noyes said public and regulatory agency concerns about the stability of financial institutions should make banks follow a conservative approach toward expansion. Otherwise, he said, the regulators could be expected to "impose more specific and rigid regulations on bank lending and on bank liability management."[7]

Expansion Since World War II

Following the depression of the 1930s, "somehow the impression gained favor that the true business of banking was to accept deposits—rather passively at that—and to concentrate on the direct extension of credit to borrowers, usually business borrowers and usually on a short-term basis."[8] Although rapid economic growth in the period after World War II led to increasing demands for financial services, bankers were slow to take advantage of their new opportunities.

The turning point came in the mid-1950s when the excess liquidity built into the financial system during the war was absorbed and banks were forced into competition for funds for the first time since the late 1920s. Banking lost its conservative image as an aggressive new generation of bank managers sought ways to expand services and develop new sources of funds. Banking expanded rapidly to meet the needs of an increasingly affluent society. Meanwhile, technological advances revolutionized banking operations and made it possible for banks to venture beyond the narrow confines of traditional banking. Bankers predicted the emergence of a "cashless-checkless" society.[9]

Perhaps the most visible aspect of postwar banking expansion has been the growth of branch banking. Nearly 2,000 new branches were opened in 1973 alone. As recently as 1963 the number of branches was about equal to the number of banks in the United States. By the end of 1973, there were 14,172 commercial banks and 26,251 branches.[10] Conveniently located branch offices are one key to a bank's ability to tap the funds of small depositors, but laws in most states impede branch banking. Branching is not just a matter of organizational form, according to banking analyst Carter H. Golembe. "It has emotional overtones with roots to be found in ancient fears over large aggregations of banking power and the loss of states' rights."[11]

After a controversy over branch banking in the 1920s, Congress set policy guidelines in the Banking (Glass-Steagall) Act of 1933. The law prohibited the expansion of banks across state lines but left the determination of intrastate branching policy to the states themselves. The result was a hodgepodge of legislation, ranging from outright prohibition of branching in some states to unrestricted branching in others. Many state legislatures recently have eased restrictions on branch banking. New York, for example, will permit statewide branch banking to begin in 1976. First National City Corp. (Citicorp) and other giant bank holding companies are scrambling to acquire small upstate and suburban banks so that they will have a foothold in new markets.[12] Although the big banks say their presence will bring increased competition, lower costs and more sophisticated banking services, there is come concern that statewide branching will lead to undue concentration.

Fundamental Change

The explosive growth of bank holding companies[13] in the past two decades has fundamentally changed the American banking system. Multi-bank holding companies began to multiply in the early 1950s. In an effort to prevent the growth of potential banking monopolies, Congress passed the Bank Holding Company Act of 1956. The act brought multi-bank holding companies under federal regulation and prohibited such companies from managing or controlling non-banking businesses. The prohibition did not apply, however, to holding companies that controlled only one bank. The exemption was made primarily to accommodate the 117 small one-bank holding companies that already existed.

Major banks that wanted to reach into activities not permitted to them as banks discovered the one-bank exemption in the late 1960s. The first of the giants to transform itself into a one-bank holding company was First National City Bank (Citibank), in 1968. Following Citibank's lead, hundreds of other banks, mostly large in size, organized one-bank holding companies that would permit them to expand geographically and provide a greater variety of services.

"[Opposition to branch banking] has...roots to be found in ancient fears over large aggregations of banking power and loss of states' rights."

—Carter H. Golembe

Many holding companies were set up by banks, which became the dominant or sometimes only subsidiary. However, some holding companies were established by major non-bank corporations, such as Macy's department stores and the Goodyear Tire & Rubber Co. They acquired banks as junior subsidiaries. By the end of 1970 there were 1,352 one-bank holding companies throughout the United States. They accounted for 38 per cent of the nation's commercial bank deposits and, because of their unregulated status, operated in every major sector of the economy. There also were 121 multi-bank holding companies, operating 895 banks that held one-sixth of all commercial bank deposits.[14]

Congress closed the one-bank loophole in the 1970 amendments to the Bank Holding Company Act.[15] The 1970 legislation brought one-bank holding companies under federal regulation and gave the Federal Reserve Board responsibility for deciding what activities were permissible for them to engage in. The law stipulated that an activity must be "so closely related to banking or managing or controlling banks as to be a proper incident thereto." It also provided a means to force bank holding companies to divest themselves of non-banking activities.

Bank holding companies have continued to expand under the 1970 law. Fed regulations have permitted them to engage in a growing list of activities—ranging from data processing and equipment leasing services to mortgage banking, consumer financing and investment management. By the end of 1973 the number of bank holding companies had grown to 1,677. They controlled 3,097 of the nation's commercial banks, with $446.6-billion—or 65.4 per cent—of all commercial bank deposits. Bank holding companies accounted for 95.4 per cent of all commercial bank deposits in Rhode Island, 93.3 per cent in California and 90.3 per cent in New York, the states with the highest concentrations.[16]

Critics of the bank holding company movement are uneasy about the risks of concentration and possible loss of competition in the financial system. They also fear that bank managers might neglect the public's interest in their pursuit of holding company profits. The Fed is concerned about the capital adequacy of subsidiary banks. Others question whether the holding companies will be able to handle their expanded domains.[17] One example of a holding company that apparently could not was Beverly Hills Bancorp, which recently went bankrupt as a result of shaky real estate transactions. Although its banking subsidiary, Beverly Hills National Bank, was solvent, the bank's assets were sold to Wells Fargo Bank in January after depositors withdrew $30-million in a few days.[18]

International Banking

The rapid expansion of international banking has transformed major commercial banks into multinational enterprises. American banks first moved into foreign operations to serve their corporate customers who were going abroad. In the 1960s these banks began to develop the gigantic Eurocurrency markets, using the funds generated both to support their own domestic banking business and to finance multinational business. U.S. banks now operate more than 700 foreign branches with total assets of more than $100-billion. Major U.S. banks also operate abroad through various affiliates engaged in leasing, factoring, investment banking, money market operations, wholesale and retail financing and other activities. With the biggest international business of any U.S. bank, Citibank derives more than half of its income from its international operations.

Although Europe is the most important arena for multinational banking, U.S. banks also are moving into other areas. At the close of 1973, 125 member banks of the Federal Reserve System operated branches in 76 foreign countries and overseas areas of the United States. U.S. banks operate widely throughout Latin America, and are expanding their operations in the Middle East. Meanwhile, foreign banks have rapidly expanded in the United States. More than 60 foreign banks maintain some banking facilities in this country and they have total assets of about $40-billion. Most are multinational giants: 90 per cent of those foreign banks that have total deposits of over $10-

New Deal Reform

Many banks that had been sound before the 1929 crash were weakened to the point of bankruptcy in the years that followed. One of Franklin D. Roosevelt's first acts after becoming President on March 4, 1933, was to declare a national bank holiday to give breathing space to rescue the collapsing system. The Emergency Banking Act of 1933, pushed through Congress and signed by the President in a single day (March 9), marked the beginning of various moves to strengthen the banking system. Among other things, the emergency law provided for reorganization of closed banks, instituted stringent control over the gold supply and over Federal Reserve member banks, and authorized expansion of Federal Reserve credit and loans.

Psychologically, at least, the most important banking reform of the New Deal era was federal insurance of bank deposits, instituted under the Banking (Glass-Steagall) Act of 1933, passed three months later. The Federal Deposit Insurance Corp., established on a temporary basis by that law, was made permanent by the Banking Act of 1935. To qualify for insurance, the banks had to meet certain standards concerning capital structure, earnings prospects and general character of management, and they had to pay an assessment to the FDIC for its reserve fund.

(Today the FDIC covers deposits in nearly 99 per cent of the nation's commercial banks and slightly over two-thirds of the nation's mutual savings banks. Congress in 1974 boosted the ceiling on federal insurance of private bank deposits to $40,000 from $20,000.)

Other New Deal banking reforms were no less significant. To prevent cutthroat competition among banks, the Glass-Steagall Act provided that commercial banks should no longer pay interest on their demand deposits. Another provision of the law effected a separation of investment from commercial banking by forcing commercial banks to divest themselves of affiliated investment companies within one year.

In 1934, Congress established the Securities and Exchange Commission to license stock exchanges and require registration with SEC of securities listed on the exchanges. The new act also gave the Federal Reserve Board authority to impose margin requirements on stock purchases. The Banking Act of 1935 reorganized the Federal Reserve System and reemphasized its power, first granted in 1933, to adjust reserve requirements of member banks. The Federal Open Market Committee, composed of the seven members of the Board of Governors and presidents of five of the 12 Federal Reserve Banks, was created to establish policy for the buying and selling of government securities for the entire system.

billion maintain banking offices in the United States. The 64th largest bank in the United States at the end of 1973 was Bank of Tokyo Trust Co., New York—up from 100th place in 1972.

The growth of multinational banking has created regulatory problems. Banks in many countries have broader powers than have been granted to banks within the United States. To increase the competitive effectiveness of

American banks abroad, the Fed has permitted them to engage in a wider range of activities than is permissible under domestic law. Foreign banks operating in the United States are subject to a complicated web of state and federal regulations, but in some cases enjoy regulatory advantages over their domestic rivals. Federal Reserve Vice Chairman George W. Mitchell, chairman of a Fed task force on international banking regulation, thinks a uniform regulatory framework is a long way off. In the interim he has proposed that foreign banks be made subject to the regulations of the host country.[19]

Sources of Borrowing

As recently as the late 1950s, demand deposits —traditionally the major source of bank funds—were twice as large in dollar volume as interest-bearing time and savings deposits. But growth of deposits at major banks lagged in the 1950s as corporation treasurers and other large investors learned how to limit holdings of idle cash and put their money into interest-earning Treasury bills and other securities. Banks could not compete effectively for these funds, partly because of interest rate constraints and reserve requirements. They also did not meet the need of corporations for interest-bearing money instruments that could be converted into cash quickly.

Then banks discovered they could profitably "buy" money to expand their limited lending capacity to meet strong credit demands. In 1961 Citibank pioneered a new kind of time deposit, the negotiable certificate of deposit. The purchaser of a CD, typically a corporation, deposited the money for a fixed period. However, the negotiable feature permitted him to sell the CD on the market to another investor if cash was needed before the CD came due. The idea caught on and by August 1966 CD volume reached $18.5-billion.

When interest rate ceilings on CDs were held below market rates during tight money periods in 1966 and 1969, money market banks stepped up their Eurodollar borrowing to compensate for the reduced lending capacity caused by CD runoff. Since Eurodollar liabilities are not subject to interest rate ceilings—and until September 1969 were not subject to reserve requirements—banks had flexibility to obtain funds through their foreign branches. When interest rates dropped in the United States and the domestic need for Eurodollars declined, overseas use of Eurodollars expanded. As monetary policy tightened during 1973, American banks began to increase their Eurodollar borrowings again. But the suspension of interest rate ceilings on all large CDs in May 1973 permitted U.S. banks to compete for domestic deposits in a way previously prohibited, thus easing the scramble for Eurodollars.[20]

"It [the banking system]... responds to changes in monetary policy with overt spasms...."

—*Treasury Secretary William Simon*

In addition to tapping corporate treasuries by selling CDs and borrowing Eurodollars, banks have utilized the banking system's lending capacity more fully through greatly increased borrowing of federal funds—reserves that otherwise would lie idle. Although federal funds, CDs and Eurodollars have remained the standbys, U.S. banks also have developed other sources of money to meet loan demand, such as sales of loans under repurchase agreements and the issuance of commercial paper by their holding companies.

And the search for new sources of funds goes on. Citicorp announced in June that it planned to seek $850-million from the public by offering 15-year notes paying a floating interest rate pegged one percentage point above average rates of three-month Treasury bills. The floating rate, the relatively small denominations and the feature allowing early redemption at full face value were designed to attract money from ordinary savers. Thrift institutions fought the offering, contending it was an evasion of interest rate ceilings on small deposits. Responding to their pleas, Congress later in the year enacted legislation that gave bank regulatory agencies authority to clamp interest rate ceilings on such obligations.

Outlook

Current strains in the banking system may not be the harbinger of financial collapse, but in the view of many experts they point to the need for substantial reforms. "Our financial system, like any system which has not been updated, needs to be brought into the 20th century," Treasury Secretary Simon told a Senate subcommittee May 13. "It is a system which responds to changes in monetary policy with overt spasms, to the detriment of both savers and borrowers." Others, like Sen. William Proxmire (D Wis.), think the banking system has failed to serve the needs of society in such areas as home financing and inner-city development.

Proxmire, prospective chairman of the Senate Banking, Housing and Urban Affairs Committee in the next Congress,[21] has described the American banking system as "the most competitive and innovative" in the world. Nonetheless, he said in a Senate speech on June 6, "there is very great room for improvement." Many bankers fear that Proxmire may join with Rep. Wright Patman (D Texas), chairman of the House Banking and Currency Committee, a long-time critic of banks, to promote legislation inimical to the industry.

The Nixon administration had its own plan for improving the banking system, which would involve greater reliance on market determination of the cost and availability of credit. The administration claimed its proposals would remove causes of rigidity and instability in the nation's financial institutions, create a more efficient and competitive financial system and promote adequate funds for consumer needs, including mortgage credit. The proposals were based on a 1971 report of the President's Commission on Financial Structure and Regulation, headed by Reed O. Hunt, retired board chairman of Crown Zellerbach Corp. They were presented to Congress in 1973 and endorsed by President Ford Oct. 8, 1974.

The proposals would eliminate many existing distinctions between commercial banks and thrift institutions. Banks would be able to offer negotiable order of withdrawal (NOW) accounts to all depositors and savings accounts to corporations. Federally chartered thrift institutions would be able to provide demand deposits, NOW accounts[22] and credit cards to all depositors and customers, and would be permitted to offer consumer, realty and construction loans in competition with banks. As reduced asset and liability restrictions enabled thrift institutions to compete more effectively for savings, ceiling rates on time deposits and preferential tax treatment for them would be eliminated. Housing finance would be strengthened by eliminating Federal Housing Administration and Veterans Administration interest ceilings.

Testifying in behalf of the administration proposals before the Senate Banking Subcommittee on Financial Institutions on May 13, Simon said the present stresses in the financial system "clearly demonstrate that it is now more important than ever for us to act. Although it might be easier to implement these changes during a period of economic and financial calm, we cannot wait for such a period to arrive. We must strengthen the system so that it can withstand the pressures whenever they arise, and we must do so as soon as possible."

Control of Corporation Stock

The extent to which stock holdings in large corporations are concentrated in the hands of bank trust departments is an issue of growing concern. Although banks generally are not permitted to hold stock for their own accounts, they have become major holders of common stock as trustees, and often have sole or partial voting rights over stock so held. Bank trust departments now manage $400-billion of other people's money and hold more than one-fifth of all corporate stocks and bonds. More than one-third of their total trust assets—about $150-billion—comes from employee pension and profit-sharing funds.[23]

Problems created by the growing stock holdings of banks and other financial institutions were the subject of a report on corporate ownership released by two Senate subcommittees in January.[24] Based on a survey of 89 large corporations, the study found a large concentration of stock holdings in a few big New York banks. The study found that Chase Manhattan held 2 per cent or more of the stock in 46 of the companies, Morgan Guaranty Trust in 29, Citibank in 28 and Bankers Trust Co. in 21. The study further showed that banks in many cases held a big chunk in two or more competing firms.

Such holdings raise obvious conflict-of-interest questions. Another potential conflict of interest involves interlocking directorships—bank officials serving as directors of other companies. There also is a potential conflict of interest in a bank serving as lender to the same corporations in which it holds stock. Although banks are required by law to maintain a separation between their trust departments and their commercial loan operations, critics question whether this "Chinese Wall" is as impregnable as bankers claim. A study group sponsored by consumer advocate Ralph Nader charged in a recent book that Citibank used billions of dollars in bank-managed trust funds primarily to benefit the bank, with little attention to the needs of its trust customers. The book also charged that Citibank made improper use of commercial banking files in making investment decisions.[25] Citibank Chairman Walter B. Wriston denied the charges.

The role of banks in the stock market also is a matter of concern, particularly the tendency of major banks to concentrate investments in relatively few big corporations—thereby making it difficult for many small companies to raise equity capital. "Contractual funds paid into pension plans now account for more than 75 per cent of the net new money going into the stock market," according to William Wolman, vice president of Argus Research Corp. "And since banks manage well over 75 per cent of all pension money, their trust departments have come to dominate the stock markets.[26]

"Must all of America's finance activities be concentrated in the banks of this country?"
—*James Needham, president of the New York Stock Exchange*

Additional federal regulations over bank investment practices are likely, but as yet there is no consensus on what they should be. The Senate subcommittees recommended that banks and other institutional investors be required to disclose more information about their holdings. The Comptroller of the Currency has proposed that officials of national banks be required to keep lists of their outside business interests and any links between those interests and the bank. The information would be available only to bank examiners, not the public.

Moving beyond disclosure, Chairman Patman of the House Banking Committee has urged that trust departments be completely separated from commercial banks. And a Senate Banking subcommittee is studying the role of banks in the securities market as part of a broad overhaul of the securities system. Meanwhile, a ruling issued by the Comptroller of the Currency on June 12 is expected to spur the entry of banks into the stock brokerage business. Comptroller James E. Smith reaffirmed a ruling of his predecessor that banks could offer their customers stock investment services through checking account deduction plans. The prospect alarms brokerage and mutual funds businesses. Sen. Edward W. Brooke (R Mass.) has introduced a bill to require banks offering the service to register as broker-dealers with the SEC.

Capital Shortage

The capital spending needs of the U.S. economy are growing rapidly, and many financial experts foresee a shortage of investment capital. In addition to increasing productive capacity, business will have to spend heavily in such areas as development of energy sources and pollution control. A study by the General Electric Co. indicates that the United States must spend $3.2-trillion, in terms of current dollars, on business fixed investment in the years 1974-85—triple the comparable figure for the preceding 12-year period.

The prospect of a capital shortage has stimulated demands for a system of allocating bank credit to meet the nation's priority needs. Former Federal Reserve Governor Andrew F. Brimmer has long advocated that bank reserve requirements be based on asset structure—that is, on bank lending—instead of deposits. He thinks the Fed should be permitted to vary asset reserve requirements to avoid unwanted effects of monetary restraint in particular sectors of the economy and to keep bank lending practices in line with the objectives of monetary policy.

In line with Brimmer's proposal, Rep. Henry S. Reuss (D Wis.) recently introduced a bill to give the Federal Reserve Board power to allocate credit by requiring banks to set aside additional reserves whenever they made loans

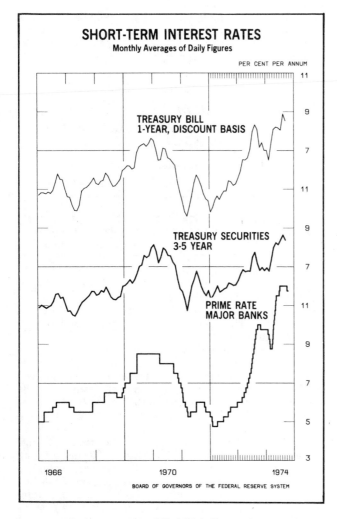

SHORT-TERM INTEREST RATES
Monthly Averages of Daily Figures

PER CENT PER ANNUM

TREASURY BILL
1-YEAR, DISCOUNT BASIS

TREASURY SECURITIES
3-5 YEAR

PRIME RATE
MAJOR BANKS

1966   1970   1974

BOARD OF GOVERNORS OF THE FEDERAL RESERVE SYSTEM

for non-priority purposes. His bill defines priority areas as the following: (1) capital investments that increase productive capacity, lower costs, control pollution or conserve energy; (2) low- and middle-income housing; (3) state and local government investment; and (4) small businesses.

Financial criteria, not social goals, traditionally have determined bank loan and investment policy. But strong pressures are building to force bankers to reshape their aims. Because of the relative importance of bank resources in the economy, banks will be called upon to play a major part in meeting the nation's future social and economic requirements. Their ability to do so, however, is contingent on the success of current efforts to bring inflation under control without causing the nation's—and the world's—financial machinery to collapse. ∎

¹ Franklin's assets were taken over by the European-American Bank and Trust Company, owned by six large European banks. The second largest bank failure in the nation's history occurred less than a year earlier. The United States National Bank, San Diego, was declared insolvent Oct. 18, 1973. That failure involved questionable loans made to companies controlled by C. Arnholt Smith, the bank's controlling shareholder. Under an arrangement worked out by federal regulatory authorities, the San Diego bank's "clean assets" were taken over by Crocker National Bank.

² Consumer prices rose 12.1 per cent from September 1973 to September 1974.

³ For background on the monetary system, see *The Federal Reserve System: Purposes and Functions* (6th edition, 1974).

⁴ "The Bruising Cost of Banking," *Business Week*, June 8, 1974, p. 20.

⁵ Federal regulations attempt to control competition for time and savings deposits by setting interest rate ceilings on deposits below $100,000. To encourage a flow of deposits to mortgage lenders, regulatory authorities traditionally have given thrift institutions a competitive advantage over commercial banks by setting their rate ceilings a half point higher. But when ceilings were raised in 1973, in recognition of rising market rates, this differential generally was reduced to a quarter point.

⁶ Quoted in *Finance Magazine*, May 1974, p. 31. Leavitt also cited figures on the growth of short-term borrowed funds in the liabilities of banks. From mid-1965 to early 1974, he said, demand deposits fell from almost 55 per cent to less than 40 per cent of the liabilities of large commercial banks, while savings deposits fell from almost 25 per cent to less than 15 per cent. Meanwhile, large CDs grew from about 8 per cent of liabilities to over 15 per cent and borrowings from others (mostly federal funds) from 2 per cent to about 13 per cent.

⁷ Liabilities are bank obligations to repay money to depositors and those from whom the banks borrow. Banks must manage their liabilities so they can be repaid or refinanced, and so they provide an adequate source of funds for loan and investment commitments. For banks to earn a profit, the liabilities must be managed so their costs are covered by earnings from loans and investments.

⁸ Carter H. Golembe, "The Organization of Modern Banking," *The Changing World of Banking* (edited by Herbert V. Prochnow and Herbert V. Prochnow Jr., 1974), p. 24.

⁹ See "The New Banking," *Business Week*, Sept. 13, 1973, pp. 88-124.

¹⁰ Board of Governors of the Federal Reserve System, *60th Annual Report, 1973*, p. 298. By comparison, there were 30,000 banks in 1920 and only 1,281 branches.

¹¹ Carter H. Golembe, *op. cit.*, p. 19.

¹² The Justice Department has taken the position that big banks should expand into other cities by starting new branches or acquiring small banks, but not by merging with big ones. In a decision that could significantly affect antitrust regulation of bank mergers, the Supreme Court on June 26 approved the acquisition of the third largest bank in Spokane, Wash., by the second largest bank in the state. In a 5-3 decision in U.S. *v.* Marine Bancorporation, the Court rejected Justice Department arguments that the move would reduce potential competition in the area.

¹³ Holding companies are set up to own or control subsidiary companies. Bank holding companies include one or more banks among their subsidiaries, and some of them also have non-banking subsidiaries.

¹⁴ One-Bank Holding Companies Before the 1970 Amendments," *Federal Reserve Bulletin*, December 1972, pp. 999-1008.

¹⁵ Certain other exemptions from the 1956 act had been eliminated in 1966. For a summary of congressional action on bank holding company legislation, see Congressional Quarterly, *Congress and the Nation* Vol I (1945-64), pp. 448-449; Vol. II (1965-68), pp. 265-267; Vol. III (1969-72), pp. 139-141.

¹⁶ *Federal Reserve Bulletin*, June 1974, pp. A 80-83.

¹⁷ See H. Lee Silberman, "Bank Holding Companies: Pros and Cons of Controlled Conglomeration," *Finance Magazine*, May 1974, p. 29.

¹⁸ See "The Gang That Couldn't Bank Straight," *Forbes*, June 1, 1974, p. 17.

¹⁹ Speech at a conference on "New York as a World Financial Center," New York City, June 10, 1974.

²⁰ See Frank E. Morris, "The Role of the Eurodollar," *The Changing World of Banking* (1974), pp. 98-125.

²¹ Proxmire is in line to succeed the present chairman, John Sparkman (D Ala.), if Sparkman makes his expected switch to the chairmanship of the Foreign Relations Committee, succeeding J.W. Fulbright (D Ark.) who suffered a primary election defeat.

²² NOW accounts already are offered by mutual savings banks in Massachusetts and New Hampshire. Since the withdrawal order is negotiable, it can be used much like a check to transfer funds to a third party. Several New York savings banks recently introduced a similar plan, but under a law enacted by Congress in 1973 they are barred from paying interest on the accounts. New York's commercial bankers are challenging the legality of the service.

²³ "Trust-Busting?" *Forbes*, July 1, 1974, p. 54.

²⁴ *Disclosure of Corporate Ownership*, prepared by the Senate Government Operations Subcommittees on Intergovernmental Relations and Budgeting, Management and Expenditures.

²⁵ David Leinsdorf and Donald Etra, *Citibank: Ralph Nader's Study Group Report on First National City Bank* (1973).

²⁶ *The New York Times*, Oct. 7, 1973.

ECONOMIC SLUMP HITS ELDERLY ESPECIALLY HARD

Recession and inflation, the twin horrors of the current economic situation, are stirring new fears among those whose working years are nearing an end. The reason is that their prospect for a reasonably comfortable income in retirement—an expectation nurtured by maturation of the Social Security system, growth of private pension plans, and rising interest on savings—no longer seems quite so secure as in the immediate past.

While recent increases in Social Security benefits, partly tied to rises in the Consumer Price Index, help meet the inflation threat, payments to many beneficiaries are still no match for the cost of living.

There are other threats arising out of the over-all economic situation: the declining value of pension trust funds and personal holdings because of the stock market slump; rising unemployment which deprives pensioners of extra-income odd jobs and reduces payments into public and private pension funds; and the expected cutback of government expenditures for public services utilized by the elderly.

It is no wonder that the trend toward early retirement, which had been building up in recent years, has begun to slow down as older workers cling to their jobs as long as possible. On the other hand, where unemployment is most severe, the retiree on fixed income may be the most favored member of his community. An ironic situation may develop in which the meagerly but regularly paid pensioner will be helping to feed the young, able-bodied worker unable to find a job.

Even if the decline in economic activity should reach depression levels, the factor of retirement will make a vast difference between the current situation and that of previous depressions, as during the 1930s. For retirement as a status has become of great significance both in the personal lives of the people and the economic structure of the nation. Currently some 38 million Americans receive regular cash payments based on public retirement programs sponsored by the U.S. government. At least 1.5 million others receive regular payments under retirement systems for state employees.

Effect of Programs

The sizable segment of the nation's population in retirement status gives the elderly leverage to impress their needs on political and social policymakers. *(Box, p. 31)*

Economic questions concerning the aged have to do not just with the adequacy or inadequacy of their public benefits but the capacity of the nation to support, out of past savings and current income, a growing part of the citizenry that is economically non-productive. Many economists, for example, point out that Social Security benefits are made at the expense of low-wage earners.

Since 1950, Social Security benefits have increased as follows: Regular cost-of-living increases in Social Security

Effective	Per cent	Effective	Per cent
September 1952	12½	January 1970	15
September 1954	9	January 1971	10
January 1959	7	September 1972	20
January 1965	7	March 1974	7
February 1968	13	July 1974	4

benefits were mandated under 1972 legislation and were revised a year later. Under current provisions of law, an increase of 3 per cent or more in the Consumer Price Index from the first quarter of the year above the first quarter of the previous year will require an automatic increase in benefits. To support the increases in benefits, the Social Security tax and the amount of earnings on which it is based have risen several times in recent years, as is shown below:

Year	Annual maximum taxable earnings	Tax rate employer and employee, each	Tax rate, self-employed
1970	$ 7,800	4.8 %	6.9%
1971	7,800	5.2	7.5
1972	9,000	5.2	7.5
1973	10,800	5.85	8.0
1974	13,200	5.85	7.9
1975*	14,100	5.85	7.9

* Becomes effective Jan. 1.

For the retired individual, the big question is how much confidence he or she can have that the system will in fact provide economic security in old age. So far the public programs have held up very well, though at levels of benefits and coverage that have still left many old people in poverty. The private pension system, far less extensive since it is voluntary, has worked well for some but fallen down for others. Some but not all of the private pension system's failings were attended to when President Ford on Sept. 2 signed the Employee Retirement Income Security Act of 1974, popularly known as the pension reform bill. *(p. 31)*

Persistence of Aged Poverty

On the whole, the economic condition of retirees and their dependents or survivors has greatly improved over what it was in the past. However, despite a current annual expenditure of possibly $100-billion in public and private "transfer" funds—pensions, disability benefits, public assistance, etc.—for the support of the elderly, there remain millions of old people who live in poverty and neglect.

A Brookings Institution analysis of the federal budget shows that in the current fiscal year $86.8-billion is being spent by the government for cash income and maintenance programs directed entirely or in great measure to the benefit of the old and the retired of all ages. In addition $28.6-billion is being spent for "helping people buy essentials," as in housing and food-stamp programs. One-half of this sum ($14.2-billion) is the outlay for Medicare. Private pension systems add another increment; in 1970 the private pension outlay was $7.4-billion.

The growth of these expenditures—Social Security payments alone having risen from $11-billion in 1960 to $64.4-billion in 1975—obviously had much to do with the reduced incidence of true poverty among the elderly. According to the Brookings study, "the incidence of poverty was cut in half [during the 13-year period, 1959-1972], as the number of people over 65 rose and the number of *poor* old people declined [from 5.7 million to 3.7 million]." Among the millions who have been saved from poverty by these programs, however, are many retired persons engaged in a desperate struggle to keep from losing the minimal security and independence for which they have worked and saved during their economically productive years. The truism about the elderly today is that those who were poor before retirement are even poorer afterward, and many who were well-off before retirement became poor afterward.

The average monthly payment under Social Security for a retired worker in July 1974 was $186.71 and for a disabled worker $204.68. The most that a worker who retires in 1974 may get is only a shade over $300. The maximum for those who retired in earlier years is less because the monthly benefit is based on the average of annual pay on which a Social Security tax was paid. In earlier years the level of pay that was taxed was lower than it has been in more recent years. If the retired person is living with a dependent spouse, the benefit amount is increased by 50 per cent.

The insufficiency of the typical Social Security payment to meet the cost of living is indicated by hypothetical budgets developed by the Bureau of Labor Statistics for a retired urban couple. At last accounting, in the autumn of 1973, the bureau said average costs, excluding personal income taxes, amounted to $3,763 "at a lower level of living," $5,414 at an "intermediate level," and $8,043 at a "higher level." Since then the Consumer Price Index has risen about 12 per cent. Furthermore, these hypothetical couples are presumed to be in reasonably good health and able to care for themselves, which is not true of all the elderly.

Beneficiaries of Retirement Programs*

Programs	Retired and Disabled Workers	Survivors
Social Security*	23,106,000	7,163,000
Railroad retirement	655,000	335,000
Civil Service	943,000	371,000
Veterans	3,243,000	2,295,000
Subtotals	27,947,000	10,164,000
Total	**38,111,000**	

Statistics as of July 1974 except for Civil Service and veterans' survivors, which date from June 1974.
**Old-age Survivors and Disability Insurance*

SOURCE: Social Security Administration

Social Security

Obviously the success of the system relies on the retiree's possession of other resources. A Social Security Administration study of private pension plans indicated that approximately 15 per cent of all aged couples or single persons receiving Social Security payments were also deriving support from private pension plans. The sums available from that source tended to be smaller than from Social Security.

Generally speaking families that draw private pensions are better off than those that do not. Most of the private pension systems were in major and highly unionized industries where pay scales were relatively high and job security was strong. Beneficiaries therefore were favored not only by receiving the extra monthly check but by their relatively high Social Security payments based on their past earnings. These industries included manufacturing, transportation, communications and public utilities.

All studies of the economic condition of the older American point to the preponderant importance of the Social Security benefit in providing cash support for the retirement years. A government survey of the situation in 1967 indicated that Social Security benefits "were virtually the only source of retirement income...for more than one-half of the aged married couples getting benefits and nearly two-thirds of the non-married aged beneficiaries."

Another report based on data from this survey indicated that one-half of the married couples had less than $2,000 in assets and two-thirds of the single persons had less than $1,500. "Clearly a majority of the elderly could not have counted on much income from such savings," the report concluded. Home ownership was common, especially among the married couples, 77 per cent of whom owned at least an equity in their homes while four-fifths of the homeowning group had already paid off the mortgage. But many older persons lack the means to keep their homes in repair and they are often the victims of rising property taxes or deteriorating neighborhoods.

The black old person is more likely to be poor than his white counterpart. Special census surveys in 1972 indicated that 40 per cent of the 1.6 million blacks above age 65 were living in officially defined poverty, in contrast to 17 per cent of the 20.1 million whites in that age group. The blacks were less likely to have other assets or second pensions and their benefits under Social Security were lower because of lower earnings in their working years.

Impact of Inflation

The big obstacle to retirement security is inflation. The current inflation is described by the Federal Reserve Board as "the most severe and prolonged that the United States has experienced since the rise in prices following World War II." The 1973 rate of price increase was double that of 1972 and further acceleration of the rate occurred in 1974. The Consumer Price Index rose faster in the first 10 months of 1974 (10.6 per cent) than it did in the entire 12 months of 1973 (8.8 per cent).

Inflation has hurt the retired person and his family in more ways than one. The chief thrust, of course, is the rise in prices of basic necessities. Food, shelter, medical care and transportation account for at least four-fifths of old people's budgets at lower and moderate levels of living, according to the Bureau of Labor Statistics. Food prices in October 1974 were 11.9 per cent higher than 12 months earlier. Transportation costs were up 16.1 per cent, housing 13.5 per cent and medical care 11.2 per cent.

America's Retired Population

One American in every ten today has passed his or her 65th birthday, the standard milestone for retirement. The 1970 Census counted more than 20 million persons in this older age bracket. Not all were retired, however; some older persons were still at work. And a number of persons had retired before they reached 65—often at age 62 when many became eligible for reduced benefits.

The retirement period is likely to last a number of years. Men at age 65 may, statistically, look forward to 13.1 more years of life; women at 65 may look forward to 17.2 more years. When death occurs, cash benefits continue to flow to the surviving spouse and dependent children.

Of the 30.1 million persons now receiving Social Security benefits, 10.6 million are under 65. Most of these younger recipients are wives or widows of retired workers or they are dependent children or disabled offspring of the primary retiree. Some 3.7 million of the younger group are themselves retired or disabled, for which benefit claims may be made at any age if the disability is severe enough.

Inflation hurts in another way by the pressure it puts on governments to curtail social services. These services are often more vitally needed by the elderly than other persons. In terms of medical care, inflation hits the elderly not only in the purchase of medicines, eyeglasses, foot and dental care, and other cost items not covered by Medicare, but it has forced the government to increase the amount charged directly to the retiree for hospitalization and the amount charged to him or her for insurance against physician fees. Inflation also puts pressure on workers to fight for wage increases, a fight in which the blows fall ultimately on the person of fixed income. Such struggles may lead to strikes, depriving the public of accustomed services that are more essential to the older segment of the population than to others.

When transit workers struck in Los Angeles in October 1974, many persons in that automobile-oriented city managed to adjust to the deprivation reasonably well. But for the elderly, the loss of bus service was devastating. Many could not drive or did not own cars and lacked the strength to walk long distances to grocery stores, doctors' offices, churches and banks. Some of those who could walk the necessary distances were afraid of being attacked and robbed; slow-moving elderly persons are targets for muggers.

"Today's inflation is the prime breeder of misery among older Americans," Nelson H. Cruikshank, president of the National Council of Senior Citizens, told the "summit conference on inflation" in Washington, D.C., Sept. 19, 1974. The American Association of Retired Persons, in a joint statement with the National Retired Teachers Association, submitted to the conference a series of eloquent excerpts from correspondence of their members.

One couple referred to themselves as "an unfortunate generation," their work history having spanned the Depression Thirties when wages were low or non-existent, World War II when salaries were frozen and mobility of workers restricted, and the period of institution of pension plans in the late 1950s when they were too old to be included. Their

claims on both public and private pension systems were therefore minimal. Others wrote of their careful planning and saving during their working years only to find "our carefully laid plans for an enjoyable and independent old age are being sabotaged by...cruel inflation."

The economic handicaps of the retirees are somewhat modified by various benefits granted senior citizens, usually available to them when they reach age 65. These include an additional personal exemption on the federal income tax, reduced fares on many transit systems during non-rush hours, discounts on tickets for shows and concerts, and various social services such as home-delivered meals, free transportation and visiting nurse services. The development of these programs has been encouraged by the availability of federal funds for this purpose, dating from the establishment of a federal agency, the Administration on Aging, under the Older Americans Act of 1965. These programs were expanded by Older Americans Comprehensive Services Amendments of 1973.

A majority of the states now provide some property tax relief to homeowners and renters among older or low-income persons. California, Colorado, Connecticut, Georgia, Iowa, Kansas, Michigan, Missouri, Nebraska, South Dakota, Virginia and Wisconsin are among the states that have adopted some form of "homestead tax relief" or have liberalized previous enactments to this effect. A bill introduced in Congress by Sens. Edmund S. Muskie (D Maine) and Charles H. Percy (R Ill.) would provide federal reimbursement to states for one-half of the property tax relief offered low-income homeowners and renters.

Growth of Pensions

Pensions originated many centuries ago as personal grants by royalty to favored individuals. The choice of beneficiary was arbitrary. Those favored might be ex-ministers or ex-mistresses, and the amounts given were equally subject to royal whim.

Formal pension systems were first instituted for ex-soldiers, then extended to other public employees. The practice of establishing private pension funds, supported by employer and employee, began to take hold during the latter part of the 19th century. Almost from the start, the principle prevailed that employees as well as employers should contribute to systems that promised to provide for workers in their old age.

A corollary of this principle was that the pension benefit was no longer to be viewed as a beneficience bestowed by the mighty or the worthy, but a deferred wage to which an aged or disabled worker was entitled as a matter of right after a lengthy period of service. Employers were induced to accept the obligation to contribute to these plans on the theory that workers would accept a lower wage and remain with the same firm, despite tempting offers from other places of work, in order to qualify for the retirement benefit. The pension thus came to be regarded as a contractual obligation.

As time went on, greater emphasis came to be placed on attainment of a certain age. However, length of service continued to bear on the amount due a worker on retirement. As pension systems grew, the need for sounder financing became apparent and this led to the introduction of actuarial expertise in devising the financial structure of the systems.

Social Security System

The first major public system of social insurance against old age dependency was introduced in Germany in 1889. Other nations of Europe soon followed suit. The United States was one of the last of the modern industrial nations to introduce such a plan. Twenty-seven other countries already had established retirement systems.

From the beginning of social insurance in the United States, a double motive prevailed—that of alleviating poverty and of replacing earned but withheld income. It is significant that the federal social insurance system and the public assistance system were born in the same piece of legislation—the Social Security Act of 1935. The need for both programs had long been apparent, but it was the magnitude of the economic crisis of the 1930s that compelled Congress to authorize so radical a turnabout of social policy. The practical necessity at that time was to create purchasing power for millions who were unable to obtain the barest necessities of life.

The 1935 act created three new systems: (1) retirement insurance for persons presumed too old to work, (2) unemployment insurance for those temporarily unable to find work, and (3) public assistance for the poor who, for reasons beyond their control (disability, infirmities of old age, blindness, responsibility for the care of young children) were unable to seek work.

Social Security began almost solely as an insurance system and it still retains many features of such a system. The 1935 act required that employer and employee in commerce and industry pay 1 per cent each on the first $3,000 of the worker's wages. The money was placed in a trust fund from which future benefits to retirees would be drawn. The system was given until 1942 to accumulate enough to begin paying out benefits. It was not long, however, before Congress began to amend the act in order to extend benefits on the basis of social need rather than merely earned right.

Changes Since 1935

The first cluster of amendments, adopted in 1939, made the first benefits payable in 1940, revised the benefit formula to increase minimum payments, and made certain dependents of retired workers and survivors of deceased workers eligible for benefits too. The 1939 amendments also established the principle of a minimum income for aged retirees; payments were to be based on the average monthly wage rather than on the size of the accumulated wage during a lifetime. The result, according to a Brookings Institution study, was that "the principle of individual equity was severely modified...to attain other welfare-oriented goals."

The "social adequacy" principle gained emphasis as the amendments piled up over the years. Coverage was extended until the system became all but universal. Benefits, tax rates and the taxable pay base were raised repeatedly. Most significantly, benefits were made available to numerous beneficiaries on the basis of social need rather than on their past contributions to the system.

An amendment adopted in 1950 not only extended coverage to additional categories of workers, but made it possible for workers who were to retire in 1954 to qualify for full benefits after only 1½ years of covered employment.

Benefits were extended to the disabled at age 50 in 1956, to the dependents of the disabled in 1958, and to all disabled persons regardless of age in 1960. Meanwhile, in recognition of the inadequacy of earned benefits to meet the cost of living, the retirement test—meaning the amount of money a retired person may earn before forfeiting at least part of his retirement benefit—was liberalized step by step. The original act provided benefits only to persons who received no earnings at all. The 1939 act permitted earnings up to $15 a month without loss of benefits. Beginning on Jan. 31, 1975, earnings up to $2520 a year or $210 a month will be permitted before the retiree forfeits $1 of each $2 above those limits.

When the Social Security Act was adopted, it was hoped that as the social insurance system matured, the need for public assistance for the aged would shrink to a residual few. Instead, the numbers on Old-age Assistance rolls grew. This situation has been attributed to the inadequacy of Social Security benefits despite the increases, to inflation and to shrinking earnings of older workers in an era of technological change. By early 1953, some 2.7 million old people were receiving welfare cash benefits. The number did decline after that, however. By December 1973, the last month of Old-age Assistance before aid-to-the-indigent-aged was to be taken over by a new program, the number on OAA rolls was 1,820,000.

Growth of Private Pension Plans*

Year	Persons receiving benefits	Amount of benefit payments *(in millions)*	Reserves *(in millions)*
1950	450,000	$ 37	$ 12,000
1955	980,000	850	27,500
1960	1,780,000	1,720	52,000
1965	2,750,000	3,520	86,500
1970	4,720,000	7,360	137,100
1971	5,100,000	8,590	151,400
1972	5,550,000	10,000	167,800

* Includes deferred profit-sharing plans.

SOURCE: Social Security Administration

New Program

The new program of assistance to the aged poor is known as Supplemental Security Income (SSI), authorized by the Social Security Amendments of 1972, effective Jan. 1, 1974. The 1972 Amendments have been described as a "major landmark in a period of extraordinary activity in the area of Social Security legislation," and of all the provisions in the amendments SSI was said to constitute "the most revolutionary shift in the Social Security structure."

SSI constitutes, in all but name, a guaranteed annual income for the aged, the blind and the disabled. It provided originally for at least $130 a month for a single person and $195 a month for a married couple. Those amounts were later raised, effective July 1974, to $146 and $219. Social Security amendments of 1973 also made SSI recipients eligible for Medicaid, the federally aided, state-administered health service for persons who cannot afford to pay their own medical expenses.

Unlike the old OAA, SSI is fully financed by the federal government from general revenues; OAA had been a joint federal-state program. This means that there is a nationally uniform floor for the aged, the blind and the disabled, rather than various standards set by states. Minimum payments under SSI are higher than the former OAA maximums in about half of the states. The new program is under the Social Security Administration, which expects to provide benefits in 1975 to more than five million persons, most of them elderly, compared with 3.2 million under the entire state-federal public assistance program that preceded it.

The result of these developments is a greater intermingling of the welfare benefit concept with the insurance principle. Of the 29.9 million people receiving benefits in December 1973 under the Old-age, Survivors, Disability and Health Insurance program—that is, the basic Social Security insurance system—only 15.4 million were retired workers, 62 or older, whose benefits were based on contributions from their earnings during their pre-retirement years. Two million were the disabled who qualified at a younger age, and the rest were wives, widows, children, parents and a special group of individuals 72 or older who have been brought into the benefit system though not qualified on the basis of contributions to the system.

Recent Growth

The years of Social Security expansion were also years of growth for private pensions. In 1940 only four million employees were covered by private pensions; estimates of the number now run up to 35 million or roughly one-half of the industrial work force. Collective bargaining had much to do with this growth.

Tax benefits also encouraged the growth of pension plans. In plans that meet Internal Revenue Service standards, employers may deduct their contributions to the pension funds and wage earners do not pay taxes on their contributions until they receive the benefits in retirement when they are then likely to be in a lower tax bracket. The Life Insurance Company Income Tax Act of 1959, by permitting tax deduction on earnings of invested pension funds held by insurance companies, provided another growth incentive. The Self-employed Individuals Retirement Act of 1962—the so-called Keogh Act—permitted the self-employed to place part of their earnings in a retirement plan and defer paying taxes on the amounts until retirement.

As the plans grew, so did concern for the security of the systems. This concern sharpened considerably in 1964 when the Studebaker automobile plant in South Bend, Ind., closed down and terminated its pension plan, affecting the retirement security of 10,500 workers. At the time, 3,600 persons were already retired or eligible to retire. To distribute the $25-million fund to meet these obligations left 4,000 vested employees between the ages of 40 and 60 with the prospect of receiving only 15 per cent of their vested rights, while 2,900 other workers under the age of 40 could expect nothing.

There followed a decade of extensive congressional investigation of private pension plans by several committees and a presidential committee. These studies showed, Sen. Harrison A. Williams Jr. (D N.J.) told the Senate, Aug. 22, 1974, that "too many workers, rather than being able to retire in dignity and security after a lifetime of labor rendered on the promise of a future pension, find that their earned expectations are not to be realized."

According to Treasury records, in 1972 alone, 19,400 workers lost their rights to approximately $49-million in potential pension benefits because the plans were terminated without enough funds to meet obligations. After many efforts to devise legislation to protect worker interests, after compromises on divergent views, the Employee Retirement Income Security Act of 1974 was approved and signed into law on Labor Day. This act represents a new major step in government regulation of private pension systems. Its impact is yet to be determined.

Prospects

How secure is the retirement future of the American worker? The current recession and inflation make all predictions precarious, but on the whole the safeguards for a solvent retirement would appear far stronger today than they have ever been and they are likely to grow stronger. Several factors account for this view: the broadened coverage of Social Security to near-universality, the improvement of Social Security benefits, the incorporation of income-floor and cost-of-living-increase provisions into the benefit system, the growth of private pensions, the growing size of the older population with its added political clout and the growth of effective senior-citizen lobbying groups.

1974 Pension-Reform Law

A major advance in retirement security is expected to result from the new Employee Retirement Income Security Act. Sen. Jacob K. Javits (R N.Y.), a leading sponsor of the legislation, described it as "the greatest development in the life of the American worker since Social Security." "For the first time in our history," he added, "most workers will be able truly to retire at retirement age and to live decently on their social security and private pensions." The legislation was made necessary, he added, by "the absence of any supervision" over private pension funds, representing assets in excess of $160-billion, and "the lack of minimum standards to safeguard the interests of plan participants and beneficiaries." Major provisions of the law are:

Vesting. Plans must include any employee who has reached the age of 25 and has had at least one year of service. Employers may choose one of three procedures for vesting.

Funding. Contributions must be made at a rate sufficient to provide reasonable assurance that adequate funds will be on hand to meet pension obligations.

Insurance. A Pension Benefit Guaranty Corporation in the Department of Labor will provide insurance to meet pension obligations in case funds are short. Employers will pay $1 into the insurance fund for every covered employee (50 cents for multi-employer plans).

Management. Standards for management of pension funds were established and limits set on transactions that might involve conflict-of-interest.

Individual Pension Accounts. Individuals not covered by a pension plan may establish their own retirement accounts with contributions that are tax-deductible. The tax-free amounts that the self-employed may contribute to their own retirement accounts (as previously provided by the Keogh Act) were raised from a maximum of $2,500 a year to $7,500, or 15 per cent of income, whichever is less. The fiduciary standards, reporting and disclosure provisions become effective Jan. 1, 1975. The law provides for delay, until January 1976, for application of the participation, vesting and funding standards to plans in existence on Jan. 1, 1974.

From the standpoint of retirement security, the greatest weakness of the private pension system is beyond the reach of legislation. It is that the plans fail to cover one-half of the employed population. Since private pension plans remain voluntary, there is nothing in law to prevent employers from terminating them, so long as they meet the obligations already incurred at the time of termination.

Some promoters of pension regulation were disappointed that the act did not include a strong portability provision to permit workers to carry full pension rights as they moved from one job to another. "While this legislation does remove some of the restrictions [on portability]...it does not entirely free an employee from the need to stay at one place of employment for a certain length of time...in order to have his credits vested," complained Rep. Michael J. Harrington (D Mass.).

Some critics object to what they consider favoritism toward the upper-income brackets in tax and pension laws. The complaint is that corporations get appreciable tax relief from contributions to pension systems that assure their top-level executives princely incomes on retirement. An amendment offered to the pension bill by Sen. Gaylord Nelson (D Wis.) would have set a limit of $45,000 on annual retirement income from tax shelter sources. It failed to win approval.

An amendment that was adopted, the one that increased the amount the self-employed can put away tax-free, is seen as favoritism toward the rich. An article in *Barron's*, a business weekly, hailed the amendment as a boon to independent businessmen and professional persons of high income. The author drew up a hypothetical case of a self-employed individual in the 50 per cent tax bracket who puts aside $7,500 a year over a 15-year period, invested at 8 per cent, for pension purposes. Under the new rule, the tax-free $7,500 annual contribution and its tax-free earnings would amount to $203,640 at the end of the 15-year period. If the $7,500 and its earnings were taxable, the individual would have saved only $3,750 a year and his accumulation in 15 years, according to this accounting, would be only $67,825.

Questions on Viability

Other questions are raised about the viability of the pension system as a whole. Writing in *Harvard Business Review*, Robert D. Paul, head of a pension consulting firm in New York, suggested that the prevailing form of private pension plans, which base benefits on averages of peak earning years, may be outmoded. "Their structures may not be suited to the kind of economy we now seem to be entering," he wrote, "and the cost...may increase to unsupportable heights." While pension plans may have worked well during periods of low inflation, they "may not fit the economy of the 1980s and 1990s."

In addition, the aging of the population will put a larger burden of support on the producing population; the proportion of the population above 65, 9.8 per cent in 1970, is projected to rise to 10.9 per cent in the year 2000 and 13.1 per cent in 2020. The growing tendency of women to pursue full-time career employment will deprive the pension funds of contributions from the wages of women as casual employees—contributions which in the past have been forfeited by women for lack of sufficient credits to qualify for benefits.

Another point is that industry is likely to give in to the demands of women liberationists for equal treatment with men as pensioners, even though women tend to live longer in retirement and hence would make heavier drains on the funds than men if their monthly benefits are the same. Still another factor is the trend in collective bargaining toward lowering the age of retirement and toward inserting cost-of-living escalations in benefit schedules. Both of these two features have already become incorporated into public retirement systems, including Social Security.

The doleful prospect envisioned for private pensions is matched by the forecasts of pessimists regarding the future of the Social Security system. The latter foresee a financial collapse when the cost of the system becomes too great a burden on the tax-paying worker. Several factors they point out, will account for a coming imbalance in the tax-benefit ratio. One is that the size of the population in retirement will grow relative to the size of the population drawing taxable income. Another factor is that benefits are based on taxable earnings in the years immediately preceding retirement, which are usually much higher than in most of the years when the retiree was contributing to the system. Adding to the tax burden are the liberalized benefits, including built-in cost-of-living increases. Thus the outgo from the Social Security fund may rise to insupportable heights.

The Board of Trustees of Social Security trust funds has made the following projections of the system's income-and-disbursement experience over the next 75 years: for the first 25 years, slowly increasing costs relative to income; for the second 25 years, rapidly increasing costs; for the third period, high but leveled-off costs amounting to about 17.68 per cent of payroll (compared with the present 10.44 per cent). The board emphasized that accuracy in such projections is hard to achieve. Factors affecting future costs include economic developments, changes in the cost of living, increase in disability awards at early ages, changes in labor force participation, unemployment rates, average earnings and future fertility rates.

New Breed

Some believe it is time to dispense with what they consider the fiction of social insurance and convert Social Security in name and in fact to a general welfare program for the aged. This would silence complaints that the Social Security tax is regressive, applying disproportionately to low-wage earners. The alternative would be to make retirement payments out of general revenues and dispense with the entire concept of a trust fund. "Is the social myth [of

(Continued on p. 122)

HOUSING: SOARING COSTS AND TIGHTER CREDIT

The housing industry served as the whipping boy for many of the nation's economic ills in 1974. It was caught by the "double whammy" effects of inflation, which forced up the cost of its product, and tight monetary policy used to fight inflation, which dried up credit for the purchase of homes.

The housing industry traditionally experienced "boom or bust" cycles because of its extreme sensitivity to changes in the availability of credit needed to build or buy homes. The 1974 mortgage credit crunch, accompanied by record lending interest rates, led to what President Ford characterized Oct. 8 as the "longest and most severe housing recession" since the end of World War II. The two previous housing slumps brought on by tight credit occurred in 1966 and 1969.

The federal government took several emergency steps in 1974 designed to pump funds into the mortgage money supply, but both the Nixon and Ford administrations generally maintained that the housing industry would recover only if efforts to fight inflation with tight credit controls were continued. The government's actions fell short of steps proposed by the housing and banking industries.

Development of Slump

It appeared early in 1974 that the housing industry would recover from the slump in new construction which had begun in mid-1973. New housing starts jumped from an annual rate of 1,464,000 units in January to 1,922,000 in February.

Starts continued to move up and down in the next few months, but in August fell to a four and one-half year low. Starts picked up slightly in September, to a seasonally adjusted annual rate of 1,120,000. This rate compared, however, to slightly over 2 million units started in 1973 and the 2.6 million units set as an annual goal in the 1968 housing act. *(Congress and the Nation Vol. II, p. 215)*

Even more significant in terms of the outlook for recovery of the housing industry was a decline in the number of building permits issued, an indication of future starts. Permits issued fell to 825,000 units in September, the lowest annual rate since December 1966 and 50 per cent below the rate for the same month in 1973.

Interest Rate Pressures

The tight monetary policy restricting credit availability and forcing interest rates up was set by the independent Federal Reserve Board. In April, the Fed raised its discount rate, the lending rate it charges member banks, to 8 per cent in an effort to curb inflation by depressing demand for loans. The rate had been increased in stages from 4½ per cent at the end of 1972.

The Fed's action had a direct effect on the "prime" lending rates banks charged their best customers for short-term loans. The prime rate charged by major banks hit a record 12 per cent from early July to late September.

Several major banks had lowered the rate to 11 per cent by late October, however, and further decreases were predicted by the banking industry.

The pressures toward higher interest rates also affected mortgage lending rates. The average effective interest rate on conventional mortgages—those not insured by the federal government—was 9.2 per cent on new homes and 9.34 per cent on existing homes in September, according to preliminary estimates by the Federal Home Loan Bank Board. The rates were more than 1 per cent higher than the same figures for September 1973.

Allowable interest rates on mortgages insured by the Federal Housing Administration (FHA) and Veterans Administration (VA) also were increased steadily in 1974. The interest ceiling was set at 9½ per cent on Aug. 14, the highest rate since the government began insuring mortgages in 1934. *(Box, p. 38)*

Savings and Loan Problems

Another key factor in the mortgage credit crunch was the outflow of savings from savings and loan associations, the major source of mortgage lending. When interest rates on other investments are high, savers tend to withdraw their funds from savings and loan associations, barred by regulation from paying more than 6 per cent on most accounts, to seek a higher return. This process was known as disintermediation because thrift institutions ceased serving as intermediaries between savers and borrowers.

The outflows were encouraged by the issuance of $1,000 Treasury bonds in August and new variable interest rate securities sold by bank holding companies, both of which offered the small saver a relatively high return on his investment. The smallest Treasury bond issued was increased to $10,000 in September, but the $1,000 bonds were reissued again in October with special safeguards against their purchase by individuals using funds withdrawn from savings accounts.

According to the Federal Home Loan Bank Board, net outflows from federally insured savings and loan associations hit $1.22-billion in August, the biggest drain since January 1970. Outflows eased slightly, to $1.1-billion, in September according to preliminary board figures. By late October, however, some major savings and loans had begun reporting deposit growth and housing industry experts predicted net savings inflows in October.

The problem of disintermediation reflects some of the differences between savings and loan associations and commercial banks. Because they are restricted under various laws in making most kinds of short-term loans, savings and loans tend to borrow short and lend long—borrow on short-term savings accounts and make long-term loans. Savings associations are required to concentrate their lending on mortgages, loans traditionally running as long as 30 years.

Because of these long-term commitments, the interest a savings and loan receives on an old mortgage loan may barely cover the interest it must pay on regular savings accounts during periods of high interest rates. To cover long-

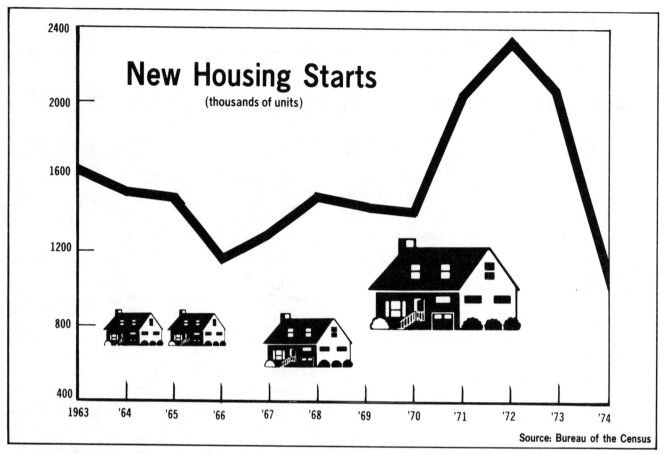

New Housing Starts
(thousands of units)

Source: Bureau of the Census

term loans, savings and loan associations may be forced to borrow massively during periods of savings outflows and sharply restrict new mortgage lending.

Effects on Buyers

While mortgage credit itself was scarce, potential homeowners faced other obstacles because of inflation. Rising costs had driven the median price of a new single-family home to $35,700 in August compared to $33,200 a year earlier, according to the Census Bureau. Average home-buying costs were much higher in many cities. *(Box, p. 37)*

In combination with higher interest rates, the higher sale prices meant increases in the monthly mortgage payments needed to finance purchase of a home. Some lenders also began to shorten the term of a mortgage to 20 or 25 years, another factor boosting monthly payments. And sellers or lenders began demanding higher cash down payments, freezing others out of the housing market.

The increases in monthly payments meant that many buyers could afford only to buy homes costing thousands of dollars less than what they could have bought a year or two earlier. Many homeowners paying off old mortgages at interest of perhaps 6 per cent literally would have been unable to buy houses they already owned at 1974 prices and interest rates.

Effects on Builders

Builders were forced to pay more for wages, land and materials. The credit crunch not only dried up mortgage lending, but also reduced the supply of construction loan money and increased capital borrowing rates for builders able to secure loans.

The construction slowdown produced both a drop in housing starts and employment. According to the Bureau of Labor Statistics, 567,000 individuals in the construction industry were out of work in October, a seasonally adjusted unemployment rate of 12.2 per cent compared to a 6 per cent general rate. Michael Sumichrast, chief economist of the National Association of Home Builders (NAHB), estimated in early October that construction unemployment could reach 16 to 18 per cent by the end of 1974.

The construction slowdown also had ripple effects on a number of housing-related industries, including the lumber business and appliance manufacturers. General Electric Co. and Westinghouse Electric Corp., for example, laid off several thousand employees in mid-1974 because of sagging sales of refrigerators and air conditioners. The American Plywood Association estimated in September that unemployment among plywood-mill workers could reach 25 per cent by the end of 1974.

The number of construction firm failures was up 23.7 per cent in the first eight months of 1974 compared to the same period in 1973. The debt held by failing firms increased 43 per cent over the same period.

A major concern to builders was their large inventory of complete, but unsold housing. While the seasonally adjusted number of unsold single-family homes actually dropped by about 30,000 from August 1973 to August 1974, the unsold homes accounted for a larger percentage of housing completed.

"Our problem now is low sales, not just low starts," remarked a NAHB spokesman.

Government Action

President Nixon had asked Congress in September 1973 to include a number of proposals designed to ease mortgage credit in pending housing and community development legislation. The new housing bill (PL 93-383), which was not cleared by Congress until Aug. 15, 1974, included some but not all of these proposals. The 1974 bill was the first piece of major housing legislation approved since 1968.

Proposals

The principal legislative proposals recommended by Nixon included:
● Increases in the dollar amounts of mortgages eligible for insurance by FHA.
● Elimination of ceilings on mortgage interest rates for FHA-insured mortgages. The limits held these rates below market levels and forced lenders to charge special payments ("points") to compensate for the below-market rates.
● Federal authority to set up flexible repayment arrangements for federally insured mortgage loans to allow lower initial payments to be increased with a family's expected income.
● Tax credits of up to 3½ per cent for financial institutions investing in residential mortgages.

Congressional Response

The housing bill approved by Congress included a number of provisions to ease mortgage credit, but did not give the Department of Housing and Urban Development (HUD) all the authority it had sought.

Key provisions of the bill increased the maximum FHA mortgage amount for single-family homes to $45,000 from $33,000 and sharply cut required cash down payments on homes financed with FHA-guaranteed mortgages. The HUD secretary also was given authority to set flexible interest rates for FHA-backed mortgages, but points were not barred specifically.

The bill also allowed HUD to experiment with flexible mortgage repayment schemes, but explicitly outlawed experimentation with repayment arrangements using "variable" mortgage interest rates which would move up and down with market rates. HUD had asked for this experimental authority.

Other provisions of the measure increased to $55,000 the maximum mortgage loan a federally chartered savings and loan could provide for a single-family home, revised some banking laws restricting mortgage credit availability, and increased the size of mortgages eligible for purchase by various government agencies which deal in secondary mortgage market operations. Low mortgage amount ceilings on FHA insurance and other government programs had rendered them inoperable in many parts of the country as the average cost of housing increased.

Nixon's tax credit proposals received a chilly congressional reception. They were not included in tax reform legislation drafted by the House Ways and Means Committee in the fall of 1974.

Administrative Action

The Nixon administration also took several steps not requiring congressional approval to increase funds available for mortgage loans. These steps used the government's authority to buy mortgage loans from lending institutions in order to free more private funds for mortgage lending.

HUD's Government National Mortgage Association ("Ginny Mae") was authorized in January to buy $6.6-billion of FHA-VA insured mortgages carrying 7¾ per cent interest rates under its "tandem plan." Under the tandem plan, Ginny Mae buys government-backed mortgages at below-market rates and then resells them at market rates, with the Treasury covering any losses from the interest subsidy. Another $3.3-billion was authorized for tandem plan use on May 10.

On May 10, President Nixon also approved commitment of another $7-billion through two other mechanisms. The Federal Home Loan Bank Board was authorized to provide $4-billion in loan advances to member savings and loans at interest rates below their usual borrowing costs. An agency connected with the bank board, the Federal Home Loan Mortgage Corporation ("Freddie Mac"), was authorized to buy $3-billion of conventional mortgages at interest rates of 8¾ per cent.

Ford Emergency Program

It became apparent by late summer of 1974 that these administrative steps would have only modest effects on the industry's problems. Singling the housing sector out for special attention in his economic program, President Ford Oct. 8 proposed emergency legislation allowing Ginny Mae to buy conventional as well as government-insured mortgages. Conventional mortgages account for over four-fifths of all mortgage lending.

The President proposed to make $3-billion available immediately for purchase of the mortgages. The Senate Banking, Housing and Urban Affairs Committee already

Average Home-Buying Costs

(Single family homes, September 1974)

Metropolitan Areas	New Homes	Effective Interest Rates	Old Homes	Effective Interest Rates
Atlanta	$47,300	9.12%	$48,100	9.18%
Baltimore	40,300	8.69	34,700	9.62
Boston	49,900*	8.82*	41,500	9.26
Chicago	48,100	9.01	43,800	9.35
Cleveland	44,800	8.60	40,700	9.27
Dallas	52,300	9.16	47,900	9.62
Denver	43,900	9.00	36,200	10.12
Detroit	44,100	8.87	36,700	9.92
Houston	47,600	9.18	83,600**	9.31
Los Angeles	53,100	9.35	44,800	10.27
Miami	38,100	9.74	44,200	9.98
Minneapolis-St. Paul	48,700	8.31	39,300	8.14
New York	54,100	8.62	51,800	8.64
Philadelphia	42,300	9.16	33,600	9.59
St. Louis	43,900	8.30	20,300**	8.31
San Francisco-Oakland	54,400	9.73	52,400	10.31
Seattle	47,300	9.67	31.700	10.00
Washington, D.C.	55,200	8.83	49,600	9.34

* August figures; September data not available.
** May reflect statistical aberrations because of sample size. According to August data, the average cost of an existing home was $50,800 in Houston and $30,400 in St. Louis.

SOURCE: Federal Home Loan Bank Board

FHA Mortgage Interest Rates

The following chart lists maximum interest rates prescribed on mortgages insured by the Federal Housing Administration since 1934. Interest rates on mortgages insured by the Veterans Administration were generally identical.

Period	Maximum Interest Rate
November 1934—June 1935	5½%
June 1935—July 1939	5
July 1939—April 1950	4½
April 1950—May 1953	4¼
May 1953—Dec. 3, 1956	4½
Dec. 4, 1956—Aug. 5, 1957	5
Aug. 6, 1957—Sept. 23, 1959	5¼
Sept. 24, 1959—Feb. 1, 1961	5¾
Feb. 2, 1961—May 28, 1961	5½
May 29, 1961—Feb. 6, 1966	5¼
Feb. 7, 1966—April 10, 1966	5½
April 11, 1966—Oct. 2, 1966	5¾
Oct. 3, 1966—May 6, 1968	6
May 7, 1968—Jan. 23, 1969	6¾
Jan. 24, 1969—Jan. 24, 1970	7½
Jan. 5, 1970—Dec. 1, 1970	8½
Dec. 2, 1970—Jan. 11, 1971	8
Jan. 12, 1971—Feb. 17, 1971	7½
Feb. 18, 1971—July 6, 1973	7
July 7, 1973—Aug. 24, 1973	7¾
Aug. 25, 1973—Jan. 22, 1974	8½
Jan. 23, 1974—April 14, 1974	8¼
April 15, 1974—May 12, 1974	8½
May 13, 1974—July 7, 1974	8¾
July 8, 1974—Aug. 13, 1974	9
Aug. 14, 1974—	9½

had approved a bill (S 3979) to create a $10-billion permanent aid program.

Sponsors of the committee bill modified their proposal on the Senate floor to reflect the President's request for a $3-billion emergency program. The Senate passed the compromise two days after the President's request and the House cleared the measure Oct. 15. President Ford signed the bill (PL 93-449) Oct. 18 and ordered commitment of $3-billion for mortgage purchases to begin immediately.

Subsidized Housing Programs

While these steps concentrated on increasing the mortgage money supply, the general housing bill also included provisions authorizing government spending to stimulate the housing industry more directly. The bill authorized new federal spending of $1.23-billion in fiscal 1974-75 for public housing programs and a new rental subsidy program (Section 23).

The Section 23 program authorized HUD to contract with developers or housing agencies for provisions of newly constructed, rehabilitated or adequate existing housing for low or moderate-income tenants assisted by a federal rental subsidy. The bill also authorized a new $800-million loan program for developers of housing for the elderly and handicapped.

But the bill did not authorize substantial new funding for homeownership (Section 235) and rental (Section 236) subsidy programs created in 1968. The administration had suspended all commitments under the two programs in early 1973, branding them ineffective and inequitable.

Critics of the moratorium pressed HUD in 1974 for release of unused funds for the two programs as a means of stimulating construction. HUD Secretary James T. Lynn indicated Oct. 18 that release of the unused funds was unlikely. "...I can't see turning on Section 236 as a way of helping the homebuilding industry," he said.

Industry Proposals

The housing industry had pressed for stronger government initiatives in 1974, specifically urging some relaxation of tight monetary policy. "We support a reasonable degree of monetary restraint and a sound fiscal policy," the executive committee of the NAHB said in a policy statement in early August, "but restraint in today's economy has fallen to an unwarranted and unnecessary degree almost solely on the housing industry and its customers."

The NAHB called for a number of legislative and administrative steps to help the industry, including:
● An income tax exemption for interest on savings deposits.
● Tax credits for investors in residential mortgages.
● Emergency legislation stepping up government purchases of conventional mortgages.
● Relaxation of the Fed's tight money policy.
● Use of the Fed's authority to encourage loan support of the residential mortgage market.
● Reactivation of the Section 235 and Section 236 subsidized housing programs.
● New federal loan programs for construction of housing financed with conventional mortgages.

Pre-Economic Summit on Housing

The homebuilders and thrift institutions aired their grievances with the government's economic policy and urged emergency relief efforts at the pre-economic summit on housing in Atlanta Sept. 12. They presented a number of proposals; ranking high on almost every group's list was a tax exemption for the first $500 or $1,000 of interest earned on savings accounts.

Alan Greenspan, chairman of the Council of Economic Advisers, warned against "palliative" measures, however. He and other administration officials continued to argue that the housing industry would recover only if efforts to fight inflation with tight money policies continued.

October Conference

Housing-related groups were pleased with Ford's $3-billion emergency program, but insisted that it would not bring the housing industry out of its slump or substantially ease the mortgage credit crunch.

At a housing "crisis" conference Oct. 17, a number of groups endorsed a resolution urging that the emergency program be made permanent whenever housing starts dropped below a certain rate. Other industry spokesmen complained that the emergency program would not deal with the large inventory of unsold, completed housing because it was geared toward new construction.

Future Alternatives

The 1974 housing situation fanned discussion of a number of proposals designed to stabilize the mortgage money supply in the future in order to hold violent swings in housing activity to a minimum.

Interest Tax Exemptions

Industry groups argued that the tax exemption for savings account interest was one of the simplest ways to guarantee savings and loan associations adequate funds for mortgage loans. Savings and loan groups estimated that a $1,000 individual exemption would swell savings inflows by $24-billion. They contended that the new housing activity supported by these inflows would generate new tax revenues exceeding the estimated $1.8-billion annual tax revenue loss caused by the exemption.

Despite administration objections, the Ways and Means Committee approved a bill (HR 16994) Oct. 8 which would authorize a $500 individual exemption for savings interest. The White House argued that the exemption would not increase total savings.

Reform

The Ford administration had endorsed President Nixon's 1973 proposals for reform of the nation's financial system. The proposals would blur the distinctions between commercial banks and savings and loans by allowing savings institutions to engage in more short-term lending and by easing restrictions on mortgage lending by commercial banks.

The administration also supported phasing out the Fed's Regulation Q, which authorized federal regulatory agencies to set ceilings on interest that banks, savings and loans and other institutions could pay on savings deposits. The administration contended that the ceilings encouraged disintermediation, thus reducing the mortgage money supply in periods of tight monetary policy.

Congress sidestepped most of these proposals in 1974. It approved extension of Regulation Q authority through 1975.

Credit Allocation

The housing crunch reopened discussion about direct allocation of credit for high-priority uses such as housing. Rep. Henry S. Reuss (D Wis.) introduced legislation (HR 15709) in June which would allow the Fed to make it more profitable for its member banks to make loans in four priority areas, including low- and middle-income housing.

Congress took no action on the bill before the 1974 election recess, but congressional discussion of credit allocation may have prompted the Fed to endorse guidelines Sept. 16 urging member banks to steer away from making loans for low-priority activities, such as speculative investment. These informal guidelines, however, were not binding on member banks.

The Ford administration contended that direct federal allocation of credit was "highly undesirable" in statements accompanying the President's Oct. 8 economic address. It argued that the government could not allocate credit "in a way that was acceptable to the American people."

Variable-Interest Mortgages

Controversy also was revived in 1974 over use of variable-interest mortgages—mortgage carrying interest rates which would rise and fall with the market over the term of the loan. Theoretically, variable-interest mortgages assure savings and loans high enough earnings during periods of high interest rates to keep returns on deposits high enough to discourage disintermediation. Almost all mortgage loans carried fixed interest rates which did not change if interest rates went up over the term of the loan.

The Federal Home Loan Bank Board began circulating a draft proposal to authorize variable-interest mortgages among key members of Congress in August and hoped to win congressional backing for the plan in 1975. The plan was accompanied by proposed guidelines which would limit any change in the interest rate to ½ per cent in any six-month period and 2½ per cent of the entire life of the loan.

Opposition to the variable-rate plan was stiff. Consumer groups and the AFL-CIO argued that it would force homeowners to pay for rising interest rates and prevent them from budgeting monthly mortgage payments. House Banking and Currency Chairman Wright Patman (D Texas) also objected to the plan.

Outlook

Because of the low level of building permits issued, housing economists predicted in October that the housing situation probably would not begin to improve until the second quarter of 1975. But by early November, there were some indications that the credit crunch had begun to ease.

Due primarily to some loosening of the Fed's tight monetary policy, prime lending rates for short-term loans began to drop in October. At the American Bankers Association in October, analysts predicted that the prime rate could fall to 10 per cent by the end of 1974 and to 8 per cent or lower by mid-1975. They also suggested that while mortgage lending rates would remain relatively high, more credit would be available by 1975.

Some expansion of the mortgage money supply was expected because declining interest rates make savings accounts more attractive investments and promise savings and loans better deposit inflows. Analysts also predicted that recessionary factors would soften business demand for loan funds and that the Fed might encourage credit expansion to keep recessionary trends from deepening.

But the key question at the end of 1974 as the nation faced the prospect of simultaneous inflation and recession was how builders and buyers would react as credit became more readily available. Would pent-up demand revive housing sales and stimulate new construction or would consumers pinched by recession forego purchase of housing at inflated prices? ∎

Sources of Mortgage Lending

Residential Loans Outstanding, July 1, 1974

(in billions of dollars)

Lender	One- to four- family	Multi-family	Total
Savings and loan associations	$197.3	$23.4	$220.7
Commercial banks	71.8	7.4	79.2
Mutual savings banks	44.4	17.1	61.5
Life insurance companies	21.8	18.9	40.7
Federal and related agencies	39.8	9.6	49.4
All others	26.9	12.0	38.9
Total	$402.1	$88.4	$490.5

Figures may not add due to rounding.

SOURCE: Federal Reserve Board

HOLLOW ECHOES FROM THE HORN OF PLENTY

The American cornucopia, that overflowing horn of plenty, has an ominously hollow air about it these days. It still is undeniably bountiful, but lately this land of material abundance has come up short of some important items—including foods, fuels, lumber, chemicals and textiles, to name just a few. Though not crippling or universal, the shortages are widespread and irritating enough to wake up the American public to the harsh fact that many traditional resources can no longer be taken for granted. Many say the shortages are merely temporary, and that the cornucopia soon will replenish its depleted supplies. But others grimly forecast a future filled with insufficiency and want, and warn that the nation should learn to cope with the new economics of scarcity.

Theoretically, a constant condition of scarcity is a basic element of modern capitalism, as the individual drive to satisfy personal want keeps the economy functioning. In practice, however, genuine scarcities—as the concept is generally defined—have been rare in the United States for nearly a quarter-century. Poverty and hunger have by no means been eliminated, but the material standard of living for the bulk of the American people is among the highest in the world. To a great degree, the scarcity phenomenon is directly related to rising affluence. Americans, who have become accustomed to seemingly unlimited supplies of diverse goods, now are suddenly shocked that some items are no longer obtainable. In much of the developing world, on the other hand, shortages are a universal condition only beginning to be alleviated. Two-thirds of the world's inhabitants find scarcity a way of life. Inevitably, the efforts of less-developed countries to raise their living standards will exacerbate scarcities in the United States.

Scarcities that have developed in this country so far in the early 1970s cover an astonishingly wide range of items. Meat and gasoline probably have been the most widely felt and publicized everyday items, along with heating oil and natural gas. But the list seems endless. It includes such basic materials as paper, plastics, metals, fertilizers, cotton, wool, wood, ceramics, leather, cement and rubber. Those scarcities led to consumer product shortages for—among other things—blue jeans, rugs, diapers, wire, toilets, rags, cardboard, belts, stationery, furniture, burial caskets, automobile parts, electric motors, musical instruments, polyester fabrics, wooden poles, fuel tanks and starch. Basic industrial products in short supply have included chlorine, soda ash, phenol, toluene, hides, newsprint, insulating material, steel tanks, ethyl alcohol, ethylene oxide and tallow. Food shortages extended to such staples as potatoes and rice, as well as to raisins, salmon, sauerkraut, shrimp, corn syrup, grapes, apples, canned fruits and vegetables, honey, goat's milk and popcorn.

Economic Factors

This inventory of shortages resulted from an array of complicated economic conditions arising, ironically, in the midst of a soaring business boom. Basically, surging demand taxed the supply of numerous items so severely that

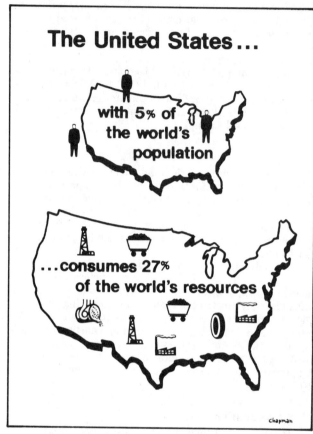

the inevitable result was scarcity, accompanied by higher prices. When supplies of raw materials and agricultural commodities fall short of demands, a chain reaction is touched off. Producers of finished products are forced to reduce their output. And when consumers turn to substitutes—buying pork instead of beef or synthetics instead of cotton—the substitute soon becomes scarce.

The solution is for demand to level off, giving producers time to increase their capacity and output. But that seems an unlikely development for the immediate future. "We are going to be continuously confronted with choices between higher prices and shortages," Herbert Stein, chairman of the Council of Economic Advisers, has said.[1] E. F. Andrews of the National Association of Purchasing Management, a trade organization that prints a monthly list of shortage items, described the situation this way: "This is the hottest seller's market we've seen since 1952-53 [during the Korean War]. There is no segment of the economy...which is not feeling it to a degree. All the classic signs are apparent—poor service, poor delivery, poor quality, rising prices—all the usual accompaniments of a period of shortages." Howard Zacher of the Singer Company added: "Shortages are more acute now than I have seen them in the past 20 years because they involve practically all basic commodities. I think this situation will be short-lived, but it is going to get worse before it gets better."[2]

The problem of fuel and energy shortages in the United States has received so much publicity that officials fear the public will think they are "crying wolf" about the "energy crisis." So far, scarcities of gasoline, heating oil, natural gas or electricity have caused few hardships. The summer passed without any disastrous blackouts. Even so, the U.S. energy supply picture for the decade ahead looks grim by nearly every accounting. And serious heating fuel shortages are in prospect if the coming winter is unusually cold. Stephen A. Wakefield, assistant secretary of the interior for energy and minerals, told a meeting of the Maryland State Chamber of Commerce on Sept. 25, 1973: "This year the comfortable words are hard to come by. The truth is that I can give you no assurance whatever that there will be an adequate supply of heating oil...."

Heating-Fuel Scarcity

In the meantime, the only immediate alternative is for the country to increase its imports of fuel from abroad. Petroleum imports accounted for less than one-fifth of U.S. consumption a decade ago but about one-third today—some six million of the 17 million barrels of oil used daily in the United States come from abroad, as is shown in the following table:

Imports from	Barrels
Venezuela and Caribbean	2.7 million
Canada	1.4 million
North Africa and Middle East	1.1 million
Elsewhere	0.8 million

While most of America's imported oil currently comes from this hemisphere, the bulk of it in the future is almost certain to come from the Middle East, particularly Saudi Arabia and other Persian Gulf states. However, the renewal of warfare between Israel and its Arab neighbors on Oct. 6, 1973, showed how precarious the dependence on Arab oil can become. By Oct. 21, oil exports destined for the United States had been embargoed by all of the major Arab oil-producing countries—including Saudi Arabia, the major producer and traditional American ally among the Arab states—in retaliation for U.S. arms aid to Israel.

America's energy worries for the coming winter extend to natural gas and propane, a petroleum product generally pressurized into a liquid form for piping or bottling but burned in a gaseous form. It accounts for about 3 per cent of the U.S. heating supply and is relied on especially by farmers and mobile home owners. It also is used in mass-transit vehicles, by hospitals and, in the case of factories and power plants, as a substitute for natural gas. The Nixon administration in September 1973 imposed a mandatory allocation plan on the wholesale distribution of propane, and then followed with similar allocation plans for heating oil, diesel fuel, kerosene and jet aircraft fuel.

Congress late in 1973 voted to extend the present allocation program for heating oil and propane to crude oil, gasoline, heavy residual oil burned by utilities and other petroleum products. The bill, titled the Petroleum Allocation Act of 1973, was passed by the House Oct. 17 and won final congressional approval Nov. 14. The Nixon administration adopted its limited allocation program quite reluctantly and argued that wider controls, as set forth in

the bill, were not needed. Nevertheless, House passage of the bill was by an overwhelming vote of 337 to 72, indicating that Congress was fearful of citizen reaction if fuel shortages worsened.

Two studies issued in September 1973, one by the Interior Department and the other by the congressional Joint Economic Committee, stressed the danger of fuel shortages in the coming winter. Both said factors beyond government control—the weather and the willingness of foreign countries to export oil—would be crucial. The Joint Economic Committee study said that a combination of import disruptions, refinery breakdowns and severely cold weather could mean supply shortages "growing rapidly towards 30 per cent; in other words an economic crisis for the United States unparalleled since the Great Depression."[3] The Interior Department study estimated that demand for oil during the winter would be 10.4 per cent higher than during the past winter because of the likelihood of colder weather and other factors.[4]

A shortage of natural gas has increased the demand for distillate oil—distilled petroleum products—for heating fuel. Demand has simply outrun the capacity of American refineries, so the nation now depends on Europe for imports of distillate oil. And Europe is heavily dependent on the Middle East for crude—unrefined—oil. Even before the last Arab-Israeli war broke out, the Common Market nations and Canada had begun to impose export restrictions on petroleum products to protect their own citizens in case of a hard winter.

Food Prices and Reserves

Next to the energy shortage, food scarcities probably have been the major concern of the American public in recent months. Many different foods were either unavailable or virtually priced out of reach in grocery stores. Reasons given by food and agricultural experts included:

Bad weather conditions at home and abroad during the growing seasons, resulting in poor crops.

Booming economic conditions in the United States which gave many families a higher income and more money for grocery budgets, thus *increasing demand.*

Devaluation of the dollar, which made it easier for foreign nations to buy American food to substitute for shortages abroad.

An unexpectedly *low catch* (one-tenth of normal) *of Peruvian anchovies*—one of the world's primary sources of protein-rich animal feed—due to abnormal currents.

A rare coinciding of the *low points of production cycles* of both American cattle and hogs, so that far fewer were marketed.

Large *grain sales to Russia.*

The meat shortage and price spiral of 1973 confused and enraged consumers who had become accustomed to a steadily increasing share of beef in their diets.[5] At first, meat boycotts were organized to protest high prices, but when President Nixon imposed a ceiling on beef prices in March and announced his Phase IV price controls in July, many consumers began to hoard beef in anticipation of still higher prices. The hoarding spree increased home food freezer sales by 300 to 400 per cent in some areas, resulting in a freezer shortage. Other consumers bought horse meat and buffalo meat. Cattle rustling and deer poaching increased in many rural areas. The beef-price ceiling was lifted at midnight on Sept. 9, three days before the originally scheduled date of Sept. 12. Despite widespread fears, no precipitous increases in prices resulted. But prices still remained higher than ever before in U.S. history and there was little hope that they would return to their former levels.

Stocks of processed foods—chiefly canned fruits and vegetables—fell to their lowest levels in 20 years. Canned fruits and vegetables were under Phase IV price controls while fresh produce was not; thrifty shoppers emptied supermarket shelves and left warehouse inventories decimated. According to the National Canners Association (NCA), the average inventory of canned vegetables over the last 10 years was 41.1 million cases but in 1973 was down to 9.7 million cases.

The connection of many food shortages to the massive grain sales to the Soviet Union in 1972 still is the subject of heated debate. The Russians bought 18 million tons of American grains and soybeans for $1.1-billion, including more than one-fourth of the total 1972 wheat crop. Agriculture Secretary Earl L. Butz hailed the sale as "good for all citizens" while former Treasury Secretary George P. Shultz said the United States "got burned" on the deal. Sen. Henry M. Jackson (D Wash.), who held congressional hearings on the sales, said: "The grain sale brought food to the Russians, huge profits to a few corporations—and more inflation to the American people."[6] The wider importance of the sale may have been its impact on world grain reserves. Worldwide wheat stocks stand at 23 million tons, about half of an average year's crop in America. Drought and disastrous crop failures in many parts of the world drained the reserves and created a situation that has aroused warnings that a severe global food shortage may be imminent.

Among the most serious conditions in terms of world food potential is a fertilizer shortage in the United States. Wheat farmers entering the fall planting season could not get enough to fill their needs. Most fertilizer is made by petroleum companies, and one primary fertilizer in liquid form—anhydrous ammonia—is made from hard-to-get natural gas. A large amount of fertilizer also is being shipped overseas for high prices, cutting into domestic supplies.

Past Periods of Dearth

In many ways, current scarcities are the outgrowth of soaring American affluence, coupled with rising prosperity in many other parts of the world. At no time in history have Americans had such copious supplies of diverse goods as in the past decade. Consequently, shortages of anything appear worse in contrast to accustomed abundance. But Americans almost certainly will have to get used to more shortage conditions in years ahead. Scarcities seem inevitable, and much can be learned from past periods of paucity, such as in two world wars.

World War I was the first conflict to demonstrate the voracious appetite of fighting industrial nations for raw materials. The United States entered the war in April 1917 without any stockpiles, and with dangerously low supplies of many essential industrial materials. In July, President Wilson prohibited further exports of coal, grains, meat, steel and other products, effectively putting the nation's entire foreign commerce under licensed control. In addition, the nation began stepping up its production of nitrogen, manganese, chrome, tungsten and other materials.

The United States developed an elaborate system of priorities, with civilians taking third place behind the military and industry. Occasional exceptions were granted for civilian morale.[7] The major responses to shortages were

Paper Shortages

A paper shortage has caused consternation in many places. John Miller of the Boise Cascade Corp., a leading paper supplier, told the *Los Angeles Times* on Aug. 25, 1973, that the market for three primary paper products—newsprint, container board and pulp—was the tightest in 25 years. So was the market for "white papers"—business forms, stationery, adding machine rolls, tablets and book and magazine stocks. The only paper products in ample supply by early autumn were disposable items such as tissue, toilet paper and sanitary napkins.

The reasons were several. A series of strikes at Canadian newsprint plants—which supply almost 70 per cent of U.S. newsprint—reduced Canada's normal output of 800,000 tons a month by one-fifth. A Canadian railway strike magnified the problem, while fuel and pulp shortages and heavy rains in the American South left normal domestic output low.

Many newspapers were forced to reduce their size by cutting advertising or editorial space or eliminating some editions entirely.

substitution and rationing. Every country sought to develop substitutes for scarce products. Aluminum and steel were substituted for copper and tin, various mechanical devices were employed to reduce rubber consumption, oils from the distillation of coal replaced petroleum lubrication, synthetic nitrates replaced Chilean saltpeter, vegetable fibers were used in woolens and glass containers were substituted for tin cans.

An American slogan in World War I was: "Food will win the war." War gardens were encouraged for produce, and sheep were grazed on the White House lawn to dramatize the need for increased meat and wool production. Coffee and chocolate were replaced by substitutes made from chicory, cereal and beets. The bread supply was stretched by use of potato flour and whole grains. Food rationing was accomplished by issuance of cards entitling holders to certain quantities. Sugar was rationed to reduce the need for raw sugar imports from Cuba and the Philip-

Even spaghetti became hard to find at times. The United States exported most of its hard durum wheat in 1973, depriving flour-milling companies of the wheat most suitable for spaghetti making.

pines. But with regard to sugar, a major reason for rationing "was to bring home to the entire population a sense of the desperate character of a war capable of pervading the tissue of daily life and placing the whole economic system on a war footing."[8]

Federal Control in World War II

World War II brought severe shortages of many items, and again the response was substitution and rationing. "During the second World War just about everything was scarce at one time or another," wrote historian Richard R.

Lingeman. "The government instituted a variety of measures to keep the factories running and the population fed and clothed. On the industry level, the War Production Board allocated scarce raw materials among factories by a priority system. Goods for the civilian populace were distributed under a rationing system or simply sold on a first-come-first-serve basis, which meant an awful lot of standing in line at times. To oversimplify, we had guns but we did not have a whole lot of butter."[9]

Finding substitutes, stretching supplies or simply doing without were ways of coping with shortages. Rationing and price controls on critical items were other ways. Tires became the first item to be rationed; the Office of Price Administration in January 1942 called for anyone owning more than five tires to turn the extras in. The Japanese takeover of Malaya and Java had cut off 92 per cent of the nation's rubber supply. The government asked citizens to gather up and turn in anything made of rubber, for which they were paid one cent a pound. The rubber drive fizzled and the government directed its effort to the creation of synthetic rubber.

Gas rationing went into effect later that year, on Dec. 1. Each driver was issued a windshield sticker and a book of gasoline coupons. The basic allotment was three gallons a week, but those who had to drive to work or use a car for business got more. There were special stamps for persons with other needs, such as attending aging or sick relatives in distant towns or planting "victory gardens" in the country. Policemen, firemen, doctors, clergymen, reporters and photographers got as much gas as they needed; they were on their honor to drive no more than necessary.

Black Markets and Stockpiling

As for food, sugar was again the first item to be rationed, quickly followed by coffee, meat, canned goods and fish. Much rationing was anticipated and a great deal of hoarding took place. Another inevitable consequence of rationing was the appearance of black markets. Black-marketeering was known during prior wars, but it reached full flower during World War II. To deal with the situation, the Office of Price Administration issued more than 600 price and rent regulations, fixing the prices of over eight million articles and 20 categories of rationed commodities, and controlling distribution of many essential products. Still, black markets steadily spread throughout the land. Enforcement by the undermanned OPA was far from complete; each inspector was responsible for more than 1,000 businesses. In a postwar study, Marshall B. Clinard [10] estimated that one out of every 15 businesses was prosecuted by the OPA for ceiling-price or rationing violations, and one in five was warned.

Another approach to wartime shortages was stockpiling, which began on a modest basis in 1938 and continued through the war years for such things as copper, nickel, rubber and chromite. When World War II ended, the United States found it had drawn heavily upon its reserves of raw materials. The Korean War set off a crash program to replenish stockpiles and for some years afterward succeeded to such an extent that the "maximum objectives" for most strategic materials were not only achieved but exceeded. By May 31, 1962, the government's hoard of minerals contained five times as much cobalt and four times as much tungsten as the objectives called for. Critics of the stockpiling program contended that it was more concerned with stabilizing commodity prices than with bolstering national security.

Dealing with Scarcities

Substitution, rationing and stockpiling were the major responses to scarcity in the past, and they are likely to be seen again. "The American consumer has good reason to feel that his fate is to be buffeted from one shortage to another," the *Washington Star-News* commented editorially on Aug. 5, 1973. "It is a state of mind we all should get used to.... Americans are getting some painful training for a future of decreasing abundance." This affects attitudes at home and relations with the rest of the world. U.S. foreign policy no doubt will be governed more directly by the need for trading with countries rich in the resources this nation needs. The United States seems destined to become less self-sufficient and more in need of economic allies as time goes on.

There are 13 major industrial raw materials other than petroleum required by advanced national economies. A country is considered import-dependent if it must import more than 50 per cent of any one of these materials. In 1950, the United States was import-dependent on only four—aluminum, manganese, nickel and tin. By 1970, two more had been added—zinc and chromium. By 1985, three more are expected to be on the list—iron, lead and tungsten. And by the year 2000, the list will probably include potassium, copper and sulfur, making the United States dependent on imports for all of the basic raw materials except phosphate.

The U.S. Geological Survey, in its first comprehensive assessment of the nation's mineral resources in 20 years,[11] found that this country now imports about one-third of the 125 million tons of iron ore it uses each year, after having been self-sufficient in this resource for most of its history. Large U.S. reserves of low-grade aluminum ores exist but cannot be mined without major technological advances or much higher extraction costs. Copper is in adequate domestic supply to last at least 25 years at current consumption rates.

Worldwide, mineral consumption has been increasing about 5 per cent a year, thus doubling about every 15 years.

Zinc is relatively plentiful worldwide, but the United States produces only about 9 per cent of the world's supply while using three times as much; between 1950 and 1970 the world used half of all the zinc ever produced up to that time. Manganese, indispensable to steel production, has been exhausted in the United States (the last mine closed in 1970) and the only prospect for relieving U.S. dependence on foreign sources is that of gathering manganese off the ocean floor. Domestic production of mercury amounts to less than one-third of U.S. requirements, and the outlook for discovering new, rich ores is rated poor. Silver used for photography alone is greater than the domestic production.

The reason for this depletion of resources is not hard to find. Since 1940, it is estimated, the United States alone has consumed more minerals than all the rest of mankind did in previous history. The National Commission on Materials Policy noted that the United States, with only 5 per cent of the world's population, consumes more than 27 per cent of the world's production of major resources. Even though world production is expected to triple in the next three decades, the U.S. share will remain about the same.[12]

Some "futurologists" place considerable hope in the discovery of new deposits of raw materials or in technological advances that will make the removal of known but marginal deposits profitable. The ocean floor and the continental shelf are storehouses of many minerals. Other experts suggest that the polar ice caps might be sources of mineral deposits accessible with new technology. For the long run, the moon and even other planets might be mined for materials scarce on earth. The $200-million Earth Resources Technology Satellite (ERTS) was scorned as a wasteful boondoggle when it was launched in 1972, but since then has been praised as a valuable recorder of the earth's mineral deposits, croplands, forests, watersheds and polluted areas. It has revealed new nickel fields in Canada and South Africa and copper ranges in Pakistan.

Mining technology already has improved the utilization of low-grade ores. Methods have been developed for drilling extremely hard minerals like taconite with plasma torches and rocket nozzles. Atomic devices may be used more extensively to open up deep deposits of various minerals or energy sources such as natural gas. Refining techniques may be improved to the point where vital minerals such as aluminum can be extracted from clay or other domestically abundant materials. Use of abundant resources in place of scarce ones undoubtedly will increase.

Raw Materials

One clear mandate of the 1970s has been a call for development of new national and international materials policies. The National Academy of Sciences and the National Academy of Engineering jointly sponsored a recent conference on "National Materials Policy"[13] to discuss the recommendations of two recent major studies on the subject. One was the final report of the National Commission on Materials Policy, and the other was the report of the NAS Committee on the Survey of Materials Science and Engineering.

Materials policy is an international as well as a national problem. The Materials Research Advisory Group of the Organization for Economic Cooperation and Development (OECD), an international body with headquarters in Paris, concluded that: "All countries are short of something or other and depend on international trade to meet their needs of raw and processed materials. International specialization and the interdependence it implies will clearly increase from now on: difficulties which have already arisen with regard to oil might be repeated for other natural resources which might be threatened for economic or political reasons."[14] The OECD report recommended that each nation formulate its own materials policy, but recognized that natural resources problems were "essentially international" and suggested that OECD might provide a platform for the study of these problems.

One of the principal elements of any materials policy almost certainly will have to be recycling—a word that has gained wider use in recent years than the practice itself. For some time, various experts have been urging more recycling of critical materials, but economic costs usually have hampered progress. A report for the Senate Public Works Committee in 1968 stated: "It is now evident that the industrial economy of the United States—and indeed the entire industrial world—must undergo a shift from a use-and-discard approach to a closed cycle of use and salvage, reprocess, and reuse. The timing of the conversion need not be precise; it is likely to go on for a century or more; it may never be total. But it must occur, or else man faces the alternative of a congested planet that has turned into a polluted trash heap, devoid of plant and animal life, depleted of minerals, with a climate intolerable to man."[15]

World Food or Grain Bank

Advocates of an international approach to world shortages also have proposed the establishment of a world food bank to meet emergency needs of starving nations in lean years ahead. One such proposal was made by Lester R. Brown, an agricultural expert for the Overseas Development Council. Another suggestion—for an international grain reserve—was made in a study by Professor Timothy Josling of the London School of Economics for the British-North American Committee. He said the contributing countries should own the grain, fix policies for its use and determine where it should be stored.[16] Addeke Boerma, director of the U.N. Food and Agriculture Organization, has proposed that national food stockpiles be accumulated in underdeveloped countries most vulnerable to natural disasters and unfavorable weather, with financing and technical assistance to come from wealthy nations.

Norman Borlaug, the Nobel Prize winner widely credited with fathering the "Green Revolution" through development of new strains of wheat, also has urged the formation of an international granary built from supplies contributed by all nations. Borlaug has said: "Only a handful of people are aware of just how close we were to having 50 to 60 million people die this year."[17] Finally, a group of economists from Europe, North America and Japan, meeting at the Brookings Institution in Washington, D.C., in September 1973, proposed the creation of an international food bank of some 100 million tons of grain, but acknowledged that building the reserve would involve sacrifices, even sometimes the denial of food to hungry people and the diversion of grain from livestock feed to direct use, thereby reducing available meat.

Protein Use

Other experts have been working on improving use of the nutritious protein contained in oilseed crops, especially soybeans. Such protein can then be used for direct human consumption either as bland supplements in other foods or in high-protein "analogs" resembling meat, poultry or fish. These products would utilize natural agricultural crop proteins at about 70 per cent efficiency, compared with the less-than-10-per-cent efficiency rate of feeding soybeans to animals for production of meat. Another promising development is single cell protein (SCP), made by breeding selected species of high-protein micro-organisms at rapid rates.

Economic and Population Growth

Closely related to the problem of scarcities is the question of continued economic and population growth. Hazel Henderson, director of the Council on Economic Priorities, has pointed out that more than 20 books on this general subject have been published in the last few years, most of them since 1970.[18] John Kenneth Galbraith, as early as 1958 in his book *The Affluent Society*, questioned the premise that the economy could continue unrestrained growth without air and water pollution and land despoliation. *Scarcity and Growth* (1963), by Harold J. Barnett and Chandler

Some Easing

As 1974 drew to a close, many of the shortages that plagued the nation in 1973 appeared to have eased. Business and industry reported that such basic materials as steel, chemicals, lumber and paper were easier to come by in recent months. "As contrasted with a year ago, we're no longer getting those loud cries about going out of business because of shortages," said Samual Rosenblatt, director of the Commerce Department's Office of Business Research and Analysis.

However, the shortage abatement apparently was more a result of the general economic slowdown than of expanded material supplies or increased production capacity. Recession and inflation combined to lessen industrial output and reduce consumer purchasing, giving supplies of many materials a chance to overtake demand. In a survey of business purchasing executives, *The Wall Street Journal* reported a "buyer's market" for some key materials. Prices of copper, cotton and lumber actually went down. "While a few raw materials continue to be in short supply and their availability is erratic, the worst appears to be over for most items," said S.T. Wepsic of the Firestone Tire & Rubber Co.

Morse, took a new look at the Malthus theory and analyzed the population-resource problem with detailed statistical data. Kenneth E. Boulding's *Beyond Economics* (1968) put forth the concept that "cowboy economics"—the idea that the earth was an unlimited frontier of exploitable natural resources—might not be suitable for "spaceship earth."

But it was *The Limits to Growth* (1972), written by a group of Forrester's colleagues at Massachusetts Institute of Technology, that brought the no-growth issue fully to public attention. Sponsored by the prestigious Club of Rome's "Project on the Predicament of Mankind," the study concluded that the earth's interlocking resource system probably could not support present rates of economic and population growth much beyond the year 2100, if that long. If current trends continue, "The most probable result will be a rather sudden and uncontrollable decline in both population and industrial capacity," the study concluded.[19]

The study was scoffed at by many economists, who questioned the data and said the report ignored technological breakthroughs that were sure to come. But some of the same economists have since begun to revise their opinions. Environmentalists argue that it would be foolhardy to place such total faith in technology as the source of salvation. Barry Commoner in *The Closing Circle* (1971) argued that the earth's resources would give out long before less-developed countries could escape from poverty.

Herman E. Daly has drawn together a collection of articles on the no-growth issue in a book, *Toward A Steady-State Economy* (1973), in which he contends that radical changes in institutions and economics are necessary if the world is to avoid disastrous scarcities and continue cultural advancement. Daly advocates a steady-state economy with constant levels of population and material wealth maintained at a chosen rate. As one step toward reaching that goal, he suggests that each person be licensed at birth to have, statistically, only 1.1 children, the figure which rep-resents zero population growth, and allow the licenses to be bought and sold on the open market.[20]

There are still other thinkers who maintain that the real dimensions of scarcity are not environmental or economic, but existential. Walter A. Weisskopf, in *Alienation and Economics* (1971), regards time, life and energy as the resources that are ultimately "scarce" because of human mortality. Weisskopf notes that economics, once based on the ethics of thrift and self-denial, now requires an ethic of "utilitarian hedonism" if it is to justify mass consumption, mass production and advanced market economics.

Yet this very hedonism, promoted by advertising, now is leading to the breakdown of industrial discipline and complaints of dehumanizing jobs. Finally, some philosophers have made the point that there is another vital resource which risks becoming the ultimate scarcity—and the final casualty—of a world in which "progress" only brings us closer to oblivion. When the British economist D. H. Robertson asked himself the question—What is it that economists economize?—his answer was "love, the scarcest and most precious of all resources."[21] Paul Samuelson quotes Robertson approvingly in the latest edition of his influential textbook, *Economics*. The human need for love, along with such accompanying amenities as peace of mind, self-fulfillment, companionship, leisure time and contemplation, is not likely to be satisfied in a future governed solely by the economics of scarcity. ∎

[1] In a speech to the American Bar Association, Washington, D.C., Aug. 8, 1973.
[2] Both quoted in *U.S. News & World Report*, June 11, 1973, pp. 28, 26.
[3] Joint Economic Committee staff study, "Prospects of Distillate Oil Shortages for Winter 1973-74," Sept. 17, 1973, p. 3.
[4] Interior Department, "The Distillate Fuel Oil Situation, Winter 1973-74," Sept. 15, 1973.
[5] Per capita U.S. beef consumption went from 55 pounds in 1940 to 117 pounds in 1972. See "Nutrition in America," *E.R.R.* 1973 Vol. II, pp. 583-600.
[6] Remarks made July 19, 1973, in opening hearings by the Permanent Investigations Subcommittee of the Senate Government Operations Committee. A recent statement of praise for the sales was made by Butz on Sept. 14. Shultz gave his appraisal at a White House news conference on Sept. 7.
[7] One ingenious tactic involved the fashion industry. When America entered the war, the Parisian couturiers had just decreed the lengthening of women's skirts. But the American government, through the French ambassador, elicited the promulgation from Paris of new fashions greatly abbreviating hemlines and thus saving millions of pounds of wool.
[8] Alvin Johnson, "War Economics," *Encyclopedia of the Social Sciences*, Vol. VIII, p. 345.
[9] In "Remembrance of Rationing Past," *The New York Times Magazine*, Sept. 9, 1973, p. 108. Lingeman is author of *Don't You Know There's a War On? The American Home Front 1941-1945* (1970).
[10] Author of *The Black Market* (1969), a definitive study of black marketeering during World War II.
[11] The 722-page report, "United States Mineral Resources," published in May 1973, examined supplies of more than 60 mineral and energy commodities.
[12] Wilfred Malenbaum (professor at the University of Pennsylvania's Wharton School of Business), "Materials Requirements in the United States and Abroad in the Year 2000," April 1973. The commission was created by the National Materials Policy Act of 1970. Its final report was issued in June 1973.
[13] In Washington, D.C., Oct. 25-26, 1973.
[14] "Needed: A Better Materials Policy," *OECD Observer*, August 1972, p. 17.
[15] Franklin P. Huddle, Science Policy Research Division, Legislative Reference Service (now Congressional Research Service), Library of Congress, report on "Availability, Utilization, and Salvage of Industrial Materials," Jan. 8, 1968, p. 1.
[16] *An International Grain Reserve Policy*, August 1973, p. 1.
[17] Quoted by Lewis M. Simmons in *The Washington Post*, Sept. 13, 1973.
[18] "Ecologists Versus Economists," *Harvard Business Review*, July-August 1973, p. 28.
[19] Donella H. Meadows, Dennis L. Meadows, Jorgen Randers, William W. Behrens III, *The Limits To Growth* (1972), p. 23.
[20] The idea was originally proposed by Kenneth E. Boulding.
[21] D. H. Robertson, *Economic Commentaries* (1956), p. 154.

MATERIALS SHORTAGES

Report—Senate Government Operations Permanent Investigations Subcommittee Aug. 29 issued a report of a survey of the nation's largest corporations on materials shortages.

Hard on the heels of the energy crisis, a crisis was emerging in the supply of minerals and other materials vital to an industrial economy, the report indicated.

A survey of the nation's largest manufacturing concerns disclosed serious shortages in everything from aluminum to zinc. Shortages of many of the materials were expected to persist from two to ten years, according to the report "Materials Shortages—Industry Perception of Shortages," released Aug. 29 by the Senate Government Operations Permanent Investigations Subcommittee.

The report was based on responses from more than 250 of the nation's largest corporations to a survey conducted by the subcommittee under the direction of Walter (Dee) Huddleston (D Ky). The report was released in the form of a committee print.

Noting that the nation consumed 40,000 pounds of materials per capita annually, Huddleston declared, "Where we are not faced with physical shortages, we are often faced with economic shortages—with prices driving a material out of reach....We simply must take a detailed look at shortages and their inflationary impact and devise some means of bringing supply and demand into better balance."

In releasing the report, Subcommittee Chairman Henry M. Jackson (D Wash.) asserted, "Materials shortages have a domino effect throughout the economy affecting the consumer price for every product for which a scarce resource constitutes a necessary ingredient."

Jackson announced that Huddleston would chair subcommittee hearings during September on the impact of material shortages.

A survey of the nation's largest manufacturing concerns disclosed serious shortages in everything from aluminum to zinc.

The subcommittee received 258 responses from the 500 corporations queried. The respondents cited seven major interrelated reasons for the shortages:

1. Stocks of resources were being depleted at a time when demand was surging.

2. High interest rates and low rates of return hampered construction of new facilities and expansion of old ones.

3. Price controls kept domestic prices abnormally low, which led domestic suppliers to export their goods to the higher priced foreign markets.

4. Environmental protection laws caused some plants to close and others to cut production.

5. Two dollar devaluations made U.S. resources less expensive than those of other nations, leading to increased exports.

6. The Occupational Safety and Health Act limited capacity by requiring costly conversions that did not increase productive capacity.

7. Energy shortages hampered production in three areas—as a source of process heat, as a fuel for transportation and as a raw material.

The survey turned up 63 different raw materials shortages that affected at least some of the industries. Some of the major ones were:

Petrochemicals

The survey found that petrochemicals were the raw materials which the most companies, 181, had trouble acquiring. Companies blamed the energy crisis and price controls for the shortages. Petrochemicals were needed to make such products as plastics, rubber, textiles, detergents, pigments and lubricants.

Steel

Steel was listed as a major shortage area by 106 companies. The problem cited was low production capacity caused by price controls, environmental controls, scrap exports and shortages of coking coal. The report said new capacity probably could not be built before 1980.

Steel Products

Shortages in a variety of steel products were reported: steel castings, 51 companies; steel forgings, 28 companies; steel plate, 10 companies; sheet steel, 3 companies; other steel products, 80 companies. The shortages affected everything from the building industry, which used reinforced concrete, to the energy industry, which needed roof bolts and plates for coal mines and tubular steel and other materials for drilling rigs.

Plastics

Energy shortages had caused severe shortages in the plastics industry. Both natural gas and crude oil were basic materials for plastics production. The report found 104 companies with supply problems related to plastics.

Paper

Shortage of wood pulp had led to paper shortages which affected 101 companies, the survey found. Wood pulp was scarce, the report stated, because of excessive exports, heavy rainfall affecting logging operations, labor problems, lack of adequate transportation and low production capacity. Price and pollution controls also were cited as major causes of the shortages.

Aluminum

Seventy-four companies reported shortages of aluminum. "The basic problem...is surging world demand versus a relatively static supply," according to the report. Production was hampered by the power shortage in the Pacific Northwest in 1973 and the industry had not fully recovered, the survey found. In addition, "aluminum scrap is very difficult to get because of the high prices available in foreign markets," the report said, and bauxite (used in aluminum production) might become a problem if an international cartel was formed by producing states, several companies feared.

Zinc

Zinc production had dropped precipitously in a few years from 1.4 million tons to 600,000 tons in 1973, one company reported to the subcommittee. The shortage was blamed on the closing of "marginally profitable smelters because of stringent environmental protection laws." Domestic demand for zinc was reported to be double the domestic production capacity. Forty-four companies reported problems in buying enough zinc. ∎

ENERGY: A STUBBORN COMPONENT OF INFLATION

As the Ford administration struggled to handcuff inflation, about half of the rate of increase in the cost of living seemed out of reach of traditional economic restraints.

That was the share of the increase caused by soaring energy prices, which accounted for around 50 per cent of the annual increase in the consumer and wholesale price indexes. Both were rising faster than 10 per cent a year.

Most of the surge in energy prices was due to a leap of almost 400 per cent in the cost of imported oil. The world price of oil soared from $3.00 to $11.65 a barrel between Oct. 1, 1973, and Jan. 1, 1974. Having raised them, all oil exporters, not just Arab nations, steadfastly refused to lower their oil prices.

Strategies normally used to fight inflation—cutting federal spending, raising taxes and tinkering with the money supply—failed to affect the world oil price, which pulled up the cost of all other forms of energy.

Grim Outlook

The economic diagnosis was almost universally gloomy.

"Devastating," said Lee C. White, former federal power commissioner, when asked about the effect of energy prices on consumers.

"It is difficult to discuss the energy problem without unfortunately lapsing into doomsday language," President Ford declared in a Sept. 23 speech to the world energy conference in Detroit, Mich.

"Exorbitant prices can only distort the world economy, run the risk of worldwide depression and threaten the breakdown of world order and safety," the President said.

Secretary of State Henry A. Kissinger told the United Nations the same day, "The complex, fragile structure of global economic cooperation required to sustain national economic growth stands in danger of being shattered."

'Recycling' Problem

The danger, though, was not so much the spiral of inflation as the inability of oil consuming nations to sustain the massive drain of money to the exporting nations.

Economists called it the greatest transfer of assets in world history. By the 1980s, they estimated, more than $600-billion would have shifted from the oil consuming nations to the producing nations.

Suggestions flowing from the White House economic summit conference on Sept. 27 and 28 were aimed mainly at the problem of trade deficits and worldwide imbalances of payments. There were no concrete remedies aimed at reducing energy prices in the short run.

World financial officials were looking beyond the high oil prices to find ways to "recycle" oil money in the economies of the consuming nations. This meant finding ways to get the oil exporters to lend money to consuming countries so they could pay for oil and other imports and avoid recession.

Sen. Henry M. Jackson (D Wash.), a leading energy expert in Congress, scoffed that recycling was nothing more

than foreign aid from Arab nations to consuming nations. Recycling would do nothing to dampen the inflation of energy prices, Jackson said at a Sept. 30 press conference.

Lack of Options

There seemed little the administration could do, with oil prices dictated by a determined cartel. The administration during 1974 veered between sweet reason and tough talk in trying to persuade oil exporters to cut prices. Nothing worked. The hopes of lower prices that bloomed with oil surpluses in the spring withered in the summer when Arab nations announced production cutbacks and increased oil taxes.

Treasury Secretary William E. Simon continued to pin his hopes on the law of supply and demand: "Underlying market forces prove that there is a large potential oil surplus which, in a free market, would be reflected in lower

---

"It is difficult to discuss the energy problem without...lapsing into doomsday language."

—President Ford

---

prices," he told the Senate Government Operations Permanent Investigations Subcommittee on Sept. 18. "If the market were free from interference, the prices would drop."

But the market was not free from interference, and probably would not be for a long time.

With little hope of reduced prices in the short run, the administration turned its attention to the longer term. In his Oct. 8 economic message, Ford brushed aside suggestions that gasoline taxes be used to force conservation. He indicated he would rely on voluntary cooperation of the auto industry and consumers to reduce the demand for oil.

Jackson preached austerity: "Let's tighten our belts now before we face disaster later."

The Fuel Price Spiral

Simon said at the Sept. 18 hearing that "the quadrupling of oil prices over the past year, when its effects are fully felt, will have contributed in the range of 5 to 8 percentage points in our wholesale price index." This amounted to about half the increase in the index in the year ending in mid-1974, he said.

In September, wholesale prices compiled by the Bureau of Labor Statistics showed a 16.2 per cent increase over a year earlier. There was a one or two month lag in the fuel component of the index.

The September index showed that energy prices had increased 63.8 per cent during the year ending in May. Petroleum led the way with a whopping 69.1 per cent surge in the price of crude oil and an 85.2 per cent jump in the price of refined products.

Consumer Prices

Energy prices to consumers increased 33.5 per cent in the year after the cost of imported oil shot upward, while consumer prices as a whole jumped 11.2 per cent, said Joel Popkin, a staff member of the President's Council of Economic Advisers.

Popkin estimated that energy was responsible for 19 per cent of the increase in the cost of living. While this differed markedly from the 50 per cent estimated by Simon, it covered a different period.

"Energy inflation in the past three months has slowed," Popkin said. "In the three months ending in August, energy prices increased 10.3 per cent, while the consumer price index was rising at a rate of 12.9 per cent."

The worst rate of increase for energy prices was in the three months ending in January 1974, when consumer prices jumped 75.5 per cent for gasoline and motor oils, 247.5 per cent for fuel oil and coal, and 40.6 per cent for gas and electricity.

The index merely confirmed what consumers already knew from visits to the gas pump or examination of their bills for heat and light.

Regular gasoline that cost 35 cents a gallon in mid-1973 had jumped to 56 cents a gallon by August 1974, according to a summary prepared by the American Automobile Association. This was confirmed by the Federal Energy Administration (FEA), which reported gasoline prices excluding state and federal taxes. In January 1973, the average before-tax price of regular gasoline was 25.31 cents a gallon. By September 1973 the price had climbed to 27.74 cents. Then it soared to 31.3 cents by the end of 1973 and to 43.1 cents a gallon by July of 1974.

Other Fuels

The price of coal, natural gas and electricity also went up with the price of oil. For example, the wholesale price index released in September showed an annual increase of 63.8 per cent for coal, 26 per cent for gas and 32.8 per cent for electricity.

Consumer prices rose more slowly. Gasoline and motor oil prices increased 38.5 per cent in the year ending in September. Heating oil and utilities were up 20 per cent but fuel oil and coal jumped 66.7 per cent in the same period.

Minor Improvement

While energy prices were increasing at a frightening rate on an annual basis, the most recent price indexes confirmed Popkin's statement that the rate of increase was slowing down. There was a decrease of 1.5 per cent in the wholesale price of gasoline.

The automobile association's figures showed that gasoline prices had leveled out, with the average nationwide price of regular holding at 56 cents a gallon from the end of May through Sept. 4.

Before the Shock

Energy prices began rising at an inflationary rate before the world price of oil went through the ceiling. The fuel shortages of 1972-74 pushed the price of all energy upward, and the oil producing countries gradually increased the price of oil during 1973. *(Chart, this page)*

"The rising trends in the price of practically all forms of energy in recent years accelerated markedly in 1973," declared a study for the Ford Foundation's Energy Policy Project by Foster Associates, an economic study group. Fuel shortages and skyrocketing import prices caused the 1973 increases, according to the study, "Energy Prices: 1960-1973."

Import prices did not go up all at once. Crude oil prices increased gradually from $1.80 per barrel in 1960 to $2.59 per barrel at the start of 1973. By Oct. 16, 1973, imported oil cost $5.12 a barrel. Then came the shocker, with the Organization of Petroleum Exporting Countries (OPEC) announcing a new posted price of $11.65 per barrel, effective in January 1974. During the Arab oil embargo, also announced in October 1973, spot prices for oil were quoted as high as $20 a barrel because consumers were willing to pay almost any price for fuel.

End of an Era

The shock of the October 1973 increase in oil prices was all the greater because energy prices had been stable for nearly 30 years. In terms of current dollars, the price of coal, oil and natural gas rose moderately from 1947 until 1970, when shortages began causing modest spurts.

However, in terms of constant dollars, the price of energy actually declined over much of the post World War II period, according to "Low-Cost Abundant Energy: Paradise Lost?", a Resources for the Future study by Hans H. Landsberg.

A barrel of crude oil was worth $2.60 in 1948 and $3.39 in 1972 "with only a slow upward trend until the very recent rises," Landsberg wrote in December 1973. "In constant (1948) dollars, however, the 1972 price reached not $3.39 but $1.85, for a decline of about 50 per cent during the quarter century. To put it differently, any 1973 price below $4.75 per barrel represented a decline in the real price of oil since 1948. At $3.30, oil in 1972 lagged about 30 per cent behind the rise in the general price level."

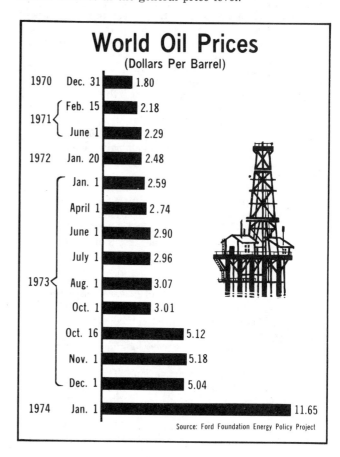

World Oil Prices
(Dollars Per Barrel)

1970	Dec. 31	1.80
1971	Feb. 15	2.18
	June 1	2.29
1972	Jan. 20	2.48
1973	Jan. 1	2.59
	April 1	2.74
	June 1	2.90
	July 1	2.96
	Aug. 1	3.07
	Oct. 1	3.01
	Oct. 16	5.12
	Nov. 1	5.18
	Dec. 1	5.04
1974	Jan. 1	11.65

Source: Ford Foundation Energy Policy Project

Landsberg said the price decline for coal was even greater than for oil—40 per cent in the postwar period through 1970 when measured in constant dollars. He showed that the price of natural gas increased gradually until 1955 and then leveled off at about 10 cents per thousand cubic feet through 1972. Natural gas prices at the wellhead reflected the fact that prices had been controlled since 1956.

"To a considerable extent, then, recent events in the price arena mark the end of energy as one of the great postwar bargains," Landsberg said.

Impact of Price Increases

The impact of increased energy prices was somewhat harder to measure than the price increases themselves. But there were some firm figures.

Income Decline

The purchasing power of workers dropped substantially in the year ending in June 1974, Bureau of Labor Statistics figures showed. A manufacturing worker with three dependents had $107.70 in 1967 dollars to spend in June 1973. A year later, the same worker had a spendable income of $102.90.

On Sept. 25, Gov. Milton J. Shapp (D Pa.) told the Senate Special Committee on Aging that rising energy prices had cut the purchasing power of the elderly for other essentials at least 20 per cent.

In Pennsylvania, Shapp said, the average cost of heating a home with oil had increased from $312 a year to $420 and with coal from $340 to $625.

"It is inhuman and malignant for a society in this wealthy nation to tolerate the specter of old people eating dog food as a trade-off for heat, light or rent money," Shapp declared.

Sen. Jackson, at his press conference, said that energy price increases had added $472 a year to the fuel bill of the average American. The increases were $180 for gasoline, $192 for electricity and $100 for heating oil.

Employment Picture

The shifts in consumer buying patterns resulting from higher energy costs also affected the unemployment rate. The auto, airline and the utilities industries have been particularly hard hit by increasing fuel costs, Simon testified on Sept. 18.

"These sudden shifts cause a loss of output and create unemployment, even when some sectors of the economy are still at full capacity," Simon said.

Mark Roberts, a research economist for the AFL-CIO, told Congressional Quarterly that "one of the reasons for lower sales is higher energy prices." But he said unemployment was caused by so many factors it was hard to know how much was due to inflation.

In the long run, many economists believe, the U.S. economy could stand a 400 per cent increase in energy prices.

"The recent price increases have been a substantial shock to the world's economies because they were compressed into only a few months," Arlon R. Tussing, chief economist for the Senate Interior and Insular Affairs Committee, said in a Feb. 15 speech. "Spread over a decade, however, their impact will at worst be swamped by the normal economic growth that ranges in different countries from 50 per cent to 150 per cent per decade," Tussing told the National Association of Business Economists.

The Secondary Impact

While federal officials were willing to estimate the direct effect of higher energy prices, they were much less confident when asked about the secondary effects. Direct effects of increased fuel prices were reflected in higher costs for fuels such as gasoline or heating oil. Indirect effects were those that showed up in the price of other products—plastics, fertilizers, food or metal products, for example.

Raw Materials

Fred Allvine, a consultant for the Permanent Investigations Subcommittee, said, "The indirect impact is coming in from all directions. The underdeveloped countries that are not able to pay for their oil imports have doubled and tripled the price of raw materials."

It was difficult to determine how much of the increases in world prices for raw materials was due to increased energy prices, how much to shortages in the materials and how much to the example of the oil cartel's success.

"How do you say how much is due to petroleum prices? I suspect it's not possible," said Bartram Massell, staff member of the Office of Management and Budget's energy group.

Food prices, which experienced inflation on their own, also were pushed up by increases in the price of fertilizer, as well as the cost of fuels farmers need to run their machinery. The wholesale price of natural gas, a prime ingredient in some fertilizers, increased 41.6 per cent in the year ending in August.

Plastics and Synthetics

Other products with important energy components, such as plastics, synthetic rubber and synthetic textiles, were affected by rising energy prices. Here, oil was the principal raw material. The wholesale price of crude oil increased 69.1 per cent in the year ending in September. During the same period, the wholesale price of plastics, resins and other materials produced by the chemical industry jumped 87.5 per cent and the price of rubber climbed 29.1 per cent.

The Role of Windfall Profits

Oil company profits were 82 per cent higher during the first six months of 1974 than for the same period of 1973. At

Energy Price Trends

1967 = 100

Year	Fuel Oil and Coal	Gas and Electricity
1960	89.2	98.6
1965	94.6	99.4
1968	103.1	100.9
1969	105.6	102.8
1970	110.1	107.3
1971	117.5	114.7
1972	118.5	120.5
1973	136.0	126.4
1974 (to Oct.)	225.5	151.5

SOURCE: Bureau of Labor Statistics

Oil Company Profits: Higher Increases In 1974

In the current furor over worldwide inflation—due in large part to increased energy prices—relatively little has been said about oil company profits.

Yet the profit picture for the oil giants in 1974 has been considerably better than during the winter of 1973-74, when lesser profit increases generated much greater outrage in Congress.

"People seem very angry and upset about windfall profits," declared Sen. Charles H. Percy (R Ill.) during January hearings of the Government Operations Permanent Investigations Subcommittee. Henry M. Jackson (D Wash.), the subcommittee chairman, branded oil company profits "unconscionable."

Rates of Increase

During the hearings, Jackson released *Business Week* figures of the increases in third-quarter 1973 profits of the seven oil companies represented at the hearing, over the same period in 1972. A later *Business Week* survey showed that five of those companies did even better during the second quarter of 1974, when Jackson released the figures.

The table shows the percentage increase in profits of the seven companies for the third quarter of 1973 over the third quarter of 1972, and for the second quarter of 1974 over the same period a year earlier.

Company	3rd Quarter 1973 Increase	2nd Quarter 1974 Increase
Exxon Corp.	81%	67%
Gulf Oil Corp.	91	28
Mobil Oil Corp.	64	99
Shell Oil Co.	23	39
Standard Oil Co. of California	51	57
Standard Oil Co. (Indiana)	37	131
Texaco Inc.	48	72

The new *Business Week* survey showed that the profits of all oil and coal companies—often the same companies—during the second quarter of 1974 were 83 per cent higher than in the same period a year earlier.

The only clearly identifiable coal companies in the survey were Westmoreland Coal Co., which registered a 952 per cent profit increase in the second quarter, and North American Coal Co., whose profits dropped by 7 per cent. Continental Oil Co., which owned Consolidation Coal Co., showed an increase of 94 per cent; and Occidental Oil Co., owner of Maust Coal and Coke Corp., increased its profits by 293 per cent in the April-June period.

In January, Percy asked seven oil executives what they thought would be a reasonable rate of return on investment. The consensus was between 12 and 15 per cent. Taken together, companies in the current survey showed a 19.3 per cent return on investment for the year ending June 30.

The oil industry did better than manufacturing as a whole, which showed a second quarter profit increase of 24 per cent and a 14.2 per cent return on investment.

Need for Perspective

In Aug. 13 hearings before the Senate Small Business Subcommittee on Government Regulation, Treasury Secretary William E. Simon conceded that the oil industry "historically as well as presently" earned a "high dollar volume of profits." But the profits should be put in perspective, Simon argued.

He said a Federal Trade Commission study showed that oil companies' return on invested capital had run around 10 per cent for the past 16 years. He also repeated the January argument of oil executives that the spurt in profits in 1973 followed several lean years.

Treasury Study

A Treasury Department survey of the 19 largest oil companies found profits increased by 76 per cent in the first three months of 1974, Simon said. He cautioned that much of the profit gain was for oil company operations other than supplying Americans with oil products.

Nearly half the increase, Simon said, was a one-time gain in the value of inventories due to the dramatic rise in prices. Currency fluctuations and profits on chemical operations and tanker operations also had to be considered, Simon explained.

When all the increases not connected with petroleum operations were subtracted from the over-all profit increase, the companies were left with a 21 per cent rise in profits during the first quarter of 1974, Simon said. He quoted one analyst as saying that rising costs, the depletion of inventories and the depletion of low-cost crude oil supplies would cause oil company profits to decline 25 per cent in fourth quarter 1974 from the same period a year earlier.

the same time, oil consumption declined 3 to 5 per cent among major consuming nations, Treasury Secretary Simon told the Permanent Investigations Subcommittee. *(Oil company profits box, this page)*

The windfall profits came about when world and domestic prices were increased more than the costs of producing oil. All domestic production received an increase in prices in the winter of 1973-74. Price-controlled oil from old wells went up $1 a barrel and uncontrolled new oil rose to the world price. In addition, oil held in storage tanks increased in value when prices went up.

Crude oil prices rose at a rate that should have caused a 38 per cent increase in the cost of refined products between March 1973 and January 1974, but the actual cost rise for refined products was 127 per cent, according to an article in the May-June issue of *Challenge* magazine by economists William Nordhaus of Yale University and John Shoven of Stanford University.

"With an increase in profit margins of this magnitude, 'breathtaking' oil company profits should come as no surprise," the two economists declared.

Tussing of the Senate Interior Committee told CQ that "the increase in prices did not reflect an increase in the real cost of producing oil, but reflected windfall profits. All oil sold at $10 a barrel was producible at $3 a barrel 18 months ago.

"Although some production costs increased, a good $6 per barrel is windfall profit."

The Ratchet Effect

According to Tussing these profits exerted a substantial secondary price effect. This "ratchet effect," Tussing said, came from oil companies' bidding up the price of other materials and from labor's determination to get its slice of the economic pie.

If the world price of oil should decline, Tussing said, the higher materials prices and labor costs would prevent fuel prices from falling to levels that prevailed before the steep increase.

Tussing said the Treasury recaptured some of the profits in record bids in 1974 for the right to explore for oil on the continental shelf. However, these higher bid prices also would be reflected eventually in higher oil prices. Most of the rest of the profits were untouchable by the U.S. tax system, he said.

The oil companies were able to use their profit bonanza to bid up the price of drilling rigs and tubular goods, which were subject to a worldwide shortage. Coal companies also had reaped huge profits and were bidding up the price of draglines and roofbolts, which also were scarce. Manufacturers of earthmoving equipment used in strip mines had a three-year backlog of orders, according to Tussing. He said the price of tubular goods had tripled.

Wage Spiral

"There is a similar phenomenon with respect to wages," Tussing asserted. "The high price of oil has pulled up the price of domestic coal."

Since the increase in coal prices did not reflect increased costs of production, there have been "enormous windfall profits in the coal industry. This puts the United Mine Workers [whose contracts were to expire in November] in a tremendous bargaining position," Tussing stated.

Even though higher prices would bring on a greater supply of coal, prices would not come down again, as normally would be expected, because increased wages and other costs would have consumed part of the producers' profits.

"The wage rate will not come down again," Tussing said. "If the mineworkers get a 35 per cent wage increase, it will be a powerful example for the steelworkers, because of their close ties with the mineworkers. And the autoworkers will be next."

Other unions also were expected to seek substantial wage boosts to catch up with increases in the cost of living.

Why Prices Kept Climbing

The continued escalation of energy prices in August reflected the shock waves of the increase in world oil prices in January. With supplies still tight, consumers were willing to pay any price for coal or natural gas to keep their fires burning.

But the world price of oil had remained stable for almost a year, and the price of "old" domestic oil had been controlled at $5.25 a barrel since December 1973. Prices for most natural gas had been controlled at the wellhead for 18 years.

What was happening?

First, the energy industry was affected by the general rate of inflation and was passing these costs to consumers. Second, it took time for the shock waves of the oil price increase to work their way through the economy, a process now expected to run its course by the end of 1974.

Oil Prices

Oil prices were increasing for consumers, although the price of crude oil appeared to remain stable. This happened because the supply of price-controlled oil was declining, forcing the consumption of more high-cost oil.

Under price controls, oil produced from existing wells at a rate equal to 1972 production was limited to $5.25 per barrel. This was "old" oil. Any increase in production from existing wells, all oil from new wells and oil from wells producing less than 10 barrels a day was not controlled and could be sold at world prices. In addition, as an incentive for increased production, prices were freed on an amount of oil produced from old wells equal to the amount produced from new wells.

Oil prices continued to increase because production of old oil was declining while imports and new oil production were increasing. The amount of old oil sold in the United States had dropped within a year from about 70 per cent of total domestic demand to 60 per cent.

At the same time, the percentage of imported oil had increased since the Arab nations ended their five-month embargo in March. During the depths of the energy crisis in February, oil imports accounted for about 30 per cent of total petroleum demand, according to Federal Energy Administration figures. For the week ending Sept. 6, FEA figures showed that imports had risen to 37 per cent of total demand. All imported oil was sold at world prices.

Natural Gas Prices

In September, the Bureau of Labor Statistics reported that the wholesale price for natural gas was 26 per cent higher than the year before. Since there was a two-month lag in the statistics, the index showed prices for July. The rate of increase had slowed down. Natural gas prices decreased 12.3 per cent between April and May.

Still, the public debate over deregulation had left the impression that all natural gas prices were controlled at the wellhead. But the Federal Power Commission (FPC) had authority to regulate only the price of gas sold in interstate commerce, about half of the 22.3 trillion cubic feet sold in the United States annually. There were no price controls on gas sold within states or on imported gas.

The FPC's latest figures showed that the price of interstate gas had increased about 13.7 per cent between May 1973 and May 1974 to 25.7 cents per thousand cubic feet. But the average price of intrastate gas was up 19 per cent to 58.6 cents per thousand cubic feet in the same time frame. The price of gas imported from Canada and Mexico was up more than 30 per cent.

While the increase in average price was dramatic, new contracts for intrastate gas were ranging from $1.20 to $1.50 per thousand cubic feet, up from about 60 cents a year ago, said David S. Schwartz, assistant chief economist for the FPC. Gas prices were rising while production slumped 4.5 per cent in the year ending in May. The commission reported that sales of the major pipelines were down 4.9 per cent while revenues increased 13.1 per cent.

Prices of Electricity

The gasoline lines of the winter of 1973-74 have been replaced by soaring electric bills as the number one cause of outrage among energy consumers.

"We in Rhode Island and we in New England have a very difficult situation. I just received my bill. I have a real modest home with seven rooms in Rhode Island. I got my bill of $97. That is my electricity bill, $97. It has almost

Salaries of Top Oil Executives

One place that inflation of energy prices could be controlled was in the salary of oil company executives, according to Sen. Thomas F. Eagleton (D Mo.).

"While the American worker is exhorted to go slow on his wage demands, there appears to be little spirit of self-sacrifice among the ranks of the oil companies' top executives," Eagleton declared in a floor speech on Sept. 6.

Following is a table Eagleton placed in the *Congressional Record*, showing 1972-73 salaries and bonuses paid to the chief executives of the 10 major oil companies:

Company and Chief Executive	1972 Salary, Other Payments	1973 Salary, Other Payments
Cities Service Co.		
Robert V. Sellers, chairman	$137,660	$231,373
Charles J. Waldelich, president	119,326	187,473
Exxon Corp.		
John K. Jamieson, chairman	539,166	596,886
Clifton C. Garvin Jr., president	327,916	395,000
Gulf Oil Corp.		
Bob R. Dorsey, chairman	345,000	490,000
James E. Lee, president	251,500	266,666
Mobil Oil Corp.		
Rawleigh Warner Jr., chairman	455,000	499,667
William P. Tavoulares, president	350,000	390,000
Phillips Petroleum Co.		
W.W. Keeler, chairman	342,000	105,593
John M. Houchin, chairman	285,000	332,548
William F. Martin, president	187,580	236,608
Shell Oil Co.		
Harry Bridges, president	325,000	365,000
J.B. St. Clair, executive vice president	179,996	203,340
Standard Oil Co. of California		
Otto N. Miller, chairman	299,620	478,432
J.E. Gosline, vice-chairman	217,833	220,667
Harold J. Haynes, president	217,833	220,591
Sun Oil Co.		
Robert G. Dunlop, chairman	250,600	262,677
H. Robert Sharbaugh, president	191,601	210,354
Texaco Inc.		
Maurice F. Granville, chairman	218,114	273,748
John K. McKinley, president	149,962	176,009
Union Oil Co. of California		
Fred L. Hartley, president	251,500	294,583
Charles F. Parker, senior vice president	137,908	134,700

doubled." This typical consumer complaint was registered by Sen. John O. Pastore (D R.I.) during Sept. 5 debate on legislation (HR 8193) to establish a cargo preference for oil.

The FPC reported that electric utilities increased their rates by 8.8 per cent in the first three months of 1974.

But the base rates did not hurt so much as extra charges passed on to the consumers in the form of fuel cost adjustments.

Bill Bevis of the Florida Public Service Commission testified on the adjustment at the hearings of the Senate Special Committee on the Aging: "In January of this year, a customer who used 1,000 kilowatt-hours—which is the average monthly residential consumption in Florida—paid a base rate of $20.87 plus a fuel adjustment of $4.45 for a total of $25.32.

"This month, the same customer paid a base rate of $22.07 plus a fuel adjustment of $15.05 for a total of $37.12."

The Role of Government Policy

The over-all impact of federal policy on energy prices has been to increase them. The government's early response to the energy crisis was a $1 per barrel increase in the controlled price of domestic oil. Jackson has maintained consistently that the increase could not be justified on grounds of encouraging exploration or on any other ground. A dollar a barrel difference in the price of domestically produced old oil amounted to $5.3-million a day during the week ending Sept. 6—60 per cent of domestic production, or 5.3 million barrels a day.

Jackson argued Sept. 30, as he has since January, that the price of new oil should be rolled back to the $7 or $8 per barrel price that Simon has maintained would be an adequate incentive to produce more oil. If the price of new oil were rolled back $3 per barrel, consumers would have saved nearly $11-million a day during the week ending Sept. 6—40 per cent of domestic production times $3 a barrel.

Decontrol Philosophy

The administration adamantly opposed wage and price controls, as Ford affirmed in his first press conference on Aug. 28.

The administration also continued a determined drive to deregulate the wellhead price of natural gas. Schwartz of the FPC disagreed with the administration position. He argued that deregulation would not only increase interstate prices, but inevitably would put upward pressure on the intrastate price as well. Decontrol of natural gas prices would increase the cost to consumers by about $9-billion a year by 1977, Schwartz estimated.

Shift on Oil Prices

Decontrol of oil prices apparently was pushed to the back burner temporarily. On Sept. 10, Simon and Interior Secretary Rogers C. B. Morton told a meeting of the National Petroleum Council that oil prices should be deregulated.

"I take the position that we will rue the day if we artificially hold down the price of oil in the marketplace," Morton told the advisory committee of oil executives. Simon listed decontrol of oil and gas prices as one of the administration's short-term energy goals.

Less than a week later, at the Sept. 16 presummit economic conference in Dallas, Texas, Morton and Simon were saying deregulation of oil prices should be delayed because of its inflationary potential.

(Continued on p. 54)

High Oil Prices: Seeds of Economic Collapse

Inflation was only part, and probably not the most serious part, of the economic problems caused by high world oil prices.

Economists and government officials were far more concerned about the one-way flow of money to the oil producing nations, primarily in the Middle East. The problem was that the largest oil exporters might not be able to spend all the money they earned, which would leave consuming nations without enough cash to buy other materials. The situation held the potential for a global economic collapse. By the end of September a worldwide effort was under way to get the oil money recirculated in the world economy.

"Today, governments are watching an erosion of the world's oil supply and financial systems comparable in its potential for economic and political disaster to the Great Depression of the 1930s," wrote Walter J. Levy, a petroleum economist, in the July issue of *Foreign Affairs.*

The rise in oil prices meant that members of the Organization of Petroleum Exporting Countries (OPEC) would receive $100-billion a year from consuming nations, Henry C. Wallich, a Federal Reserve Board member, told the House Banking and Currency Subcommittee on International Finance on Aug. 13. About $25-billion would come from the United States.

"Even after allowing for a steep rise in their expenditures for imported goods and services, the OPEC countries will be left with a surplus of funds available for investment of some $60-billion," Wallach stated.

Impact on Poor Nations

The impact of this one-way cash flow would be especially devastating on poor countries, Wallich said: "Food prices are now rising generally, and the added problems of paying for fuel and fertilizer may well reach the point of depriving some countries of their minimal subsistence needs, posing very harsh alternatives."

The trade and investment of OPEC members would be concentrated in five or six wealthy industrial nations, mostly in the United States, Levy said Sept. 5 at the White House meeting of economists leading up to the economic summit meeting President Ford held on Sept. 27 and 28.

In this case, Levy said, the United States would have to supply all other importing countries with massive funds if it wanted to avoid a large increase in the dollar's value, a resulting decline in U.S. exports, heavy inflationary pressures and the bankruptcy of other nations.

Levy said exporting nations would be reluctant to lend money to any of the poor nations and some wealthier ones because it was unlikely that the loans ever could be repaid. The problem was to find a mechanism to "recycle" the oil money among all nations, not just the wealthy ones. World finance ministers meeting in Washington and at the United Nations were looking for just such a mechanism, which would depend for success on the cooperation of OPEC countries.

The International Monetary Fund (IMF) meeting on Oct. 3 named 20 finance ministers to draft a plan to recycle the oil money.

Conservation efforts by western nations would not be undercut by production rollbacks in Saudi Arabia and Iran, spokesmen for the two Arab nations promised on Oct. 4. Saudi Arabia and Iran are the two largest oil exporting nations.

Another possibility under active consideration was for importing nations to clamp down on oil consumption and cut imports. France announced in late September that it would limit imports. Sen. Henry M. Jackson (D Wash.) proposed Sept. 30 that the United States do the same thing. Levy suggested at the economists' conference that the United States limit the investment of OPEC oil funds.

Trade Deficit

The U.S. balance of payments showed the impact of the oil price increase. In August, the United States spent $1.13-billion more for imports than it received for exports. Import costs rose to $9.5-billion, with a third of the jump caused by high-cost oil and raw materials. Wallich said the trade deficit was running at an annual rate of $4.2-billion.

The United States, which imported only 20 per cent of its energy supply, seemed to have some alternatives—conservation, increased coal production, limited oil imports.

But many poor nations with no energy sources of their own seemed to have no choice but to buy fertilizer, or to buy oil and starve.

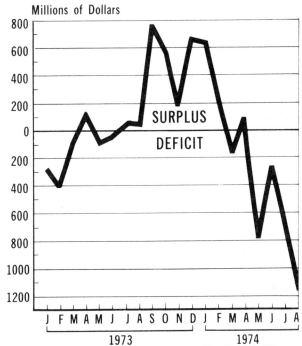

U.S. Trade Balance
Millions of Dollars

Rising prices for imported fuels and other raw materials widened the U.S. trade deficit in 1974, even though U.S. exports remained high. U.S. imports for August were valued at $9.5-billion, with one-third of the total due to fuels and other crude materials.

Source: Department of Commerce, Council of Economic Advisers

Deregulation in the face of current world oil prices could have a dramatic effect on the cost of living. If prices of the 60 per cent of the 8.9 million barrels of domestic oil produced daily during the week ending Sept. 6 were allowed to rise from $5.25 to $10.25 a barrel, it would add $15-million a day to the cost of oil.

Long-Range Policy

It seemed certain that administration figures would continue to preach a free, but not too free, market for energy prices. High-cost alternative fuels—such as oil from shale and oil and gas from coal—were likely to cost more than oil produced by conventional means. Thus, if Arab nations saw they were losing their markets to alternative fuels, they could reduce prices and wipe out the fledgling industries.

The government would have to build in some kind of market interference to protect these industries. The protection could include import quotas, tax breaks, price supports, government purchases or price guarantees.

"The price that prevails for energy in the United States five or 10 years from now will not be a free market price, but will be directly or indirectly determined by interferences in the market mechanism, either by the United States or by foreign governments," Tussing said Feb. 15.

Hopes for Price Cut

In the spring and early summer, federal officials expressed optimism that the oil producing countries would lower prices somewhat. For example, at a June 9 hearing on his confirmation as federal energy administrator, John C. Sawhill told the Senate Interior Committee that world oil prices should decline because of a slight surplus. (President Ford fired Sawhill Oct. 29 and named Andrew E. Gibson to succeed him. Ford withdrew Gibson's nomination Nov. 12 and named Frank G. Zarb instead.) *(Box, p. 9)*

But the decline did not happen. Instead of selling the surplus, the Middle East countries reduced production by some 500,000 barrels a day. Then, at a September meeting in Vienna, the Organization of Petroleum Exporting Countries, which included non-Arab nations, voted to increase oil company taxes by 5 per cent.

Until then, U.S. officials had tried to persuade the exporters that a price cut was in their best interests. When that failed, a tough line was tried.

The Hard Line

Ford fired the first salvo in a Sept. 18 speech at the United Nations when he hinted that consuming nations could retaliate against high oil prices by raising food prices.

On Sept. 23, Ford and Kissinger made tough speeches about oil prices, including allusions to the use of force.

"Throughout history nations have gone to war over natural advantages such as water or food, or convenient passages on land or sea," Ford said at the World Energy Conference. "But in the nuclear age, when any local conflict may escalate to global catastrophe, war brings unacceptable risks for all mankind."

Kissinger told the United Nations that the United States might have to re-evaluate its efforts to help Iran and Saudi Arabia improve their economic position.

But the tough talk and efforts to unite consuming nations did not have much effect. The Arab nations angrily retorted that oil prices were raised because of price increases for products they bought from the industrialized nations.

At the International Monetary Fund meeting Oct. 1, western countries urged the United States to abandon its efforts to roll back world oil prices.

Jackson's Response

Jackson said it did no good to try to bluff the oil exporters unless the United States was prepared to back up its words with action.

He offered a program to limit energy consumption, curtail imports and to crank up standby emergency machinery to deal with the results. A determined energy conservation program could save 2,000,000 barrels of oil a day, Jackson asserted. He advocated leaning on the auto industry to speed up production of small cars.

Imports should be limited to the amount bought by the current $25-billion a year the United States was spending for foreign oil, Jackson said. He urged the President to roll back domestic oil prices to $7 to $8 a barrel, and opposed any further increases in the price of old oil.

Jackson said the Arab nations would never cut oil prices unless the United States did so first. "I don't know if it would work," he said. "But it would be the beginning of a concrete program to put the onus on them as far as prices are concerned."

Ford's Program

As expected, Ford did not buy Jackson's proposal to cut oil prices. During the week of Sept. 30, the administration increasingly talked conservation, possibly enforced with a stiff tax on gasoline. Ford rejected both price controls and gasoline taxes in his Oct. 8 economic message.

His major proposal was to reduce oil imports by one million barrels a day by the end of 1975, making up the difference with new supplies and energy saving. But the saving effort would be voluntary. Ford exhorted the auto industry to improve gasoline mileage and consumers to "enlist" as "energy savers."

The President's proposals seemed unlikely to have much impact on energy prices.

Outlook

With the oil exporters holding firm, there was not much chance that energy prices would come down. If there were no further price increases, energy prices eventually would begin to level out, but with labor struggling to catch up with the cost of living, the impact of energy price inflation would linger on.

Simon appeared to be convinced that conservation and discovery of new energy supplies would bring down oil prices in the long run. Oil demand would be down sharply in the 1980-85 period, forcing the Arabs to reduce their prices to keep their share of the market, Simon said at the Sept. 18 subcommittee hearings.

He added, "Of course, 1980 is six years away, and consuming nations cannot absorb the economic impact of current oil prices for that length of time."

A hopeful note was sounded by economists Nordhaus and Shoven in their *Challenge* article. They found that the rise in commodity and wholesale prices during the Korean war boom period and 1973-74 were identical—65 per cent and 18 per cent respectively.

Commodity prices fell sharply after the Korean war boom, they wrote. "We would be surprised if commodity prices over the next couple of years do not recede from their current level. If this happens, their decline should act as a significant brake on future inflationary tendencies." ∎

PRESSURE MOUNTS FOR OIL TAX REFORMS

Oil and taxes—two subjects that most Americans would prefer not having to worry about—are uppermost in many people's minds as the nation approaches the April 15 income tax filing deadline amid high gasoline prices and soaring oil company profits. That coincidence may help bring about the first changes in oil taxation in nearly five years, and perhaps the first substantial changes in nearly 50 years. Citizens who find themselves paying higher taxes have read or heard that major oil companies earned extraordinarily high 1974 profits on which they will pay traditionally low taxes. Demands for action focusing on the federal government have become so strong that, in the words of *Business Week* magazine: "Today, the oil industry is facing the greatest threat from Washington since the breakup of the Standard Oil monopoly 63 years ago."[1] *(Footnote sources, p. 61)*

Proposals have been made in Congress and elsewhere to nationalize the oil industry, to create a competing national oil company, to split apart the major companies in antitrust action, to bring the companies under strict federal controls, to roll back crude oil prices and to eliminate or modify the industry's various tax benefits—"loopholes" to some. Of all these possibilities, the last appears almost certain, although the form which oil taxation reform will take still is an open question. Sen. Charles H. Percy (R Ill.) summed up the mood of many members of Congress when he said in January: "Changes in the federal tax law applicable to the oil industry are clearly necessary so as to encourage investment in domestic exploration, production and refining...and to assure the American public that its sacrifices have not been undertaken merely to add to already overflowing corporate coffers."[2]

Record-setting 1973 profits of many of the major U.S. oil companies were the primary impetus to calls for federal controls. Profits of the 10 largest firms increased by an average of 48 per cent over 1972 levels. Oil industry spokesmen contended that 1973 was a year of recovery from poor profit levels of the past several years. Annon Card, senior vice president of Texaco, argued: "In seven of the last 10 years the rate of return on investment in the petroleum industry was below that of all manufacturing companies." In 1972, he said, the oil companies' rate of return was only 10.8 per cent compared with a 12.1 average for all manufacturing concerns.[3] Bob R. Dorsey, chairman of Gulf, insisted: "Our returns are just pulling even with the rest of American industry. If that's an excess profit, I'll eat my hat."[4]

Nonetheless, the mood in Washington was to restrict large oil profits, and the industry found itself being criticized for what traditionally has been considered a major goal of the capitalistic system—making a high profit. Charges of "excess" or "windfall" profits were heard with increasing frequency, along with accusations that the industry was taking advantage of fuel shortages brought on by the Arab oil embargo to raise prices sharply and earn extortionate profits.

Action on Taxes

Initial congressional attempts to deal with the situation were confused and ineffectual. An emergency energy bill that finally cleared Congress on Feb. 27 drew President Nixon's veto on March 6. He specifically objected to a price "rollback" provision. At a White House news conference that night, he congratulated the Senate for having sustained his veto a few hours earlier and thus killing a bill that "mistakenly was aimed...to get down the price of gasoline."

Sen. Henry M. Jackson (D Wash.), who led the floor fight for the bill, said of the President's veto: "He's drawn an issue which frankly I welcome.... Prices are going to go up and up. The rollback provision is going to be an ongoing fight." Rollback refers to a proposed ceiling of $5.25 a barrel on crude oil, which already is the controlled price at most long-developed fields, accounting for about 70 per cent of U.S. production. The bill would have applied that ceiling to most "new oil" prices. Market prices currently exceed $10 a barrel for new oil and average about $6.50 for all domestically produced crude oil.

A provision for an equally controversial "windfall profits" tax on the oil industry fell by the wayside before the bill ever reached the President. As he proposed, it would be a temporary graduated excise tax on increases in crude oil prices above the levels of Dec. 1, 1973. President Nixon asked for this tax on Dec. 19, in a message to Congress on his forthcoming legislative proposals. Nixon said his plan was "carefully designed to avoid completely depriving producers of a legitimate return on the major investments they will have to make in order to produce the additional supply we need."

He proposed a tax rate of 10 to 85 per cent on crude oil price increases—depending on the size of the increase. After three years, the minimum 10 per cent tax would be applied only to crude oil selling for more than $7 a barrel—the Treasury's estimate of the average price needed to prompt development of long-range supplies. Defending the phase-out feature, Nixon said: "As prices return to the long-run supply level and as the potential for windfall profits disappears, a continuation of the tax would result in higher prices for consumers, with no concomitant increase in oil supplies."

The Nixon proposal was praised by some members of Congress, including Rep. Al Ullman (D Ore.), acting chairman of the House Ways and Means Committee, who termed it a "tough interim tax on the petroleum industry." On the other hand, committee member Charles A. Vanik (D Ohio) called it "a sham approach to the problem." Nonetheless, the committee appeared to be leaning toward the administration approach in legislation it began writing in February *(see p. 61)*. In an analysis of oil industry profits and taxes, *Time* magazine said: "Congress has to choose between either rolling back oil prices or eliminating some oil tax shelters. It cannot do both and expect the industry to provide the nation with enough energy. For its

Profits of Largest U.S. Oil Companies

	1973	1972	Per cent increase
	($ millions)		
Exxon	$2,440	$1,532	59.3
Texaco	1,292	889	45.4
Mobil	843	574	46.8
Standard of California	844	547	54.2
Gulf	800	447	79.0
Standard Oil (Indiana)	811	375	36.4
Shell	333	271	23.0
Atlantic Richfield	270	193	40.3
Phillips	230	148	55.3
Continental	243	170	42.6

SOURCE: American Petroleum Institute, from company reports

part, the industry has to choose between retaining high prices and preferential tax treatment. It cannot expect the public to tolerate both."[5]

Mineral Depletion Allowances

The U.S. oil industry long has been the beneficiary of tax advantages that have been lucrative for the companies and costly for the Treasury. Several major provisions have been objects of criticism over the years and are likely targets for congressional action. They include:

Percentage Depletion. The controversial percentage depletion allowance permits the owner of oil- or gas-producing property to deduct from his taxable income up to 22 per cent of the gross revenues from his wells. The allowance was originally enacted in 1926 and set at 27½ per cent *(see p. 58)* in an effort to establish a rule-of-thumb measure for the depleted value of a well as oil or gas was pumped out. The concept resembles property depreciation, but while other businesses depreciate the value of buildings or equipment to help recover capital costs, mineral depletion is an arbitrary percentage of income. It bears no relation to costs and in some cases vastly exceeds the amount invested in the property. Percentage depletion is limited to 50 per cent of net income before the allowance is calculated. For example:

If gross income is	$100,000
And costs are	60,000 (including royalty payments)
Net income is	40,000
Percentage depletion	22,000 (22% of gross income)
Deduction allowed	20,000
Taxable income	20,000

Because of the 50 per cent limitation, the determination of what constitutes an oil or gas property is quite important. The general rule is that each separate interest in each deposit in each section of land is a separate property. However, all interests in a single area may be treated together or separately, and each taxpayer with a direct interest may take percentage depletion on his share of gross income. For instance, the well operator may deduct royalty payments he makes to the landowner before computing his depletion allowance. And any royalty holder may take depletion on the share represented by his royalty.

Cost Depletion. Although percentage depletion is more widely known and used, cost depletion is another method available to the oil and gas industry. It closely resembles depreciation. A recent Library of Congress study offers an explanation why it is little used. "Percentage depletion usually results in a faster recovery than most depletion does, and the cost may be recovered many times over since percentage depletion is not limited to original cost. In practice almost all depletion is taken as percentage depletion rather than cost depletion."[6] Professor J. Reid Hambrick of George Washington University Law School estimated in testimony before the House Ways and Means Committee in 1973 that the total value of percentage depletion deductions was about 16 times that of cost depletion deductions.[7] Tax Analysts and Advocates, a private research group and public interest law firm, estimated in January 1974 that the oil and gas depletion allowances would cost the Treasury about $2.6-billion in fiscal year 1975.[8]

Intangible drilling costs, or "I.D.C.," deductions allow the operator of an oil or gas well to take an immediate tax deduction for "intangible" drilling and development expenditures. These include certain expenses incurred in bringing the well into production, such as labor, fuel and power, materials and supplies, tool rental and repairs. The deduction is not applicable to "tangible" costs of assets such as pipes, tanks and pumps. Intangible costs can be deducted for most kinds of industrial or business construction, but they must be capitalized and spread over the useful life of the building or project. Intangible drilling costs, in contrast, may be deducted entirely in the year expenditures are made. In addition, a percentage depletion may be claimed; or intangible drilling costs may be capitalized and recovered under cost depletion.

Whatever method is chosen, it is binding for all future years. For example:

Gross receipts from oil sales	$100,000
I.D.C.'s deducted currently	10,000
Taxable income	90,000
or	
Gross receipts from oil sales	$100,000
I.D.C.'s of $10,000 capitalized on a 20-year basis	500
Taxable income	99,500

The intangible drilling cost deduction was not enacted by Congress but was introduced into the U.S. tax code through a series of administrative rulings by the Treasury Department. Congress gave its approval to the practice, however, in the Revenue Act of 1954. In fiscal year 1975, according to Tax Analysts and Advocates, intangible drilling cost deductions will reduce potential federal revenues by about $800-million.

"Dry hole" expensing is another deduction available to oil and gas operators. They may write off the expense of drilling dry holes in the year the losses occur or they may elect to capitalize these costs over several years. This kind of tax option is not unusual in other businesses. However, some tax experts argue that the treatment provides a special subsidy to oil and gas because of the nature of the industry. The average rate of success for wildcat, or independent, oil drilling is about one hole in nine. Thus, the expenses incurred in drilling the eight dry holes may be considered part of the capital costs of the single producing well—and the producing well generally provides enough income to recover all drilling costs.

Mineral Depletion Rates

All minerals mined in the United States, including those mined offshore, are eligible for depletion tax deductions at varying percentage rates. The Tax Reform Act of 1969 reduced depletion on minerals then receiving 23 per cent to 22 per cent, raised molybdenum from 15 to 22 per cent, and reduced minerals then receiving 15 per cent to 14 per cent, except for silver, gold, copper, oil shale and iron ore.

Among those now receiving 22 per cent depletion are uranium, asbestos, bauxite, fluorspar, graphite, mica, cadmium, cobalt, lead, manganese, mercury, nickel, platinum, tin and zinc. Among those receiving 14 per cent are potash, feldspar, garnet, borax, fire clay, quartzite and limestone. Several others receive 5 per cent depletion, including sand, gravel, slate, stone, oyster and clam shells, granite and marble. No percentage depletion is granted to soil, sod, dirt, turf, water, mosses or minerals derived from sea water, the air or similar inexhaustible resources.

Foreign Tax Credit. Perhaps the most lucrative tax provision to the oil industry is the foreign tax credit, under which an American taxpayer may deduct foreign taxes paid on foreign income from his U.S. tax liability. The aim is to prevent double taxation, and it reduces U.S. taxes dollar for dollar.

Still another major benefit to the oil industry concerns the labeling of royalty payments to foreign countries as income taxes. In most oil-producing countries, the government holds land rights and charges royalties on each barrel. If these royalties were treated as part of the cost of doing business—as they are for other U.S. companies operating abroad—the oil companies would have to pay taxes on them.[9]

The Treasury Department, in response to requests from Congress, released figures in January 1974 showing that American-controlled oil companies used foreign tax credits to reduce their U.S. taxes by more than 75 per cent in 1971. The companies defend this practice by saying that they are competing abroad with government-owned oil companies of France (Compagnie Francaise des Petroles) and Italy (Petrofina Societe Anonyme), and with Royal Dutch Shell and British Petroleum, which are partly owned by government. All of them receive favored tax treatment in their home countries. The immediate effect of denying U.S. tax credits on foreign-earned income, according to this reasoning, would be to reduce these earnings.

Incentives for Energy Development

Critics and defenders of the oil industry generally agree that there is a great need for development of energy sources—old and new—in the near future. The Library of Congress study suggested that the oil industry's tax advantages were inefficient in stimulating exploration and development of new supplies: "It is customary to claim that production is encouraged by the percentage depletion and intangible drilling costs. Yet, quantitative studies...suggest that they encourage producers to rely on overdrilling in existing fields...."

There is little evidence that the oil and gas industry has trouble obtaining needed capital. In March 1973 the Senate Interior Committee held hearings aimed at determining the adequacy of normal market channels in meeting the capital needs of energy industries. The Federal Power Commission, the Interior Department and the Treasury all agreed that these industries had not experienced any unusual financing problems in the past and that they relied primarily on internal sources of financing. Data derived from Chase Manhattan Bank's annual studies[10] of a group of 30 major petroleum companies showed that cash earnings provided 71 per cent of the required working capital in 1971 and 69 per cent in 1972. The total amount available for new investment, repayment of debt, additional projects and dividends was $21.4-billion, 2.6 per cent more than in 1971.

The Chase Manhattan Bank study concluded that no changes in oil taxation were desirable. It reported that the 30 companies paid 112 per cent more taxes than they did four years earlier but that combined net earnings increased by only 2.9 per cent. Over the same period, "capital expenditures rose by no more than 16.6 per cent—far less than the amount necessary to keep pace with the expanding needs for petroleum." The report concluded: "No wonder petroleum is in short supply."

The American Petroleum Institute has estimated that if it were possible to find new petroleum reserves in the 1970s at the same cost per barrel as in the 1960s, the industry would have to spend about $9-billion annually. But inflation, the added expense of pollution control and exploration difficulties will run the costs much higher, the institute estimated. "Any reduction in petroleum tax incentives would either make price increases necessary or severely impede the search for domestic supplies of oil and gas," the study stated.[11]

The Federal Power Commission and the Interior Department reported in 1973 to the Senate Interior Committee that repeal of the provisions for percentage depletion, intangible drilling costs and dry holes would reduce the cash flow before adequate adjustments could take place, and that during "this interim critical period impairment of funds would be most untimely." The Library of Congress, in its study, said that this argument "must be given substantial consideration...."

Evolution of Oil Tax System

In 1866, when the U.S. oil industry was in its infancy, a proposed federal tax on crude oil was abandoned after aroused producers from the fledgling Pennsylvania oil fields brought pressures on Congress. They claimed that such a tax would cause undue harships for their struggling industry. "From that time, oil interests knew they could never abandon vigilance in the legislative halls if they were to maintain their defenses against taxation and publicly defined responsibility," Robert Engler wrote in *The Politics of Oil.*[12]

When the 16th Amendment to the Constitution was ratified in 1913, the implementing legislation, the Revenue Act of 1913, established the principle of allowing deductions for mineral depletion—although it did not use the term "depletion." The statute provided "a reasonable allowance for the exhaustion, wear and tear of property arising out of its use or employment in the business, not to exceed, in the case of mines, 5 per centum of the gross value at the mine of the output for the year...." From then on, the concept of "reasonable allowance" has changed considerably, but almost without exception it has been increased and extended to include more minerals.[13]

The Revenue Act of 1916 retained the 1913 provisions but removed the 5 per cent limitation. It also allowed the deductions for depletion at cost or fair market value as of March 1, 1913. Then came the Revenue Act of 1918, revising the depletion allowance by permitting taxpayers to use as the basis for depletion the fair market value at the time of discovery or within 30 days thereafter. Thus, "The basis for depletion no longer was the amount originally invested, and the depletion allowance lost some of its similarity to the depreciation allowance."[14]

An important aspect of discovery depletion was that it allowed deductions for depletion in excess of original cost. The size of the depletion allowance and the law's enforcement soon became objects of concern. The Treasury Department proposed in 1921 that depletion deductions be limited

> *"...Oil interests knew they could never abandon their vigilance in the legislative halls if they were to maintain their defenses against taxation and publicly defined responsibility."*
> —Robert Engler, *The Politics of Oil*

to 50 per cent of net income from the property, and the Revenue Act of 1924 included that limitation. A report from the Senate Select Committee on the Investigation of the Bureau of Internal Revenue said in 1926 that the depletion law was poorly administered and grossly discriminatory, that allowances were generally excessive and often arrived at by bargaining, and that the industry frequently hired away bureau employees to gain inside information on rulings.

Fixed Percentages

Acknowledging this criticism, Congress changed the depletion rules, adopting *percentage* depletion for the first time. The Revenue Act of 1926 set the rate at 27½ per cent, a compromise between what the House wanted (25 per cent) and the Senate wanted (30 per cent). The principal innovation was that percentage depletion was made applicable to income from *all* oil and gas production, whereas discovery value depletion had *not* been applicable to income from properties acquired by purchase. "Percentage depletion was thus less specifically an exploration incentive device than discovery value depletion had been," one analyst wrote, "a fact that did not go unnoticed by opponents of the 1926 legislation."[15] Nonetheless, little change of any significance was made in percentage depletion for more than four decades.

The comprehensive Tax Reform Act of 1969 lowered the depletion rate to 22 per cent. Again the figure represented a compromise between the House (20 per cent) and Senate (23 per cent).[16] The House Ways and Means Committee report on its version of the bill stated:

> Your Committee believes that even if percentage depletion rates are viewed as a needed stimulant at the present time, they are higher than is needed to achieve the desired beneficial effect on reserves....

The 1969 law has produced conflicting claims as to its effect. Joseph A. Ruskay and Richard A. Osserman at In-

diana University wrote the following year that depletion "escaped virtually unscathed under the Tax Reform Act of 1969." On the other hand, the American Petroleum Institute said the law had made it more difficult for oil producers to raise needed capital.[17]

Secret Ruling on Foreign Royalties

The history of the Treasury Department's ruling on foreign tax credits—that royalties paid to foreign governments would be regarded by the United States as taxes—was revealed in hearings conducted Jan. 30-31, 1974, by the Senate Foreign Relations Subcommittee on Multinational Operations. Sen. Frank Church (D Idaho), subcommittee chairman, said in an opening statement that the secret tax arrangement was made to prevent oil-producing Arab states from going Communist in the Cold War. "The Department of State made a basic foreign policy judgment that the rulers of these countries should receive revenue at the expense of the U.S. Treasury," Church stated. He said the source of his information was George C. McGhee, former assistant secretary of state.

As an example, ARAMCO, the consortium of international oil companies which operates in Saudi Arabia, originally paid both U.S. income taxes and royalties to the Saudi government. The company could use the royalties only for a tax deduction, not a tax credit. But in 1951, the year after the secret ruling went into effect, payments to the U.S. Treasury from ARAMCO dropped to $6-million from $50-million the year before, while payments to Saudi Arabia rose to $110-million from $66-million. Church and Sen. Charles H. Percy (R Ill.) agreed that the oil companies had done nothing illegal, but they objected to the fact that the companies had amassed untaxable profits on the basis of a secret arrangement with the U.S. government.

It also was pointed out at the hearings that the posted prices on which the oil companies figured their foreign

Tax Status of Natural Gas

Discussions of the impact of tax provisions generally lump oil and natural gas together. Oil and gas exploration efforts usually are conducted jointly and much natural gas is found in conjunction with oil and produced from the same well. Also, the 14 largest oil companies provide 75 per cent of the nation's natural gas supply.

However, the effect of tax incentives on gas production is insignificant when compared to the impact of regulated prices. Natural gas prices have been below the market price for several years by Federal Power Commission regulation. The average price of gas in the regulated interstate market is 22.5 cents per 1,000 cubic feet, according to the FPC, while in the unregulated intrastate market it ranges from 55.7 to 71.4 cents. *(Deregulation controversy, p. 69)*

So long as the regulated price of natural gas is so far below the market price, tax incentives probably will not have much effect on increasing supply. The incentives would have to be increased several times to have any impact on natural gas supply. On the other hand, it is unclear just what effect the deregulation of prices would have on supply and demand, although it is generally presumed that a price rise would increase supply and reduce demand.

SOURCE: Congressional Quarterly Service

payments were higher, sometimes double, the actual prices they paid for the oil they extracted. This would tend to increase the amount of tax credits they could claim on their U.S. tax returns. In February 1974, Rep. Les Aspin (D Wis.) began circulating a petition among all House members urging Internal Revenue Director Donald Alexander "to close this huge loophole" by revoking the agency's ruling. Aspin said that bills he and other members of Congress had introduced to make the change by statute were unnecessary—that IRS could make the changes through agency regulations. He estimated that the oil companies had escaped $3-billion in U.S. taxes through the device. "The worst aspect of the foreign tax credit is that it encourages oil companies to explore and develop oil overseas instead of in the U.S. because the tax breaks are greater for foreign operations," he added.[18]

Outlook for Changes

Proposals for changing the oil and gas taxation systems have proliferated and some alterations in the tax structure now appear inevitable. But any changes will be vehemently contested. The oil industry and various interest groups are bitterly divided, even among themselves, over what should be done. The percentage depletion allowance has drawn the most criticism of any tax provision, and proposals to abolish it are heard with increasing frequency. According to an estimate by Tax Analysts and Advocates, with the rising prices of crude oil the percentage depletion tax write-off for 1974 will increase to $2.2-billion from $1.5-billion in 1972.

"If we do not change percentage depletion," Sen. Gaylord Nelson (D Wis.), a member of the Senate Finance Committee, has said, "the public is going to be outraged if not astonished to discover that oil companies have received huge increased tax deductions because of increased prices. Since the percentage depletion is calculated at 22 per cent of the price of crude oil...the higher the price, the higher the tax write-off."[19] But in an editorial, *The Wall Street Journal* declared that higher taxes on oil companies probably would mean even higher prices at the pump. The newspaper said "changes in the tax law would be harmful at worst and cosmetic at best."[20]

"We are sufficiently worried to think that something might be done in anger, recrimination and haste."
—Shell Oil President Harry Bridges

Treasury Secretary William E. Simon has suggested that changes in the percentage depletion allowance might be possible without hurting oil exploration and production. While he was federal energy chief early in 1973, Simon wrote to Senator Jackson: "...in the short run, changes in percentage depletion rates should have little effect on the rate of expenditure for discovery efforts." He continued, "In the long run, a change in percentage depletion should have no effect, *per se*, on the rate of production."[21] The Library of Congress study also reckoned that "present tax provisions such as percentage depletion, expensing of intangibles and expensing of dry holes have a relatively small effect on in-

vestment in oil and gas production." "If we are to have tax incentives they ought to take the form of encouraging the producers to explore and to more efficiently operate their wells," the study recommended.

One way to accomplish this, it said, would be to reduce taxes on drilling operations that were consolidated in block leases to form more efficient producing units. This would reduce the costs of competitive drilling for discovery purposes. However, the study acknowledged, it might pose some administrative problems deriving from state property rights and might be outside the framework of tax law. The study also suggested a tax incentive for exploratory drilling in addition to the expensing of dry holes. The Treasury Department in April 1973 suggested a tax credit based on exploration costs, similar to the investment credit.

As for the effects of changing the petroleum taxation, many experts believe that the price system will take care of any problems that might arise. Thomas F. Field, executive director of Taxation With Representation, a public-interest tax lobby, told the House Ways and Means Committee on Feb. 7, 1974:

> The price incentives and financial resources generated by the recent increase in the price of crude oil are so large...that we are likely to see very sharp increases in petroleum production over the next few years. Indeed, if these prices hold at or near present levels, there is a distinct possibility of an oil glut by the middle of this decade. There is no need to further increase this coming glut by means of tax incentives that have outlived whatever usefulness they ever had.

Another prominent critic of the present oil taxation system is Gerard M. Brannon, an economics professor at Georgetown University and research director of Tax Analysts and Advocates. In testimony before several congressional committees, Brannon has argued that the best way to improve the system is to remove the percentage depletion allowance and the deductions for intangible drilling costs. "These provisions made some (but not much) sense when we were, for national security, protecting a high cost U.S. industry against low cost foreign competition," Brannon told the House Ways and Means Committee on Feb. 6, 1974. "With the U.S. oil price below world prices, this special relief is entirely inappropriate."

Resistance to Major Change

Despite the hostile climate it has encountered, the oil industry still has friends in Congress and the White House. Many knowledgeable analysts agree with Charls E. Walker, a former Treasury Department official and now a Washington business lobbyist, who has said: "When it all shakes out, I think we'll see a lot of rhetoric and some action but not that much in terms of radical change affecting the industry." On the other hand, some oil industry spokesmen have expressed genuine concern about the prospect of painful tax revision. "We know perfectly well there'll be some tax legislation," said Harry Bridges, president of Shell Oil, "and we are sufficiently worried to think something might be done in anger, recrimination and haste."[22]

Oil company executives maintain that if an excess-profits tax were imposed, reducing profits below the level of previous years, they would be prompted to cut spending that is now planned for expansion and exploration. One proposal is to exempt from any excess-profits tax the earnings that a company reinvests in the production of domestic energy. But some experts see a major flaw in this plowback provision. It would virtually mandate that the

Arguments Over Oil Tax Breaks

AGAINST	FOR
In no other industry can the investor recover tax-free more than his original investment costs—as with depletion allowance.	In other industries the value of the original investment normally can be recovered through depreciation. But depreciation of the original cost of oil and gas—that is, the cost of discovery—bears no relationship to the market value of the source in the ground.
There is no justification for the oil investor recovering value not just once, but many times over—through a combination of intangible drilling-cost deductions and percentage depletion with no time limit.	Capital asset—oil in the ground—is exhausted in the course of production. Special allowances are needed to encourage the search for new oil reserves. Investment in other industries does not involve the same high risk.
These tax bounties are enjoyed not only by the risk-takers, but by the owner of royalties and others who are not exposed to the personal liability or cash commitments that oil or gas drillers face.	That may be true but the percentage depletion represents a long-standing national policy of encouraging capital investment in oil to build up reserves for national security.
Oil's tax incentives artificially stimulate a hasty, inefficient and wasteful exploration of a scarce national resource, leading to misapplications of capital that could be employed more effectively elsewhere in the economy.	If the percentage depletion allowance were abolished or reduced, those who discover and develop oil deposits—especially small independent producers—would sell out to larger companies. This would hurt competition and hasten the trend toward concentration of economic monopoly and power.
Depletion is inherently discriminatory, to the advantage of a privileged group of taxpayers.	Gasoline prices would go up more if tax advantages were withdrawn.

companies spend their profits to avoid the tax, and it might mean their plowing money into more corporate jet aircraft, expense account budgets and other wasteful things.

In testimony before the House Ways and Means Committee, top petroleum executives maintained that any boost in oil industry taxes would worsen the nation's energy supply situation. Under the banner of the American Petroleum Institute, the spokesmen supported present tax incentives—particularly percentage depletion and the expensing of intangible drilling costs—for both foreign and domestic operations. W. L. Henry, executive vice president of Gulf Oil Corp., contended: "If the tax laws cannot be changed to help solve energy problems, then surely they should not be altered in any way that will contribute to greater shortages."

The American Petroleum Institute, in an analysis of industry tax policy, acknowledged that because of percentage depletion and other provisions, the impact of federal income taxes on the industry was lighter than on most other industries. But it argued that opponents of percentage depletion "usually ignore all other taxes, such as severance taxes, property taxes, and excise taxes," and that although the industry is favored by low effective rates under the federal corporate income tax it is not favored by the tax system as a whole.[23] According to figures from the Petroleum Industry Research Foundation, an industry-sponsored group, the petroleum industry paid about $3.5-billion in domestic taxes in 1970. But it noted that $10.5-billion of motor fuel and other excise taxes were paid by users of motor vehicles.[24]

The API analysis conceded that: "It has been said that it is improper to treat excise taxes on petroleum products as part of the industry's tax burden because the consumer pays these taxes. It is generally true that consumers pay these taxes but this does not justify the conclusion that such taxes are not properly considered as a tax burden of the petroleum industry. As a general rule, *all* taxes must be passed on to consumers through the price of goods sold. In this respect, there is no fundamental difference among income taxes, payroll taxes, property taxes, severance taxes and motor fuel taxes."

On the percentage depletion allowance, the oil industry has shown some signs of internal division. In December 1973, Thornton F. Bradshaw, president of Atlantic Richfield Co., recommended that the tax provision be scrapped in exchange for free-market pricing. "It's an albatross around our neck, and far more trouble than it's worth," he said. Stephen Stamas, vice president for public affairs of Exxon, was quoted in *Time* magaine as saying the industry might be better off now if some years ago there had been a gradual rise in prices accompanies by a phase-out of the depletion allowance. And Exxon Chairman John K. Jamieson said that "what you have to do is look at the total tax package."[25] On the other hand, many independent oil producers are incensed at suggestions by the major oil companies that percentage depletion could go. Unlike the majors, the independents attract much of their drilling capital from wealthy outside investors. They say that

Measuring Oil Industry Taxes

Are the oil companies paying their fair share of federal income taxes? The answer seems to depend on the accounting method used. *U.S. Oil Week* published data in 1971 based on company reports filed with the Securities and Exchange Commission showing an 8.7 per cent effective tax rate in 1970.

In response, the industry issued a study in 1972 by Price Waterhouse, the accounting firm, based on tax data provided by 18 major oil companies corresponding to those in the *Oil Week* study. Price Waterhouse calculated the effective rate at 21.8 per cent.

Taxation With Representation, a public-interest tax lobby, studied the two sets of figures and told the House Ways and Means Committee in 1973 that, depending on how certain elements of income were compiled for tax purposes, the rate could be 8.3, 12.3, 14.7 or 21.8 per cent. "But in any case," according to a Congressional Research Service analysis, "the tax burden of the corporate income tax appears to be substantially lower for oil companies than for other corporations."

without the quick depletion write-off much of that financial backing would disappear.

After struggling with the oil tax issue throughout 1974, the Ways and Means Committee finally sent to the House floor a bill that would deny the percentage depletion allowance on most oil production effective in 1975.

A tougher version of oil tax provisions that the committee earlier had approved in two bills that never reached the House floor, the measure would cut the depletion allowance to 15 per cent for all oil in 1974 and limit its use to relatively uncommon oil production—such as oil from Alaska's North Slope—in the years 1975-78. After 1978, no oil depletion allowance would be available.

To make the depletion phase-out more attractive during House floor and Senate action, the committee packaged those provisions with politically appealing tax cuts for low- and middle-income groups.

In reporting the bill after the Nov. 5 election, the committee was yielding to congressional pressure for legislation to toughen taxes on the oil industry after bottling up such legislation for most of the year. In part, the committee was trying to head off efforts by Democratic liberals to revamp the committee's make-up or curtail its powers.

In earlier versions of oil tax legislation—one reported as a separate bill and another included in a general tax bill that never was reported—the committee had approved a three-year phase-out that would have dropped the depletion allowance to 15 per cent for 1974, 8 per cent for 1975 and to zero thereafter.

Like the earlier versions, the committee's final 1974 bill imposed a temporary graduated excise tax on crude oil sold for more than $4.50 a barrel. But this "windfall profits tax" would be phased out along with the depletion allowance.

The measure also restricted use of foreign tax credits to reduce the U.S. taxes paid by multinational oil companies.

Even if the bill passed the House, however, it was likely to be opposed in the Senate by Finance Committee Chairman Russell B. Long (D La.) and other oil-state senators. It appeared that the question of oil tax revision would pass unresolved to the 94th Congress. ∎

Petrofina Societe Anonyme, Phillips Petroleum, Royal Dutch/Shell, the Signal Companies, Skelly Oil, Standard Oil of California, Standard Oil (Indiana), Standard Oil (Ohio), Sun Oil, Superior Oil, Texaco, Union Oil of California.

[11] "Income Tax Policy for the Petroleum Industry During the 1970s," American Petroleum Institute, May 1972, p. ii.

[12] Robert Engler, *The Politics of Oil* (1961), p. 372.

[13] Susan R. Agria, "Special Tax Treatment of Mineral Industries," in *The Taxation of Income from Capital* (1969), Arnold C. Harberger and Martin J. Bailey (eds.), p. 79.

[14] *Ibid.*, p. 80.

[15] Stephen L. McDonald, *Federal Tax Treatment of Income from Oil and Gas* (1963), p. 14.

[16] For detailed discussion, see Congressional Quarterly *1969 Almanac, pp.* 589-649.

[17] "Income Tax Policy for the Petroleum Industry During the 1970s," American Petroleum Institute, May 1972, p. 2. Ruskay and Osserman's views are presented in their book *Halfway to Tax Reform* (1970).

[18] Press release, Feb. 14, 1974.

[19] Statement to the House Ways and Means Committee, Feb. 7, 1974.

[20] "Big Oil's Taxes," *The Wall Street Journal*, Feb. 7, 1974.

[21] "Financial Requirements of the Nation's Energy Industry," Senate Interior and Insular Affairs Committee print no. 93-5, March 6, 1974, pp. 240-244.

[22] Both quoted by Albert R. Hunt in *The Wall Street Journal*, Jan. 25, 1974. For a description of the oil lobby in Washington, see *p. 82.*

[23] "Income Tax Policy for the Petroleum Industry During the 1970s," p. 21.

[24] "The Tax Burden of the Domestic Oil and Gas Industry, 1967-1970," Petroleum Industry Research Foundation Inc., p. 17.

[1] "The New Shape of the U.S. Oil Industry," *Business Week*, Feb. 2, 1974, p. 50. The Supreme Court, in an antitrust action in 1911, ordered the breakup of the Standard Oil of New Jersey, a holding company of diverse oil interests controlled by John D. Rockefeller.

[2] *Congressional Record*, Jan. 21, 1974, p. S 37.

[3] Quoted in *Time*, Feb. 4, 1974, p. 32.

[4] Quoted in *Business Week*, Feb. 2, 1974, p. 55.

[5] "Oil Profits Under Fire," *Time*, Feb. 4, 1974, p. 33.

[6] Leroy Dunn and Jane Gravelle, "An Analysis of the Federal Tax Treatment of Oil and Gas and Some Policy Alternatives," Congressional Research Service, Library of Congress, prepared for the Senate Interior and Insular Affairs Committee, January 1974, p. 3.

[7] "General Tax Reform," House Ways and Means Committee, Part 9 (Natural Resources), Feb. 26, 1973, p. 1369.

[8] "Fiscal Year 1975 Tax Expenditure Budget," *Tax Notes*, Jan. 21, 1974, p. 11.

[9] Up to a maximum of 48 per cent—the highest U.S. tax rate on corporations.

[10] "Financial Analysis of a Group of Petroleum Companies, 1972," The Chase Manhattan Bank, Energy Economics Division, August 1973, p. 17. The companies analyzed in the study were: Amerada Hess, Apco Oil, Ashland Oil, Atlantic Richfield, British Petroleum, Champlin Petroleum, Cities Service, Clark Oil & Refining, Compagnie Francaise des Petroles, Continental Oil, Exxon, Getty Oil, Gulf Oil, The Louisiana Land and Exploration Company, Marathon Oil, Mobil Oil, Murphy Oil, The Oil Shale Corporation,

CHANGING TIDE: FOREIGN INVESTMENTS IN AMERICA

Only a few years ago a flood tide of American investments abroad brought anguished cries from Europeans who feared that their national economies would be engulfed in Yankee dollars and dominated by faraway home offices. These cries have since been muffled, if not entirely silenced, by grave new economic problems on both sides of the Atlantic—and by a reverse flow of investments from overseas into the United States. This flow has risen in recent years from a trickle to a sizable current.

Foreign investment in the United States takes two forms: private "portfolio" investment in corporate and government securities, and "direct" investment by foreign companies that set up or acquire American subsidiaries. Foreign portfolio investment amounts to considerably more than direct investment,[1] but the latter poses problems because it involves foreign managerial control as well as ownership of American assets. Furthermore, the growth of direct foreign investment has shown a marked increase since 1967 and especially in 1973.[2]

Foreign-owned assets in the United States are still only about one-sixth of the amount that American corporations hold overseas. But since 1968 the rate of increase has surpassed that of U.S. direct investment overseas. A spate of purchases in the past year gave rise to comments in the press and in Congress as to the effects of foreign ownership and control of assets in the United States. *(Box, p. 63)*

While there seems to be little support in Congress for prompt enactment of restrictive legislation, many lawmakers are disturbed at the possibility of vast sums of Arab oil money being used to buy into and perhaps control large segments of American industry. Such fears are strikingly similar to those that have been voiced in recent years by other countries about the extent of American business penetration into their national economies.

There has been concern in Congress that the true extent and impact of foreign investment is not known.[3] After having made a survey of direct foreign investment in the United States, Drs. Jeffrey S. Arpan of Georgia State University and David Ricks of Ohio State University told a House Foreign Affairs subcommittee in February 1974 that "perhaps the most curious aspect" of foreign investors here is that "virtually no one knows anything about them: who they are, or what they are doing." Arpan and Ricks said they found 200 to 400 more firms owned by foreign companies than the Department of Commerce was then aware of. The two estimated that the book value of foreign direct investments amounted to $38-billion, twice as high as the official figure.

In an effort to get a better understanding of the scope and size of foreign investments—both direct and portfolio—President Ford Oct. 28 signed into law a bill sponsored by Sen. Daniel K. Inouye (D Hawaii) to authorize an 18-month, $3-million study.

Increase in Takeovers

The vast majority of foreign companies that establish a foothold in the United States do so by creating an entirely new subsidiary rather than acquiring an existing firm. This practice shows signs of changing, however. David Bauer, an international economist, reported in May 1974 to The Conference Board in New York that about one-third of the new foreign investment decisions during the first three quarters of 1974 involved acquisitions, compared to 8 per cent in the period from March to November 1973.[4] According to an estimate published in the *Financial Times* of London on June 24, British companies alone had spent more than $1.3-billion acquiring American businesses in the preceding 18 months.

Such acquisitions provide an immediate entry into the vast and profitable American market. In high-technology

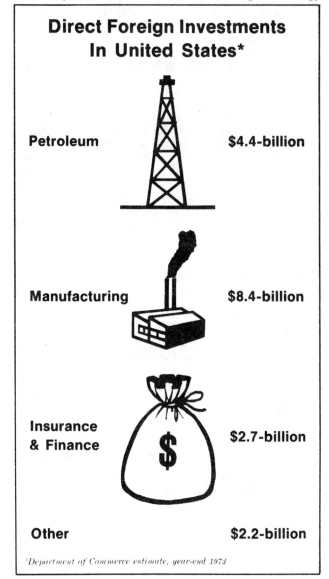

**Direct Foreign Investments
In United States***

Petroleum	$4.4-billion
Manufacturing	$8.4-billion
Insurance & Finance	$2.7-billion
Other	$2.2-billion

Department of Commerce estimate, year-end 1973

fields such as computers and chemical engineering, acquiring control of an American company can also provide the quickest access to American know-how. Where consumer products are involved, buying up a company with an established brand name and sales network can be vital. Environmental, civil rights and social-responsibility pressures, especially in the confusing American context of overlapping state and federal authorities, can prove disastrous to a newcomer. An established company provides expert knowledge of everything from prospective customers to local safety regulations.

A decline in the value of many American stocks on major markets made takeover opportunities tempting for foreign companies wanting to gain control of U.S. corporations at bargain prices, despite the premiums they sometimes had to pay shareholders in takeover bids. *The Economist* of London advised during a stock market downturn in June 1973: "Now is the time to invade the United States." *Barron's*, the American financial weekly, observed in an editorial at about the same time: "Not since World War II—or perhaps since World War I—has so much venture capital crossed the Atlantic from East to West."

Two successive devaluations of the dollar—in December 1971 and February 1973—were not solely responsible for these takeovers. British companies provided a disproportionate amount of the foreign interest in U.S. mergers and acquisitions despite the fact that British currency gained far less in dollar value than did French, German, Dutch or Japanese. Most foreign takeovers in the United States are reported to be financed by dollar loans which are repaid out of the acquired companies' earnings. Since no currency conversion is involved, this type of investment is not affected by parity shifts. Ironically, the main source of funds enabling foreigners to "buy American" is the vast pool of "Eurodollars," the product of U.S. investment in Europe since World War II.

Not all takeover bids have succeeded. America's own experience with takeovers at home led to the flowering of defensive legal skills in the 1960s. The unsuccessful bid by British Land for control of the Uris Buildings Corporation in the spring of 1973 cost it more than a quarter of a million dollars. Slater Walker, a London investment company renowned for its aggressiveness, abandoned a chain of deals in the United States and finally sold its American interests in May 1974, at a cash loss reported to be some $5-million.[5]

Stateside Plants and Branches

Fully two-thirds of the foreign direct investment in the United States from March 1973 to March 1974 involved the construction of new manufacturing facilities or the expansion of existing facilities. Many plants in the United States can produce goods more cheaply than those abroad. Moreover, they provide the foreign manufacturer a chance to tap the vast U.S. market and the base for expansion into Canada and Latin America. Labor costs in recent years have risen far less rapidly, in dollar terms, in the United States than in other industrial countries. From 1967 to 1973, Japan's unit labor costs rose 82 per cent and West Germany's 85 per cent, compared to only 16 per cent in the United States.[6]

Moreover, plant site costs in the United States may be lower than in more densely populated countries. Access to U.S. technology and marketing techniques, to money markets and to a relatively secure domestic supply of energy and raw materials are all powerful attractions. In addition, many foreign companies anticipate the growth of

---

Investments: U.S. and Abroad

The Department of Commerce estimates that there are about 1,300 manufacturing plants in the United States owned and controlled by foreign companies among the 316,000 plants in this country. The book value of these factories, together with petroleum facilities, insurance companies, banks and other entities owned in the United States by foreigners, is estimated at about $17-billion or more.

In contrast, American-based multinational companies own or control nearly 100,000 manufacturing plants and about 23,000 affiliated companies abroad, and these are valued at about $100-billion, according to the department.

Some investigators contend that foreign holdings in the United States are considerably larger than official figures show.

---

protectionist sentiment in Congress and are eager to establish U.S. subsidiaries which would not be subject to import restrictions.

Foreign companies that consider building factories in the United States often find themselves being wooed by federal, state and local boosters. In 1961, the Department of Commerce began actively promoting the United States as a good place to invest, and since then the department has worked closely with state industrial development offices, the National Association of State Development Agencies and with local chambers of commerce. The department sponsors "Invest in U.S.A." conferences around the world; more than 170 representatives from 36 states participated in a conference in Japan recently.

At least 14 states maintain full-time industrial development branch offices overseas, and their efforts to lure important foreign investors are inevitably compared to those of college recruiters vying for an all-star quarterback. Such a contest resulted in a decision of Volvo, the Swedish automobile manufacturer, to build a $100-million Volvo assembly plant in Virginia; all told, the state has attracted 36 foreign firms in the last five years. They hired 8,200 workers.[7] The Southeast, the most popular area, was the locale for 13 of 37 foreign-financed plant construction or expansion sites announced in the first quarter of 1974, while California alone landed seven.[8]

Benefits to Localities

On the local level the benefits are greatest where new manufacturing facilities arise. They create jobs, payrolls and tax revenues, although some taxes may be waived as a condition of getting the plant at that locale. Arpan and Ricks estimated that throughout the United States, foreign concerns employ some 975,000 workers, 99 per cent of them American, a figure representing 1 per cent of this country's labor force. Direct foreign investments stimulate other parts of the economy through "ripple effects" as they increase demand for supplies and raw materials, transportation and services.

The transfer of technology is another benefit. Thirty-one per cent of the patents granted by the U.S. Patent Office in 1972 were issued to foreign persons or companies. Designs and inventions that originate in other countries are often put to use in mass production in America. The boom crane, pre-stressed concrete, the radial tire and tape casette are among the thousands of items of foreign origin on the American market. Apart from the particular advantages of such innovations, they increase the competitive forces within the marketplace.

As most foreign investments are funded from abroad, they offer immediate benefits for the U.S. balance of payments. In the long term dividends flow back to foreign shareholders, but according to a Chamber of Commerce Task Force Report this net outflow will more than likely be offset by other factors. Unlike American firms overseas, which tend to begin repatriating profits quickly, foreign companies tend to reinvest at least half their U.S. earnings for the first six or seven years, according to Frank Shaeffer, director of Domestic Investment Services at the Department of Commerce's Bureau of International Commerce.

Finally, increased foreign investment in the United States helps to reduce the criticism of American investment overseas. Criticism of foreign investment in the United States echoes many of the objections voiced by foreign countries where U.S.-controlled multinationals have a stake. There are fears that foreign companies operating in the United States might not act in America's best interests, since they respond to "a flow of commands from the outside, including the commands of the parent and the commands of other sovereigns."[9]

Foreigners' Role

These worries have been intensified by the surge of foreign investment, especially takeovers. At present most foreign-owned firms are small by U.S. standards, and they dominate no American industry. They do, however, have a significant position in a few industries such as pharmaceuticals (Bayer) and nickel production (International Nickel Co.).[10] The question is whether American autonomy in key areas is threatened, and whether federal and state laws restricting or prohibiting foreign investment in certain sectors are comprehensive enough to deal with a vast influx of foreign capital.

According to an informal survey of legal provisions affecting foreign investment in the United States, published by the Department of Commerce in March 1971, aliens are excluded from ownership of enterprises engaging in coastwise or freshwater shipping, domestic radio communications and domestic air transport, and may not obtain licenses to operate atomic energy facilities. In addition some states restrict alien involvement in real estate, banking, insurance and the various aspects of the alcoholic beverage industry.

Even where national security is not concerned, critics point to areas where they say foreign influence has not been benign. Senator Inouye, in a Senate speech Dec. 20, 1973, said large injections of Japanese capital had "grossly inflated already high real estate prices to the point where very few Hawaiians can afford new housing." Japanese businessmen, Inouye added, had mishandled their public relations and irritated several local groups. Some experts say an adverse reaction to foreign investment comes about when the investment is directed toward "non-productive" or speculative assets rather than investments which create jobs.

Labor representatives, long critical of American companies that "export jobs" by going overseas, have not yet passed judgment on foreign firms coming to the United States. The AFL-CIO has adopted no official policy, and many of its member unions represent workers at foreign-owned concerns. However, the unions clearly dislike the new image of "cheap U.S. labor." There is concern that foreign investment, rather than increasing employment, simply provides new bosses for old jobs—new bosses who might not respond to local problems nor conform to established patterns of American labor-management relations. There is also some fear that foreign-owned firms, granted special advantages by local communities and supported by earnings or subsidies from abroad, might drive out of business American firms and cause net unemployment.

One source of protectionist fear, according to the Chamber of Commerce Task Force Report, is "a latent form of xenophobia, ethnic resentment, or more bluntly, racism." The source of the investment has been an important element in determining the acceptability of foreign investment. While foreign ownership of American assets has traditionally rested in Canada, Britain and other European countries, Japan has become a leading investor and the Arab countries may follow suit. *(Box, p. 66)*

"Our consistently liberal attitude toward foreign investment has undoubtedly been a positive factor in convincing other nations to adopt similar policies with respect to our investment."

—William J. Casey, under secretary of state for economic affairs, Jan. 23, 1974

Background

The United States has been a net exporter of capital only since World War. I. For the preceding 140 years foreign investment in America steadily increased, while U.S. holdings abroad remained negligible by comparison. The American colonies were founded and developed with the aid of European capital, not only British but French, Dutch and Spanish. France, and to a lesser extent Holland and Spain, helped finance the War of Independence.[11] When the peace treaty came to be negotiated, a major issue was whether British investors would lose the three to five million pounds they had invested in the former colonies.

The end of the Revolution marked the beginning of a new flow of foreign funds into the United States which has continued down to the present time despite the interrup-

States With Most Foreign-Owned Companies

New Jersey	295	South Carolina	53
New York	258	Connecticut	47
Pennsylvania	102	Louisiana	42
California	87	North Carolina	41
Illinois	74	Michigan	40
Massachusetts	61	Ohio	37

Source: Jeffrey S. Arpan and David A. Ricks, congressional testimony, Feb. 21, 1974

Some U.S. Companies Under Foreign Control

Parent Company	American Subsidiary	Location	Product
PEZ International (Austria)	Haas Food Mfg. Co.	Conn.	Pez Candies
Canadian Devpt. Corp.	Texasgulf Inc. (35%)	Texas	Minerals
Bayer A.G. (Germany)	Cutter Laboratories Inc.	Calif.	Pharmaceuticals
Siemens (Germany)	Computest Corp.	N.J.	Test eqpt.
Jardine Matheson & Co. Ltd. (Hong Kong)	Theo. Davis & Co.	Hawaii	Sugar cane
Unilever Ltd. (U.K.)	Lever Bros.	N.Y.	Soaps and oils
	T. J. Lipton Co.	N.J.	Food products
	Good Humor Ice Cream	Calif.	Frozen dairy foods
Tube Investments Ltd. (U.K.)	Raleigh Industries	Okla.	Bicycles
Rawlplug Co. Ltd. (U.K.)	Rawlplug Co. Inc.	N.Y.	Masonry tools
J. Lyons & Co. (U.K.)	Beech Nut	N.Y.	Tea and coffee
Cavenham Ltd. (U.K.)	Beech Nut	N.Y.	Baby food
British Petroleum Co. Ltd.	Standard Oil (Ohio) (25%)	Ohio	Gasoline retail
Sandoz Ltd. (Swiss)	Sandoz Pharmaceuticals	N.J.	Pharmaceuticals
Nestle Alimentana (Swiss)	Libby, McNeil & Libby	Ill.	Canned foods
	Stouffer Foods	Ohio	Frozen foods
Wasabrod AB (Sweden)	Wasa Rye-King Inc.	Conn.	Crisp bread
Jac Jacobsen A/S (Norway)	Luxo Lamp Corp.	N.Y. Calif.	Lamps
Danubia Ltd. (S. Africa)	Danubia Knitting Mills	S.C.	Textiles
Clarion Co. Ltd. (Japan)	Muntz Stereo Corp	Calif.	Stereo sets

Source: U.S. Department of Commerce

tions of panics, crises and wars. As the nation developed, its need for capital increased, and with little cash available domestically for lending purposes, Europe was the obvious source. British merchants, who had grown rich and were to grow richer on foreign trade, were eager to find new outlets for investment. Though their legal monopoly of American trade had ended, their economic monopoly was resumed soon after independence. It was said, "We had striven to be free from Westminster but we remained tied to metropolitan London."[12]

Foreign trade, particularly imports, made up the primary demand for capital in the years following the Revolution. But with the Louisiana Purchase in 1803 (funded by $11.25-million from London, Paris and Amsterdam) and the opening of other new territories, there was an enormous increase in the requirements for European capital. Cotton and sugar farming demanded large sums for the purchase and upkeep of slaves, plantation supplies and equipment. Planters were habitually in debt to their local banks and merchants, who in turn required equally long credit from others, and this chain usually led back to Lon-

don. The government-backed Bank of the United States, which supplied much of the credit needs in the South and elsewhere, was 56 per cent foreign owned in 1841.[13]

As the nation grew, its roads, bridges, canals, banks and finally railroads were largely financed by state bonds sold overseas. The Erie Canal, the first American canal to achieve commercial success, was made possible by the first state bonds to be quoted on the London market, in 1817. Europe was eager for investments such as these, and a group of Anglo-American banking houses was established in London—led by Baring Brothers—which specialized in American finance. They bought up entire issues for resale in England. In their eagerness for foreign capital, American states and private enterprises sent their agents to Europe. Generals and congressmen turned to bond selling.

British Funding

By 1854, foreign investors held approximately one-half of the federal and state and one-quarter of the municipal debts.[14] Their interest in private enterprise was much smaller. The discovery of gold in California, however, sparked activity in trade, manufacturing, and railroad building which started a new flow of European capital to America. The regularity of such investment was sometimes interrupted by panics and disclosures of the folly of American promoters; in 1869, for example, representatives of the Memphis, El Paso and Pacific Railroad sold some $5-million worth of bonds on the Paris Bourse, having widely advertised their great transcontinental line which turned out to be just three miles long.

After that fiasco, French investments in American railroads were negligible, but the English and Dutch remained enthusiastic and for a long time held controlling interests in the Illinois Central, the New York and Erie, the Philadelphia and Reading and others. For more than three-quarters of a century British investors were the principal buyers of American railway securities. By 1914, when securities and direct investments by Europeans in America totaled $7-billion, well over half of it was in railroads; in the same year, U.S. investments overseas came to about $3.5-billion.

From 1820 to 1840, with the coming of industrialization, capital investment in U.S. factories rose from $50-million to $250-million. Most of the money came from abroad, especially London.[15] The first large corporations emerged in the latter half of the century. These were communications companies which were followed by utility companies and the industrial giants, all popular with foreign investors. "No field for the employment of capital is superior to that of the United States," the London *Times* observed in 1857. When the transatlantic cable was laid in 1866, one of its first uses was to carry New York Stock Exchange prices to London.

American real estate was another area of vast direct foreign investment. New York, Maine, Florida, West Virginia, Pennsylvania and Iowa were among the states where Europeans acquired substantial holdings in a variety of ways: one English company was granted three million acres of Texas land by the state government in payment for erecting the new capitol building at Austin.[16]

"Rather than be judged a rival, it [foreign investment] ought to be considered an auxiliary...."

—Secretary of the Treasury Alexander Hamilton
Report on the First Congress, 1791

When in 1880 a Parliamentary committee reported on the high profits of the American cattle business, a wave of speculation swept England and Scotland. In the next 10 years no fewer than 18 companies were registered in Great Britain to engage in American ranching. The Scottish-American Mortgage Company alone controlled three large properties in Colorado, New Mexico and Texas, with more than 140,000 head of cattle grazing on almost 7½ million acres. Titled Europeans such as the French Marquis de Mores, the German Baron von Richthofen and the British Earl of Dunraven sought to create baronial estates in the West.[17]

At the turn of the century, with the invention of the automobile, foreign oil companies gained a substantial place in the United States. One of the largest was Royal Dutch-Shell, which as Shell Transport and Trading Com-

Sources of Foreign Investments

As recently as 1971, Britain was the source of almost half of the new investment capital flowing into the United States. Europe as a whole provided 85 per cent of the new funds and Japan accounted for only 7 per cent.

The following year new investments by the Japanese increased more than fivefold, to $105 million. Of the 188 foreign investment plans announced from March 1973 to March 1974, according to the Department of Commerce data, Japan accounted for 59, followed by Canada (30), West Germany (28) and Britain (20).

pany, incorporated in England in 1897, began buying up American properties early in this century. French and Belgian capitalists also acquired American oil interests, but Shell (which joined forces with Royal Dutch in 1905) grew most prodigiously.

Reversal

World War I worked a sudden and drastic change in capital flows to the United States. In order to supply their wartime needs for American wheat, cotton, oil, munitions and other commodities, the creditor countries of Europe disposed of a large part of the American investments they had accumulated during the preceding century. Foreign investment of all kinds was reduced from about $7.2-billion in the summer of 1914, to about $4-billion at the close of 1919.[18] At the same time, U.S. loans to the Allies moved vast sums of American capital to Europe. Thus in the space of a few years America's role shifted from debtor to creditor nation, a position it has retained.

Nevertheless, direct foreign investment in the United States increased gradually in the half-century following World War I, amounting to about $7.6-billion in 1962. Then in the next decade it almost doubled, reaching $14.4-billion at year-end 1972.[19] One important reason for the rapid increase during the sixties was the creation of the European Economic Community (the Common Market). It was crucial in creating an arena for mass corporate mergers both within and across the national boundaries, enabling European countries to achieve the giant size necessary for success as multinational corporations. It also created a "home" market comparable in size to the United States, large enough for profitable application of American techniques of production and marketing.

While American multinationals invested abroad largely as a defense measure to retain the market positions they had established through exporting, European companies have located in the United States as an offensive measure, not to sustain their parent company's role in the U.S. market but to strengthen their capacity to compete with the United States in the world and the enlarged European market. This different approach, along with the physical isolation of the United States, has meant that European subsidiaries in the United States tend to be more independent from their parent companies than are U.S. subsidiaries overseas.[20]

The traditional vehicle for the regulation of foreign investment between nations is a Treaty of Friendship, Commerce and Navigation. The U.S. has entered into 130 of these bilateral agreements since 1778. But whereas in the early days the government principally was interested in attracting foreign investment, its concerns more recently have been securing rights for U.S. investors abroad. Reciprocity is the basic principle of these treaties, and the rights the United States seeks for American investors overseas it is also willing to accord to foreign investors in the United States.

Outlook

Worldwide inflation and increased oil prices have already had a devastating effect on the economies of countries that have been the main sources for foreign investment in America. By one estimate Britain faces a massive balance of payments deficit of some $11-billion in 1974, more than three times higher than the previous year's record; Italy and Japan are expected to end the year with $8-billion deficits, while the French deficit is likely to exceed $6-billion.[21] Share prices in London have halved in less than 18 months, with the market index reaching a 15-year low.

In the face of these conditions, and with predictions of worse to come, foreign businessmen are less likely to consider substantial new investments now than in the boom conditions of a few years ago. The fast-growing Japanese investment is likely to level off, and Japanese businessmen are receiving "administrative guidance" from their government to keep away from speculative "fringe" investments in hotels and real estate, according to a spokesman for the U.S.-Japan Trade Council.

On the other hand, depressed business conditions elsewhere make investment in the United States look more attractive by comparison. Eurodollar financing for international acquisitions may be harder to come by, but "it may well be that the recent lull in overseas acquisitions by the U.K. companies has more to do with tighter liquidity at home and in the international money markets than with any sudden change in investment strategy," the *Financial Times* reported June 24, 1974.

Even if exchange control restrictions are imposed by countries concerned about capital outflows, these can be circumvented by investors able to borrow dollars directly in the Eurodollar or U.S. capital markets. As raw material prices become inflated, it becomes more economical for foreigners to exploit American resources. The Japanese, for example, have lent money to reopen abandoned coal mines in the United States and take repayment in coal.

Some monetary experts foresee the shifts in world financial tides created by higher oil prices as leading to a period of ruinous economic isolationism. Already some foreign investors in the United States have been discouraged by indications that their incursions will be greeted by suspicion by American agencies, stockholders and competitors. In some cases, the Federal Trade Commission started proceedings against foreign acquisitions months after the deals were completed.

Difficulties with FTC

Probably more than any other case, Nestle's lengthy tangle with the FTC has aroused foreigners' suspicions of official harassment. Early in 1973 the company acquired Stouffer Corporation from Litton Industries, and American lawyers for the Swiss food giant spent 3,000 hours putting together a 116-page "white paper" and voluminous documents to satisfy the federal agency. In November 1973 the FTC requested additional information in 73 categories, "most of it extremely confidential in nature," *The Wall Street Journal* reported, and involving serious legal risks under Swiss laws which prohibit divulging manufacturing and commercial secrets to a foreign power.[22]

In another example recently, British Oxygen Corporation's bid to take over Airco was blocked by the FTC two months after the British company had paid $80-million. According to the *Financial Times*, June 24, 1974, BOC has no complaints about xenophobia. American companies resisting foreign takeovers have skillfully used laws prohibiting alien involvement in certain sectors. For example, General Host Corporation successfully resisted a $20-million British bid on the ground that aliens may not control domestic shipping—one of General Host's subsidiaries ran tourist boats in the Florida Everglades.

Protectionism in Congress

Already several bills to limit foreign investment have been introduced in Congress. One of the most restrictive has been sponsored by two Pennsylvania Democratic congressmen, John H. Dent and Joseph M. Gaydos. It would limit foreign ownership to 5 per cent of the voting or 35 per cent of the non-voting shares in an American company. Such legislative measures are almost certain to be delayed at least until Congress can collect more detailed information. Senator Inouye has said that "an erroneous decision at this time could have the effect of choking off new and badly needed funds as well as aggravating our international economic relations with our allies."

William J. Casey, under secretary of state for economic affairs, testified Jan. 23 before the Senate subcommittee on International Finance: "To abandon our traditional hospitality toward foreign investment would make it difficult to resist restrictions against our own economically much more significant foreign investment. Even more important, it would bring into question the U.S. commitment to the type of open world economy which we are trying to achieve through the current international monetary and trade negotiations."

Some observers fear a premature change in U.S. policy might cause a proliferation of restrictive national policies toward foreign investment, from which the United States would stand to be the biggest loser.

"The Arabs may end up in control of the big companies of this country. It's a very serious possibility."

—Henry Ford II, chairman of Ford Motor Co.

Potential Influx of 'Petrodollars'

The oil-producing countries of the Middle East are becoming important international investors as they seek profitable outlets for their new wealth. The race already has begun in business, financial and government circles for access to the billions of "petrodollars" and the United States, with its highly developed capital markets, is expected to attract more than other countries.[23] Estimates vary widely as to how much the Arabs will want to invest, after taking into account their domestic goals for development, but Saudi Arabia, Kuwait, Abu Dhabi and Libya have small populations and little opportunity to absorb excess income. They could accumulate anywhere from $15-billion to $50-billion a year by 1980.[24]

Such vast sums have given rise to fears of a wholesale economic takeover. Henry Ford II was quoted in *Fortune* magazine in May 1973 as saying: "The Arabs may end up in control of most of the big companies of this country. It's a very serious possibility." Petrodollars already have been used to buy shares in many gigantic American firms.[25] However, most experts think the U.S. economy and capital market are large enough to absorb billions of dollars without difficulty. The flow of petrodollar investments would presumably help to offset America's own rising bill for oil imports and perhaps avert what is now being foreseen as a scarcity of capital in the years ahead. Donald Regan, chairman of the American brokerage firm of Merrill Lynch, Pierce, Fenner and Smith, was quoted as saying in *The Times* of London on July 4, 1974, "Between now and 1980 American industry will need to make capital investments of at least a trillion dollars."

"It takes capital in monumental quantities to feed the world economy, but today there is an increasingly criticial shortage of long-term capital," *Business Week* observed on July 6, 1974, in an article titled "The Worldwide Liquidity Shortage." The magazine noted that with stock prices disappointingly low in markets everywhere and with short-term interest rates temptingly high, "investors all over the world are wary about equities and chary about commitments to long-term debt."

In this situation, the Arab billions that await investment assume added importance and are coveted in every major Western nation. The United States and Saudi Arabia signed an agreement on economic cooperation in Washington on June 9. By July 20, Secretary of the Treasury William E. Simon called on King Faisal and other Saudi officials to discuss plans for investing their country's oil money in American enterprises.

Arab investment, it is argued, whether in stocks, bonds or real estate, would give the Arab world a stake in the fate of America's economy, and by encouraging economic interdependence protect U.S. interests and world stability. It would pose serious new questions, however, since unlike investments by private firms, these investments would be directly controlled by foreign governments with strong political commitments. Potential large-scale Arab investments in the U.S. epitomize the

problems of foreign investment and attempts to regulate it: how to prevent undue foreign influence over domestic political and economic affairs without discouraging desirable capital inflows or inviting retaliation from abroad. ∎

---

[1] Some $44.4-billion versus $17.7-billion book value in 1973, the last year for which figures have been compiled and published by the Department of Commerce. Portfolio investments suffered from declining stock market prices during 1973.

[2] From 1962 through 1966, direct foreign investment grew at an annual average of $330-million, while for the years 1967 through 1972 the yearly average exceeded $800-million. The 1973 figure was almost $3.5-billion.

[3] See *Congressional Quarterly Weekly Report*, Feb. 2, 1974, pp. 227-229.

[4] Part of a continuing study conducted for The Conference Board, issued Feb. 18 and May 16, 1974. The Conference Board describes itself as a private, independent non-profit research organization for business.

[5] *The Wall Street Journal*, June 14, 1974.

[6] "Bait for Foreign Firms: 'Cheap' American Labor," *U.S. News & World Report*, July 9, 1973, pp. 41-42.

[7] Timothy Larkin, "The Benign Invasion," *Manpower* (U.S. Department of Labor publication), May 1974, pp. 14-17.

[8] "Announcements of Foreign Investments in U.S. Manufacturing Industries," reported by The Conference Board, May 16, 1974.

[9] Raymond Vernon, "The Multinational Enterprise: Power Versus Sovereignty," *Foreign Affairs*, July 1971, p. 736.

[10] *Survey of Current Business*, February 1973, p. 32.

[11] Cleona Lewis, *America's Stake in International Investments* (1938), p. 8.

[12] Ralph W. Hidy, *The House of Baring in American Trade and Finance* (1949), p. xvii.

[13] Lewis, *op. cit.*, pp. 14-15.

[14] Edward C. Kirkland, *A History of American Economic Life* (1939), p. 330.

[15] Alex Groner and the editors of *American Heritage* and *Business Week*, *The American Heritage History of Business and Industry* (1972), p. 84.

[16] Lewis, *op. cit.*, p. 84.

[17] Hidy, *op. cit.*, pp. 423-424.

[18] Lewis, *op. cit.*, p. 114.

[19] *Survey of Current Business*, February 1973, p. 29.

[20] Arnold W. Sametz and Jules Backman, "Why Foreign Multinationals Invest in the United States," *Challenge*, March-April 1974, pp. 44-45.

[21] Confidential working paper discussed by the economic policy committee of the Organization for Economic Cooperation and Development (OECD), reported in the London *Observer*, June 23, 1974.

[22] *The Wall Street Journal*, June 14, 1974.

[23] See Lawrence A. Mayer's "Oil, Trade, and the Dollar," in *Fortune*, June 1974, pp. 197-198.

[24] Robert Mabro and Elizabeth Monroe, "Arab Wealth From Oil: Problems of Its Investment," *International Affairs*, January 1974, pp. 18-19.

[25] The Treasury Department Oct. 30 announced that during the first nine months of 1974, the oil-producing countries had invested about $8-billion in the United States, the majority of it in government and agency securities.

PUBLIC POLICY

C_Q

NIXON'S STRATEGY: EXPECTING THE UNEXPECTED

Federal economic policy went through marked transformations during Richard Nixon's presidency, changes both in philosophy and purpose.

In both the beginning and the end of his five and one-half years in the White House, Nixon's basic economic strategy coupled fundamentalist fiscal and monetary restraints to curb inflation with a hands-off posture toward private wage and price decisions.

In between, notably during the 15 months preceding Nixon's overwhelming re-election victory, those traditional Republican policies were abandoned in favor of stimulative tax cuts and planned budget deficits coupled with mandatory wage and price controls.

In response to those swings in policy, and to changing world economic conditions as well, the U.S. economy dipped into mild recession in 1969-70, took off in a booming recovery in 1971-73, and was plunging toward a possibly severe recession when the Watergate scandal forced Nixon from office in August 1974.

And inflation, after abating only temporarily under Nixon's controls experiment, had spiraled upward at double-digit rates during the tenure of a President who had made control of inflation his most consistent economic policy objective.

1969

Three months after taking office, Nixon sent Congress a general message on his domestic legislative program. The President said that one priority which had emerged "clearly and compellingly" since he took office was to halt the inflationary surge, then in its fourth year.

To combat inflation, Nixon chose at first to maintain an official hands-off policy on wage-price increases. Instead, in 1969 he looked to restrictive fiscal and monetary policies.

The President's fiscal policies to bring inflation under control were, first, restriction of federal expenditures to keep the government increment of total spending low and, second, maintenance of federal revenues to divert funds from private spending and to hold down government borrowing in the money market.

In pursuit of the first goal, the President in April proposed successive cuts in the fiscal 1970 budget that President Johnson had sent to Congress in the final days of his administration. The cuts totaled $8-billion; the revised budget was to bring in a surplus of $5.8-billion.

Vanishing Surplus

By the end of the fiscal year, the surplus had vanished. Congress' failure to enact presidential requests on items such as postal rate increases, coupled with increases in uncontrollable spending such as Social Security payments, helped throw the budget into deficit instead.

The budget deficit finally totaled $2.8-billion. This was caused only in part because Congress did not go along with restriction of federal expenditures. The other part of the President's fiscal policy—maintenance of the current level of federal revenues—also did not work. The President had asked Congress to help continue the level of federal revenues by extending a 10 per cent income tax surcharge enacted in 1968. Congress agreed, but did so only as part of an unusual congressionally initiated tax reform bill which carried a substantial net revenue loss. On top of this, federal revenues were lower than expected because of the recession which set in by November 1969. Profits were down, and government tax receipts were therefore lower than had been anticipated.

In the area of monetary policy, the Federal Reserve Board in 1969 continued the policy of tight money and high credit it had begun late in the Johnson administration. It held the money supply almost constant through 1969 despite warnings by some economists that inadequate monetary expansion was likely to cause a recession. Despite those stringent policies, the average inflation of consumer prices was 5.4 per cent. Thus, at the end of his first year, President Nixon had had no success at all in meeting his number one domestic goal—control of inflation.

1970

In his first State of the Union address, delivered in January 1970, Nixon said, "When I speak of actions which would be beneficial to the American people, I can think of none more important than for Congress to join this administration in the battle to stop the rise in the cost of living." He specifically avoided blaming either business or labor, but said U.S. deficit spending in the 1960s was the primary cause of inflation: "Millions of Americans are forced to go into debt today because the federal government decided to go into debt yesterday."

To fight inflation, the President again called for the restrictive fiscal policies he had supported in 1969—a budget in surplus with federal spending held down. The Federal Reserve Board, however, moved to a more expansive monetary policy.

Budget Struggle

As proposed, the President's fiscal 1971 budget called for a surplus of $1.3-billion. When the fiscal year came to an end, however, he had a deficit of $23-billion instead. There were a number of reasons for this. Tax revenues were $13.7-billion lower than projected because of the continuing recession. The economy had begun to pick up slowly in mid-1970, but was thrown back again by a two-month General Motors strike. In addition, late in the year the President indicated that he was converted to the theory that deficit spending was a valuable tool for countering recession, and the administration relaxed its efforts to control spending.

There was, however, as in 1969, a continuing struggle between the President and Congress over federal spending priorities. The President vetoed five bills on economy grounds; two of the vetoes were overridden. There was no major request or action on taxes in 1970. Congress did pass an administration bill extending excise taxes and speeding up collection of gift and estate taxes.

Monetary policy in 1970 was quite different from the restrictive tight money policy of 1969. The Federal Reserve Board permitted the money supply to expand at a relatively high average of about 5.5 per cent during the year. Both the discount rate at which the Federal Reserve System lends money to member banks and the prime rate—the interest rate banks charge their best customers—underwent successive reductions. Mortgage interest rates stabilized, and other interest rates fell sharply. The Federal Reserve Board continued this kind of expansionary monetary policy for the rest of Nixon's first term.

Controls Opposed

During the year as the recession and inflation continued and unemployment began to climb, a number of critics urged the President to adopt some sort of system of wage-price controls. The new Federal Reserve Board Chairman, Arthur F. Burns, publicly supported adoption of an "incomes policy," a term which came into fashionable use. It referred to a broad range of activities, from guideposts to wage and price controls. It connoted an effort to influence incomes through wages and prices parallel to other policy efforts to influence the money supply through fiscal and monetary policy.

On June 17, in a televised address to the nation, the President declared: "I will not take this nation down the road of wage and price controls, however politically expedient they may seem... Wage and price controls only postpone a day of reckoning, and in so doing they rob every American of an important part of his freedom."

In August, the Democratic-controlled Congress added to a Defense Production Act extension an amendment empowering the President to freeze salaries, rents and prices. The President opposed the amendment and said he would not use it.

However, during 1970 the President did change his economic policies somewhat. He moved toward "jawboning" (administration persuasion of business and labor to hold price and wage lines) with the issuance of two "inflation alerts" to publicize excessive wage and price increases. In December, he announced measures to offset oil price increases and plans to intervene in wage negotiations in the construction industry if strikes and rising costs were not abated.

At year's end, the economic figures for 1970 were dreary. General dissatisfaction with the economic situation was reflected in the mediocre Republican showing in the November 1970 congressional elections.

1971

Nixon in 1971 switched the economic issue from the foremost of his liabilities into a potential asset when the major new economic policy of controls was announced in August. Before that, the President had attempted to silence critics and end the recession with a switch to expansionary fiscal policy in the budget proposed in January.

The President began his third year in office with the new fiscal policy and a new secretary of the treasury—John B. Connally, Democratic governor of Texas from 1962 to 1968. He had long and varied experience in law and business, particularly in the oil and gas industries, but limited background in banking and finance. During the year, the highly persuasive Connally became the administration's chief economic spokesman, and was responsible for development of a new incomes policy.

Budget Deficit

The new fiscal policy was a "full-employment budget," which meant that the budget, with large deficits projected for both fiscal years 1971 and 1972, would have been in balance if the economy had been at full output and employment. The actual deficits represented the loss of federal revenues caused by economic performance below potential. In essence, the concept was the same as the deficit federal spending used by Presidents Kennedy and Johnson to stimulate the economy; President Nixon avoided that term because it was anathema to some Republicans. However, he did admit that he had been converted to new economic attitudes. To those economic conservatives who thought they had elected a proponent of fiscal orthodoxy, the President had a quick reply. He told an interviewer in January 1971: "I am now a Keynesian in economics."

The projected deficit for fiscal 1972 was $18.6-billion (the actual deficit when fiscal 1972 ended was $23-billion). The need for a large deficit was widely accepted in Congress but there was substantial Democratic criticism of the President's handling of the economy, because unemployment and the cost of living continued to rise. The consumer price index rose in May at an annual rate of 6 per cent and in June at a rate of 7.2 per cent. The nation's balance-of-payments deficit hit a record high at mid-year. The Harris Survey reported that, in a sampling taken in June, only 26 per cent of those questioned thought Mr. Nixon was doing a good job in economic matters while 70 per cent did not.

New Economic Policy

During the year the President was urged with increasing frequency by Democrats and Republicans to adopt some sort of incomes policy which would include use of wage and price controls. For the first seven months of the year Nixon continued to publicly oppose controls, although in March he did invoke the unwanted power Congress had given him in 1970 to impose controls on the construction industry. Congress in May extended the authority for controls until April 1972. The administration at that time said it did not intend to use it again, but the act eventually provided the authority under which Nixon imposed a price-wage freeze Aug. 15.

The sweeping program announced in August came largely as a surprise. To combat inflation, it called for a 90-day wage, price and rent freeze to be followed by a "Phase II" program of controls. To bring the U.S. balance of payments under control, the President suspended convertibility of the dollar to gold and announced a temporary 10 per cent surtax on imports. This led to a series of major foreign currency negotiations with other countries and culminated in what the President described as a "historic" December international agreement, signed at the Smithsonian Institution in Washington, in which the surtax was

Nixon's Budgets

(millions of dollars)

Fiscal Year	Outlays	Revenues	Deficit
1970	$196,588	$193,743	-$ 2,845
1971	211,425	188,392	- 23,033
1972	231,876	208,649	- 23,227
1973	246,526	232,225	- 14,301
1974	268,343	264,847	- 3,495
1975 (Feb. est.)	304,445	295,000	- 9,445

dropped and the dollar in effect devalued 8.57 per cent in return for concessions by foreign countries.

The Aug. 15 program also called for a number of cuts in federal expenditures. But to get the economy growing more rapidly, the President asked for a tax cut for business and individuals and for reinstatement of a form of the business investment tax credit which had been used intermittently since 1962. Congress agreed to both requests. The 1971 Revenue Act cut taxes by an average of $8.6-billion a year over the 1971-73 period and the restoration of the tax credit amounted to a tax cut of an estimated $2.4-billion in fiscal 1972, rising to $4-billion by 1974.

The Phase II program which replaced the wage-price freeze was announced Oct. 7. It involved establishment of a Pay Board and a Price Commission with authority to set guidelines for wage and price increases, issue orders and hear cases. The largest businesses and unions were to be controlled most stringently and required prior approval for pay and price increases. The Pay Board set a general guideline of 5.5 per cent per year for wage increases and 2.5 per cent for price increases.

1972

Administration economic policy in 1972 continued along the lines established in 1971. The President submitted another "full employment" expansionary budget and the Phase II controls continued throughout the year. The rate of inflation was reduced substantially and unemployment dropped a little. The economy expanded rapidly, earning approval for the wisdom of the President's domestic economic policies.

On the international side, however, the devaluation had not improved the balance-of-payments situation as much as had been hoped. On an official settlements basis, the deficit was $10.1-billion, the second largest in the nation's history (after 1971). A major contributor to this was a tripling (from $2.7-billion to $6.9-billion) in the deficit in the U.S. balance of trade (the excess of imports over exports).

Budget Battles

The budget submitted in January 1972 called for a $25.5-billion deficit to stimulate the economy. But the President emphasized in his State of the Union message that the deficit was not "irresponsible" and would disappear under full employment conditions. He asked Congress to "resist the temptation to overspend" and for the rest of the year he battled with Congress on the spending issue. By mid-year Congress had added almost $7-billion to the budget and was considering programs which could add billions more. This led the President to threaten a tax increase and to ask Congress to fix a federal spending limit of $250-billion. The request was turned down in the final floor fight of the session.

Congress and the President also confronted each other over presidential impoundment of money. At session's end, the veto of an expensive water pollution bill was overridden, but the President said he would not spend that other unwanted money. The battles over economic priorities left considerable bitterness between the President and Congress as the first Nixon administration ended.

But if Congress had quarrels with the administration over fiscal policy, the general public seemed satisfied with economic policy as a whole. It was not an issue in the November 1972 elections, and approval of the President's decisive 1971 policies was undoubtedly a factor in his huge re-election victory.

1973

Hopes were high at the beginning of the year that 1973 would inaugurate a period of balanced economic growth with reduced inflation.

Instead, the administration lost control of soaring prices. At the same time, American leadership in the international economy suffered a severe blow, as confidence in the dollar dipped to new lows, forcing a 10 per cent devaluation in the currency's worth on Feb. 12, followed by further sharp depreciation in market trading. However, the dollar was rising strongly by the end of the year.

Continuing disclosures related to the Watergate break-in sapped the administration's ability to deal with these issues, eroding the leadership that was urgently needed and consuming much of the attention and time of the White House. At the same time, the administration's economic woes were exacerbated by challenges from a Democratic-controlled Congress over spending priorities, the President's authority to impound funds appropriated by Congress and his handling of economic controls.

Added to these problems was the energy crisis, which was dramatically aggravated by the Arab oil export embargo, production cutbacks and huge price increases in petroleum products.

With the value of the dollar continuing its downturn in the world market and with inflation soaring, Nixon vacillated between employing economic controls and honoring the conservative concept of allowing free market forces to regulate the economy.

Phase III

In an announcement nearly as unexpected as his Aug. 15, 1971, order putting the U.S. economy under a wage-price freeze, President Nixon Jan. 11, 1973, terminated mandatory wage and price controls over most of the U.S. economy, leaving fiscal and monetary policies as the principal weapons to continue the nation's fight against inflation.

Most businesses and unions were freed from mandatory restraints, but controls were left in force in three "particularly troublesome" areas: food prices, health costs and the construction industry. For the rest of the economy, the President set up a system of largely voluntary guidelines backed by the threat that the government would intervene to roll back wage and price increases it considered inflationary. As he revamped the economic stabilization program by executive order, Nixon formally asked Congress to extend his authority to impose economic controls for one year past the April 30 expiration date of the Economic Stabilization Act of 1971.

The President made a number of structural changes in the stabilization program, abolishing the Pay Board and Price Commission, and transferring their functions to the Cost of Living Council (CLC).

By early March, Phase III was coming under increasing attack by economists and members of Congress who warned that the largely voluntary controls were too weak to head off another round of costly inflation.

Faced with spiraling food costs, Nixon March 29 ordered the imposition of price ceilings on meat for an indefinite period (the meat price ceilings were removed by stages, with beef left under the ceiling until Sept. 9).

History of Controls: Promises and Pitfalls

Considerable precedent existed for the sweeping program of economic controls that President Nixon imposed on Aug. 15, 1971. Stiff controls were in effect during World Wars I and II and during the Korean War. And a peacetime precedent stemmed from the years between World War II and Korea, when controls were imposed on rents and consumer credit.

In each case, the controls worked well although they produced considerable public grumbling (with the exception of World War II, when they were better accepted). Removal of the controls was always followed by inflation, except at the end of the Korean War.

World War I. In August 1917, four and a half months after the United States declared war on Germany, President Wilson ordered price controls on the sale of wheat and coal under authority derived from acts of Congress and from his war powers as commander-in-chief. From then until the end of the war the price controls were gradually extended to a wide range of commodities. These controls were lifted soon after the Nov. 11, 1918, armistice and prices rose rapidly during the following winter and spring.

World War II. Increased demand, coupled with a scarcity of commodities, forced the consumer price index up nearly 10 points during 1941. This prompted Congress to pass the Price Control Act on Jan. 30, 1942, which provided the legal foundation for a network of price controls.

As for wages, an executive order issued by President Roosevelt on Oct. 3, 1942, under the Price Stabilization Act, signed the previous day, instructed the War Labor Board not "to approve any increases in wage rates prevailing on Sept. 15, 1942, unless such increase is necessary to correct maladjustment or inequities...or to aid in the effective prosecution of the war."

Controls over consumer credit (minimum down payments, maximum maturities) were established by Roosevelt under an executive order in 1941 and were administered by the Federal Reserve Board (Fed) throughout the war. On Dec. 1, 1946, the Fed lifted controls on everything except a dozen consumer durables, including automobiles.

The controls were highly effective. The consumer price index rose a total of only five points between April 1943 and June 1946, when most of the controls ended. Prices then shot up until, in December 1948, the consumer price index was 70 per cent higher than its level in the 1935-40 period.

Post-World War II. Because of an acute shortage of housing, President Truman asked and received authority to extend the World War II-era rent controls to Feb. 28, 1948. At the President's request, the controls were subsequently extended in stages through the outbreak of the Korean War, after which they became a part of the new structure of controls established during the war period.

On June 12, 1947, President Truman asked for specific legislative authority to impose credit controls, saying that without such authority he would rescind the 1941 executive order on that subject. Congress responded by passing a bill declaring that all existing credit controls should end Nov. 1, 1947, and could not be reimposed by the President except in a future state of war or emergency. But in 1948, Congress passed legislation authorizing the Federal Reserve Board to impose controls at its discretion. (The Fed imposed restrictions in 1948 but eased them in March and April 1949, before they expired on June 30 of that year.)

Korean War. President Truman asked Congress on July 19, 1950, for authority to freeze wages and prices and to impose a variety of other controls designed to ease adjustment from civilian to military production. The Defense Production Act (PL 81-774), signed into law Sept. 8, 1950, authorized the President to assign priorities, allocate materials and facilities, and requisition property for defense production; to regulate consumer credit and to impose selective or general wage and price controls.

Controls on consumer installment credit were ordered on Sept. 18, and in mid-December, the President's Economic Stabilization Agency ordered a rollback in auto price increases and a freeze in auto wages. Further controls were ordered in 1951. And rent control authority, scheduled to expire in early 1951, was lumped together with the remainder of the stabilization program under an extension of the Defense Production Act. Rent control in non-critical defense areas was repealed as of July 31, 1953, while authority to control consumer credit was repealed as of June 30, 1952.

Under full impact of the controls, the cost of living rose 4 per cent in the last 11 months of 1951—a mark that was less than one-third the annual rate in the last half of 1950. In 1952, it rose less than one per cent. By the end of March 1953, the Eisenhower administration had removed all price and wage controls, and the legal authority behind them lapsed April 30. The general price level remained stable through 1955.

In a radio and television address to the nation, the President pointed to meat prices as "the major weak spot in our fight against inflation." Nixon's decision came amid meat boycotts by shoppers caused by record high prices for those products.

Barely two weeks earlier, on March 15, the President had stated at a news conference that price controls on food products would be counterproductive, leading to black market operations and rationing.

Controls Debate

Acting under the pressure of a midnight deadline, Congress April 30 completed action on legislation extending for one year the President's authority to impose wage and price controls. Without final action on the bill, his authority to control wages and prices would have expired less than three hours later.

Two days later, Nixon ordered new price controls on the nation's largest business firms.

Neither the administration, House Republicans nor Senate advocates of tougher controls were satisfied completely with the form of the extension measure cleared by Congress.

The President had requested a simple extension of his authority without congressionally imposed conditions. House Republicans earlier had defeated attempts of House Democrats to amend the bill to force tougher wage and price controls and had threatened to oppose the conference report because House conferees accepted four substantive Senate amendments.

The threat that even the remaining Phase III voluntary controls would expire if action on the extension were delayed caused all sides of the controls debate to reluctantly accept the conference report.

The most significant Senate amendments retained in the final version gave the President authority to ration petroleum products and required public disclosure of certain information reported to the Cost of Living Council by companies that raised the price of any product by more than 1.5 per cent.

Harried by surging prices, a falling dollar and an uncertain stock market—and by congressional pressures to do something about them—President Nixon huddled with his economic advisers during the first week in June to consider revising his economic strategy.

In many quarters—the stock markets, the international monetary exchanges and the halls of Congress—the economy was viewed as approaching a crisis point requiring urgent action. And their fears were heightened by the President's inaction.

Phase IV

Resorting to a freeze as shock treatment for an inflation-plagued economy, Nixon June 13 ordered a 60-day freeze on prices to buy time for toughening the nation's economic controls system.

In announcing the 60-day freeze—which he applied to all prices except on unprocessed food products at the farm level—the President promised to devise in the interim "a new and more effective system of controls...to contain the forces that have sent prices so rapidly upward in the past few months."

"Everybody thinks that Phase III was a failure," Treasury Secretary George P. Shultz admitted at a White House press briefing before the President's announcement. "We are not arguing about that."

The President's order froze prices at levels in effect the week of June 1-8, thus requiring roll-backs in prices increased since that week. By limiting the freeze to prices, Nixon left wages under existing Phase III controls. Rents were left free from federal controls.

Nixon July 18 lifted the freeze on food prices except for beef and laid out complex plans for toughened Phase IV controls on the economy.

To moderate inflation while fiscal and monetary restraints made an end to controls possible, the President proposed the most complicated peacetime controls system the nation had ever experienced.

As an initial step, the President July 18 exempted most segments of the food industry from the freeze and set up a two-stage program for controlling food prices. With the exception of the health industry, other economic sectors were left under the freeze until Aug. 12.

The post-freeze proposals, tailored to conditions in varying economic sectors, in general put stricter limits than did Phase II controls on businessmen's ability to translate rising costs into higher prices. Like the Phase II system, moreover, the Phase IV controls were mandatory, backed up by civil penalties.

The Phase IV proposals retained the Phase II and Phase III standards for wage and benefit increases: 5.5 per cent for wages plus 0.7 per cent for benefits.

Under Phase IV, the Cost of Living Council was given authority to grant exemptions from controls if inflationary pressures were relieved, if inequities developed or if supply shortages were threatened. The council retained power to reimpose controls if necessary.

1974

The policies that were established during 1973 continued into 1974. Preoccupied by the Watergate revelations that eventually forced his resignation in August, the President made no bold economic policy moves despite a weakening in output and unprecedented peacetime inflation.

With no initiatives undertaken by the executive branch, the Federal Reserve Board bore most of the burden of fighting inflation through efforts to hold down growth of the money supply. Its restrictive policies sent interest rates to record levels before being eased late in the year.

Federal fiscal policy remained moderately restrictive, with the fiscal 1974 deficit of only $3.5-billion. In the last budget sent to Congress by his administration, Nixon projected a fiscal 1975 deficit of $9.4-billion and federal spending that would top $300-billion.

Although Nixon preserved the option of shifting toward greater stimulus for the economy if necessary, the administration's emphasis was on spending reductions to avoid an inflationary deficit.

Controls finally were abandoned, except for oil price restrictions, when Congress refused Nixon's request for continued controls on health and construction and for monitoring authority for the Cost of Living Council.

By that time, the industry-by-industry decontrol process that started under Phase IV in 1973 had nearly been completed anyway, and both business and labor as well as Congress were opposed to continuation of controls even in limited or standby form.

The Watergate scandal drove Nixon from office, but his handling of the economy was perhaps the most glaring policy failure of his administration.

In his last months in office, Nixon's economic strategy had returned to the fundamentalist anti-inflationary approach that he had pursued at the start of his White House tenure. But in part because of the stimulative measures he had adopted in 1971-72, the time-honored restraints of tight money and budget cutting were having even less effect on inflation than before.

Nixon's last speech on economic matters, delivered to business leaders in Los Angeles barely two weeks before his resignation, restated his "old-time religion" beliefs and ruled out tax cuts, wage and price controls and other initiatives. Less than three years after he had sprung his new economic policy on a surprised nation, Nixon criticized calls in Congress "for swift, spectacular action" and pledged continued restrictiveness in monetary and fiscal policy.

When he resigned, Nixon left to his successor the task of balancing the tradeoff between slowing inflation and countering the recession that had taken hold of the economy. ∎

FORD'S STRATEGY: TRYING FOR A BALANCED POLICY

With his inflation-fighting options limited by a deepening recession, President Gerald R. Ford tried a down-the-middle approach in the economic strategy he adopted two months after taking office.

In trying to balance steps to counter unemployment with restraints on inflationary demand, however, the President was constrained from launching an all-out effort against either of the twin "stagflation" problems that were sapping the U.S. economy.

Ford insisted that the 32-point program he outlined to Congress on Oct. 8, 1974 was designed to cope with both inflation and the recession that was taking hold as he took over the presidency in August.

But by the end of 1974 it was plain that both Congress and economic trends would dictate changes in an administration program that coupled limited proposals to counter recession with an unpopular federal income tax surcharge to offset their cost.

The 93rd Congress paid scant attention to Ford's program, preferring to defer action on its major components until 1975, when the new 94th Congress, top-heavy with Democrats, convened.

Whatever course the economy took, there seemed little chance that Congress would enact the most controversial Ford proposal: a 5 per cent surcharge during 1975 on federal taxes paid by corporations and by middle- and upper-income families and individuals.

Ford maintained that the surcharge, which would be imposed on the taxes paid by individuals earning about $7,-500 or more and families earing $15,000 or more, was a fair way to raise revenues to keep the federal budget from running up an inflationary deficit.

But neither Republicans nor Democrats embraced the surcharge—which was proposed less than a month before the Nov. 5 congressional elections—arguing that it would only increase already heavy tax burdens on inflation-plagued middle-income groups.

In the expanded program he announced on Oct. 8, Ford stuck by the basic inflation-fighting strategy he had inherited from President Nixon. Even with the special measures to help certain groups deal with economic problems, administration policy still was primarily designed to restrain inflationary pressures.

Accordingly, the President's package was built around a restrictive fiscal policy. Key elements were the surcharge and federal spending cuts to trim the federal budget deficit.

By proposing measures to help the housing industry, encourage business investment, toughen anti-trust enforcement and combat unemployment—and by endorsing a tax revision bill that would cut taxes at lower income levels—Ford urged actions that had been backed in Congress to supplement the administration's basic fiscal and monetary policies.

As outlined to Congress in his Oct. 8 message, Ford's new economic proposals sought a balance between restraint on inflation and assistance to industries and individuals

who were suffering most from the combination of inflation and recession.

That implied a cautious approach, with assistance to some groups offset by demands on others, and as a result none of the measures was as strong as advocates of the different actions would have liked.

Ford presented his proposals as a package of interrelated measures that must be implemented as a comprehensive program, maintaining that "none of the remedies proposed...stands a chance unless they are combined in a considered package, in a concerted effort, in a grand design."

Among his major initiatives, Ford announced or proposed:

Federal Taxes

●A 5 per cent surcharge in 1975 on taxes paid by corporations, by families with incomes in the $15,000 range and by individuals with earnings around $7,500. The surcharge would increase 1975 taxes by about $2.6-billion on families and individuals and by about $2.1-billion on corporations. *(Box, p. 77)*

● An increase in the business investment tax credit to 10 per cent, up from 7 per cent for most businesses and 4 per cent for utilities, reducing business taxes by about $2.7-billion a year. *(Box, p. 78)*

● A tax deduction for corporations for dividends paid on new issues of preferred stock, reducing their taxes by an estimated $100-million a year.

● Enactment of a tax-revision bill then under consideration by the House Ways and Means Committee, including provisions that would lower taxes on low- and middle-income taxpayers by about $1.6-billion, cut capital gains taxes and phase out the oil and gas depletion allowance.

Federal Spending

● Enactment of a target $300-billion ceiling on fiscal 1975 federal spending before Congress recessed Oct. 11.

● Congressional approval of a package of spending deferrals and appropriations recisions to cut spending to $300-billion that would be submitted after the November recess.

Food

● Removal of remaining acreage limits on rice, peanuts and cotton.

● Authority to allocate fertilizer to farmers.

● Review of agriculture marketing orders, federal regulations and private and public restrictions that raise food prices.

● Voluntary monitoring of grain exports.

● Authority to waive certain restrictions on food shipments under the Food for Peace (PL 480) program.

Energy

● Creation of a National Energy Board headed by Secretary of the Interior Rogers C. B. Morton, with a goal of reducing petroleum imports by one million barrels a day by the end of 1975.

● Legislation to require use of coal and nuclear fuel to power new electric plants and conversion of existing oil plants to eliminate oil-fired generating plants by 1980.

● Action by the automobile industry, required by law if necessary, to increase gasoline mileage by 40 per cent within four years.

● Legislation to deregulate natural gas prices, tap naval petroleum reserves, amend the Clean Air Act and regulate strip mining.

Restrictive Practices

● More effective enforcement of antitrust laws, including laws against price-fixing and bid-rigging and elimination of non-competitive professional fee schedules and real estate settlement fees.

● Creation of a National Commission on Regulatory Reform to consider repeal of federal rules and regulations that increase prices.

● Scrutiny by the Council on Wage and Price Stability of the inflationary costs of federal government actions.

Housing

● Enactment of Senate legislation that would make most conventional home mortgages eligible for purchase by federal housing assistance agencies.

● Immediate obligation of at least $3-billion to finance about 100,000 homes once the legislation was in effect.

Unemployment

● An expanded public service jobs program that would provide temporary work with state and local governments whenever the national unemployment rate averaged 6 per cent or more over three months.

● An additional 13 weeks of unemployment insurance benefits for persons in high-unemployment areas who had exhausted their regular and extended benefits provided by existing programs.

Economic Setting

With the Watergate crisis removed from center stage by Nixon's resignation, the economy once more became the nation's most pressing concern. While Nixon had been almost totally distracted by the scandal that eventually forced him from office, Ford made control of inflation his new administration's "high and first priority."

In the three months before Ford took office, the consumer price index had risen at an annual rate of 11.7 per cent while the wholesale price index went up at an annual rate of 24.1 per cent. At the same time, a recession was taking hold, as real gross national product (GNP) fell by 1.6 per cent during the April-June quarter. In the first three months of the year, real GNP had fallen by 5.8 per cent.

Initial Request

While insisting that fiscal and monetary restraint remained necessary to curb inflation, Ford indicated that he was willing to go beyond the Nixon policies and consider congressional proposals.

Ford's first economic policy proposal was to renew Nixon's request that Congress re-establish an agency to

Ford's Proposed Tax Surcharge

President Ford's proposed 5 per cent income tax surcharge would require about 23 million families and single taxpayers to pay $2.6-billion more of their 1975 incomes to the federal government.

While aimed at increasing taxes on families with incomes of $15,000 or more and individuals earning $7,-500 or more, the administration's proposal actually would apply the 5 per cent surcharge to taxes owed after incomes were adjusted to reflect exemptions and deductions. Whether or not a taxpayer would pay the surcharge therefore would depend on expenses and family responsibilities as well as on total income.

As proposed by the President, the surcharge would increase taxes on a taxpayer filing a joint return by 5 per cent of the amount of his normal tax bill that exceeded the usual tax on a $10,000 income. In other words, if the taxable income left after deductions was more than $10,000, the taxpayer would pay an extra amount equal to 5 per cent of his taxes in excess of the tax on $10,000. At existing income tax rates, the surcharge would be 5 per cent of taxes owed in excess of $1,820.

According to Treasury calculations, an average family of four living on $15,000 a year would escape paying the surcharge. As income increased above that level, so would the surcharge, assuming that personal expense deductions stayed constant as a percentage of income:

	$15,000	$20,000	$50,000
Wages (adjusted gross income)	$15,000	$20,000	$50,000
Four personal exemptions ($750 per person)	−3,000	−3,000	−3,000
Personal expense deductions (assumed 17 per cent of income)	−2,550	−3,400	−8,500
Taxable income	9,450	13,600	38,500
Normal tax bill	1,699	2,660	11,465
Tax on $10,000	−1,820	−1,820	−1,820
Tax subject to surcharge	0	840	9,645
5 per cent surcharge	0	42	482
Tax including surcharge	1,699	2,702	11,947
Effective percentage tax increase	0	1.6	4.2

For a taxpayer who filed an individual return, the surcharge would be applied to the amount of tax he owed above $994.50, the tax on the first $5,450 of income. Under Treasury calculations, by exempting taxes on the first $5,450 of a single taxpayer's income the proposal would apply the surcharge to individual incomes of $7,500 or more.

According to Treasury estimates, the surcharge would apply to taxes owed on about 16 million joint returns and about seven million individual returns, which together account for about 28 per cent of all returns filed with the Internal Revenue Service. About 35 per cent of all joint returns and 21 per cent of individual returns would be subject to the surcharge.

Business Taxes

While proposing a 5 per cent federal tax surcharge that would raise corporate income taxes by about $2.1-billion for 1975 only, President Ford's economic program would ease federal taxation on business by widening the investment tax credit and by introducing a deduction for cash dividends paid out on preferred stocks.

Treasury officials estimated that the enlarged business investment credit would reduce business taxes by about $2.7-billion a year and the dividend deduction by about $100-million.

Investment Credit

To encourage business and industry to expand productive capacity, Ford proposed that the existing investment tax credit for business investment in plant and equipment be raised to 10 per cent. A part of the tax laws on and off since 1962, the credit allows a business to subtract a percentage of its investment in new plant and equipment from the taxes it owes the federal government.

As reinstituted by Congress in 1971 after a two-year suspension, the credit was set at 7 per cent for most businesses and 4 per cent for utilities.

In addition to asking that the credit be raised to 10 per cent for utilities as well as other businesses, Ford proposed refinements in existing law that would:

● Make the full credit available for investment in all property that for tax purposes was expected to be used for more than three years. (Under existing law, the credit was limited to one-third of the value of investments with useful lives of three to five years and to two-thirds of value of investments with useful lives of five to seven years. The full credit was available only on equipment with useful lives of seven years or more.)

● Refund to the company any excess credits that had not been used three years after investments were made. A business that made substantial investments compared with existing income—or that had no tax liability because of financial difficulties—thus would get more benefit from the credit.

(Under existing law, the maximum credit taken by a single company in any one year was limited to $25,000 plus half of its tax liability over $25,000. Credits above that limit could be carried back against taxes for three previous years or forward against taxes for seven subsequent years, but after seven years the unused credits expired.)

● Reduce depreciation deductions taken on the same assets by requiring that the cost of the property be reduced for tax purposes by the amount of the credit.

Dividends Deduction

In a proposal offered to assist funds-starved industries, particularly utilities, the administration suggested a tax deduction to corporations for dividends paid to holders of qualified stocks.

The deduction would be available only for dividends paid on preferred stock sold after Dec. 31, 1974. The corporation would be required to announce its intention to take the deduction when it issued the stock.

monitor inflation. But he took pains to make clear that he would not request authority to use wage and price controls.

Congress quickly complied with that request, establishing a Council on Wage and Price Stability. But that agency had few powers, and its activities in the following months were limited to public hearings on particularly rapid price increases such as for sugar.

Summit

Taking advantage of a period of good will following the transfer of power, Ford tried to enlist Congress in the search for other ways to fight inflation. In his first address to Congress as President, he accepted Senate Majority Leader Mike Mansfield's (D Mont.) call for a domestic summit conference on inflation.

Through a series of pre-summit meetings leading up to the Sept. 27-28 conference, administration officials solicited views from a broad cross-section of economic interests. After sifting through proposals made at the conference, which he personally chaired, Ford came up with the expanded program that he outlined on Oct. 8.

But as the summit discussions made clear, recession by that time was rivaling inflation as the top concern among Democrats, labor and many economists.

Those concerns were heightened by third-quarter figures showing that real gross national product dropped again in July through September, this time by 2.1 per cent.

By one conventional definition, a reduction in real GNP in two consecutive quarters constitutes a recession. And real GNP fell in each of the first three quarters of 1974.

Those figures notwithstanding, the administration kept insisting that controlling inflation was the nation's top priority, refusing to describe the decline in output as a recession. In releasing preliminary third-quarter output figures, for instance, Secretary of Commerce Frederick B. Dent said that the nation was experiencing a "spasm" or "sideways waffling" rather than recession.

Recession or Not

But signs of recession mounted. Auto sales plummeted, prompting widespread lay-offs, and a nationwide coal strike in November threatened to curtail operations in the steel and other industries.

In an Oct. 29 news conference, Ford insisted that his proposals could cope with both inflation and "some deterioration in some parts of the economy."

"Whether it is a recession or not a recession is immaterial," Ford insisted. "We have problems. The plan I submitted is aimed at solving these problems...."

On Nov. 1, the Labor Department reported that unemployment had risen during October to 6 per cent for the first time since 1971.

With those trends continuing, administration officials were backing away from Ford's earlier pledge to balance the federal budget. Lagging corporate profits were expected to undercut revenues, and the administration was revising its fiscal 1976 tax receipt projections to levels far below expected spending.

Anticipating more bad news on the economic outlook, presidential Press Secretary Ron Nessen Nov. 12 told reporters that economic statistics indicated "that this month we are moving into a recession."

While thus acknowledging the recession, Ford still maintained that his program could handle both it and inflation. With doubts growing in Congress, however, changes were expected. ∎

FORD'S ECONOMIC TEAM: A FIRM WITH ONE CLIENT

They came with good references. If, instead of joining the U.S. government, they had decided to hang a shingle on Wall Street as a consulting firm, Seidman, Simon, Burns & Greenspan might have had to rent a hall to hold all their clients. As it is, each has a formidable title trailing his name: L. William Seidman, assistant to the President for economic affairs; William E. Simon, secretary of the Treasury; Arthur F. Burns, chairman of the Federal Reserve Board; Alan Greenspan, chairman of the Council of Economic Advisers. They have only one client: the President of the United States.

Since Gerald Ford is a politician, and they are conservative economists, the advice this prestigious team is giving him is not very pleasant. The message, as reflected in Ford's Oct. 8 economic proposals, is that the American economy is sick from too much government spending for too many years. The only way to restore health is to reduce spending. Recovery, they say, will take years, just as the illness took years to reach its present stage of ravage.

They have said it so often that it has become as much their private cliche as their battle cry: there are no quick and easy remedies.

Of the many obstacles to recovery, Ford's top economic advisers recognize that one of the greatest is the 1976 election. The most elementary political wisdom tells them the President will have to be able to point to some substantial improvement in the economy if he is to stay in office. The team faces many complexities, but this paradox looms largest. The economy needs a long-term prescription; their client needs to keep his job.

Yet, interviews with members of the team and others reflect a confidence that they are on the right course, and more than a little optimism that Ford will allow their ideas a fair trial.

"The President's [Oct. 8] program is looking more sound every day," Seidman told Congressional Quarterly three weeks after Ford delivered his economic message to Congress. "It's a soft economy, and fiscal restraint is what's needed. I wouldn't call it the centerpiece of the program, because all parts of the program are important. The problem we have was caused by a whole pile of things, as the economic summit meetings we held indicate. But fiscal restraint is very important."

Another White House economic aide added: "There is a lot of talk of 'returning' to the 'old-time religion' [fiscal restraint]. Well, for a lot of reasons, this is not a return because we never had it during the Nixon years. Nixon preached it a lot but he never gave it a try. This will be the first time fiscal restraint has really been given a chance, and we'll have to be very tough. We'll have to be prepared to take the heat, because it's a complicated idea and it's not easy to sell to the public. We can't afford to worry about the short-term political gain we'd get by spending an extra $50-million here, a half-billion there."

Observers trying to gauge Ford's determination—in his own words, to "bite the bullet" and pursue economic policies that may be political liabilities—view his two major actions

as President to date with mixed feelings. Some believe Ford's pardon of former President Nixon and his amnesty plan demonstrate Ford's willingness to take the correct action as he sees it regardless of the political damage. Others are afraid that Ford's disregard for the political fallout, particularly of the pardon, reveals an ominous flaw in his ability to conduct long-range policy such as fiscal restraint.

Whether the Nixon pardon will seriously undermine Ford's economy cure is another aspect of Watergate that will have to await the judgment of history. In the meantime, Ford's economic advisers are shaking out the kinks from their new organization and turning their efforts to making the plan work.

Structure

"We have now an active, over-all policy-making machinery to provide the President with options," said Seidman, the man on the team closest to Ford personally and the management whiz who was most responsible for its structure.

"People who have been around Washington for a while say the preparation of the President's [Oct. 8] address after the summit meetings would have been very difficult if not impossible if the team hadn't been able to function as well as it does," Seidman said in a rare moment of relaxation in his gold-carpeted office. He sipped from a plastic cup containing his favorite drink, Pepsi-Cola. "We have a central focus; the key people involved in this are in place. In my judgment, given time it can be an effective organizational pattern."

The White House announced the formation of the team Sept. 28. Executive Order 11808 established an Economic Policy Board to "oversee the formulation, coordination and implementation of all economic policy." The same order established an executive committee of the board. Both the board and the committee are chaired by Simon, with Seidman serving as executive director of both. Simon was named the "principal spokesman" for economic policy.

"We now have an active, over-all policy-making machinery to provide the President with options.... We have a central focus, the key people involved in this are in place."

—L. William Seidman

Members of the board include: Treasury Secretary Simon; Presidential Assistant Seidman; Secretary of State Henry A. Kissinger; Interior Secretary Rogers C.B. Morton; Agriculture Secretary Earl L. Butz; Commerce Secretary Frederick B. Dent; Labor Secretary Peter J. Brennan;

Health, Education and Welfare Secretary Caspar W. Weinberger; Housing and Urban Development Secretary James T. Lynn; Transportation Secretary Claude S. Brinegar; Council of Economic Advisers Chairman Greenspan; Roy L. Ash, director of the Office of Management and Budget, and William D. Eberle, executive director of the Council on International Economic Policy.

Although he is not an official member because he belongs to an independent agency, Federal Reserve Chairman Burns also attends some meetings of the board and the executive committee. Members of the executive committee, which meets daily, include: Simon (chairman), Seidman (executive director), Greenspan, Eberle and Ash.

It was widely assumed that Ash, the dapper co-founder of the giant conglomerate, Litton Industries, would be leaving the White House soon after Ford came into office. But Ash was asked to finish preparation of the fiscal 1976 budget. Since then he has made a favorable impression on Ford's men, and there is some speculation he will be urged to stay on.

Eberle is a former chief executive of American Standard Inc., an industrial conglomerate with roots in the field of plumbing and heating equipment. He had served as Nixon's special representative for trade negotiations, with the rank of ambassador, since 1971.

Liaison with Bureaucracy

As of early November, a key element of the structure was not yet in place: regular contact with the federal bureaucracy. "We have the top part done, but we have not done the total job in setting up the contact and coordination with the agencies and the rest of the government," according to a White House source.

This part is vital because Seidman believes the White House must make skillful use of the bureaucracy to make the plan work—a view that is shared by a former ranking member of Richard Nixon's economic team, who asked not to be identified.

"In my own view, one of the real mistakes Nixon made in economic policy—and a lot of other things—was he didn't get a grip on the bureaucracy," said the former official. "A lot of people perceived Nixon as ruthless and think he fired a lot of people after he came into office, but during the first year or year and a half he was just a big old softie. It was unbelievable that just nothing was done. Too many of the holdovers [from the Johnson administration] stayed in, people deliberately did not carry out policy instructions and sometimes sabotaged programs deliberately. Nothing was done, and the word spread that you could pretty much do what you wanted and get away with it."

This source believes that after the first two years of Nixon's first term he overreacted to the frustration of not being able to control the bureaucracy by centralizing power in the White House through H.R. Haldeman and John D. Ehrlichman; and this led more or less directly to the abuses of power uncovered in the Watergate scandal.

The source places another part of the blame for Nixon's failure to control the economy on the former president's political advisers. Again, the Nixon experience contains clear warnings for Ford.

"There were various economic interest groups that wanted things done, and Congress passed laws calling for over-spending, and various people on the White House staff didn't exercise the control they should have. Often it would come down to where you either okayed an expenditure or you incurred a short-term political loss. There were a lot of

people who thought the thing to do was to take the short-term political loss. But political figures are not generally prone to do that."

The former adviser was "optimistic" that Ford will do better "in the sense that the President is going to be getting from his team the best advice I think he could pull together in the country at this time. I think the unknown in the equation is how he takes that advice and what other pressures are going to be on him, and what he feels is the right thing to do. We'll have to wait and see."

Different Approach

Seidman, at least, is determined to try to avoid the mistakes Nixon made with the bureaucracy.

"There's a tremendous capability and horsepower in the departments and agencies of government," said Seidman, who spent most of his career building a fortune in his accounting firm in Grand Rapids, Mich. "They need to be given back the work and the policy-making input they previously had. I'd say this is different than the Nixon approach."

As Seidman envisions the system, ideas and suggestions will come from the agencies to the policy board, where the "options are put into shape" and passed along to the President. Ford will act on them and they will be returned to the agencies to be carried out.

Seidman has two basic functions: making sure the policies are put into action, and acting as the liaison between the policy board and the President. He reports to Ford on meetings of the executive committee and accompanies the President to other meetings related to the economy in order to report back to the committee.

For a time, Seidman also is acting as an ad hoc liaison between the executive committee and members of the Cabinet, all of whom serve on the full board. Seidman said this arrangement is temporary until regular channels are established, at which time contact with the agencies outside of board meetings will be divided among members of the executive committee.

"The mission is not to eliminate the agency part, but to get it back," Seidman reiterated.

Congressional Problems

If sticking to the canons of the "old-time religion," and making sure the bureaucracy works, are one side of the problem facing the White House, the other side is convincing Congress that it belongs in the same church.

Ford's economic advisers are not so concerned with the fact that there will be more Democrats in the 94th Congress as they are with the kind of Democrats—and Republicans—they will be.

"There has been a lot of talk in Congress about fiscal responsibility," said one presidential aide who is familiar with Capitol Hill. "We can only hope that this will be the kind of Congress that will put individual constituent pressures in second place of the overriding concern, the national interest."

He pointed out that Ford still commands considerable respect on Capitol Hill and that he is intimately knowledgeable of its workings. However, the White House knows that Ford might have to resort to a string of vetoes to keep spending in line with his policies.

Seidman: Unknown Quantity

In its predictable battles with Congress in 1975 over the economy, the Ford White House will have to turn to persons outside the economic team for legislative strategy. Not one of the members of the policy board's executive committee has any particular claim to congressional expertise—although Burns appears on Capitol Hill frequently and has good relations.

Seidman himself is a newcomer to Washington and is considered by many to be a relatively unknown quantity.

His politics, which are moderate-to-conservative Republican in the mold of former Michigan Gov. George

Romney, are something of a mystery to those who know him. Seidman's parents were both liberal Democrats. His politically active father was a strong supporter of Democratic Gov. Frank Murphy (1937-39) during the 1930s and worked with him to establish a number of New Deal-inspired programs in Michigan such as the state's first unemployment compensation act. The elder Seidman also served as a dollar-a-year consultant to President

L. William Seidman

Franklin D. Roosevelt during the Depression and traveled to Washington on occasion to attend advisory meetings.

Frank Seidman, a Russian Jewish immigrant, founded the family accounting firm, Seidman & Seidman, in New York during World War I along with his brother, John. During the war he represented the federal government in Grand Rapids, where he audited the furniture plants there that had contracts to build airplanes. Despite his liberal politics, the conservative furniture executives were impressed by Seidman's ability and they persuaded him to open a branch office in Grand Rapids after the war.

The firm began specializing in the furniture industry. During the post-war years, when the Grand Rapids plants balked at mass production, the industry moved South, to such places as High Point, N.C., and Memphis, Tenn., where labor was cheaper. Seidman & Seidman followed close behind, opening branch offices. The firm grew steadily.

The Seidmans were not ostentatious with their wealth, but the family did establish the Seidman Foundation, a philanthropic fund in memory of Seidman's brother, who died at the age of seven. The foundation is well known in Grand Rapids for its work in the inner city and with youth programs.

Seidman grew up in this well-off, politically active family. He picked up degrees from Dartmouth (1943), Harvard Law School (1948) and the University of Michigan graduate school of business administration (1949). He fought the Japanese during World War II in between studies.

Returning to Grand Rapids, Seidman became a Certified Public Accountant and eventually took control of Seidman & Seidman as the elected managing partner. During the six years before he came to Washington he moved it from a middle-sized operation with 18 branch offices to an international firm now ranked among the 10 largest accounting businesses in the nation. Along the way he became a millionaire.

Insensitive?

Friends rate Seidman as instinctively competitive and extremely able in the fields of accounting, tax law and

organizational structure. However, critics claim he tends to be unsympathetic toward social problems.

"I shuddered when Bill was asked on a TV interview about the unemployment rate going up to 6 per cent," says one close observer of Seidman. Seidman answered that although unemployment was "regrettable," it was a price the country would have to pay for defeating inflation.

"I don't think he's yet realized that to the average American having a job and earning some money is more important than getting prices down without any money to buy anything," said the observer, who is a Democrat. "I think there is a lack of understanding or sensitivity that isn't very good, and I'm afraid he is feeding Ford's natural inclination to be insensitive to some of these problems."

Seidman grew up within a few blocks of Gerald Ford's home in Grand Rapids and met Ford once while in school. But he first attracted Ford's attention in the early 1960s when Ford was seeking to recruit capable people to the local party. Seidman had become active in politics through his efforts to organize and fund a new state college system in the Grand Rapids area. Nominally a Democrat, Seidman was working closely on the project with the state legislature and with Democratic Governors G. Mennen Williams (1949-61) and John B. Swainson (1961-63).

Seidman became involved in the state constitutional convention of 1961-62 and came out of it a strong supporter of automobile executive George Romney.

Romney persuaded Seidman to run for Michigan's auditor general's office when Romney ran against Swainson in 1962. But Seidman's Democratic background came back to haunt him. It was discovered that in 1958 Seidman's wife, Sarah—who is more liberal than her husband—had hosted a tea for Richard Vander Veen, a Democrat who then was challenging Ford for his congressional seat. (He now holds the seat.) Ford won the race anyway, and he stepped into Seidman's campaign in 1962 to assure Michigan Republican regulars that he did not bear any ill will toward Seidman because of the tea incident. During the State Republican convention Ford took Seidman around to the various congressional district caucuses to assure them that he was Ford's man.

Saving Millions

Romney defeated Swainson, but Seidman lost his race by a narrow margin. However, Romney put him to work in his new administration setting up a management consulting group to analyze the state government. The group proposed a sweeping consolidation of state agencies that saved "millions of dollars," according to Romney.

Seidman signed onto Romney's inner campaign staff when Romney decided to make his ill-fated bid for the 1968 presidential nomination.

Close observers note that there always has been a strong anti-labor streak running through Seidman's politics, ever since his early days as a Grand Rapids accountant. The major theme of Romney's campaign against Swainson was that the incumbent was a representative of a single special interest group—organized labor. Some critics see this, along with Seidman's alleged "insensitivity" to the human problems of the Ford economic program, such as higher unemployment, as a major fault in Seidman's perception of the economy.

"Things have come easily for him, particularly because of the natural ability he has," says one critic. "I suppose there's a tendency not to understand why everybody can't be like that."

Washington Career

Seidman's track record in official Washington has been short but impressive. He received his first public notices as part of the Ford vice presidential team, which he joined Feb. 1, 1974. Soon after his arrival, Seidman was assigned the job of examining the structure of Ford's staff. He drew up a plan for streamlining the office and widening access of staff members to Ford. Despite reported opposition from then chief of staff Robert T. Hartmann, who had been with Ford since 1966, major parts of the Seidman plan were adopted by Ford.

Seidman and White House Counsel Philip W. Buchen, an old friend of Ford and the President's former law partner in Grand Rapids, participated in some of the planning sessions conducted by Ford's four-man transition team during the early weeks of Ford's administration. And Seidman planned and operated the economic summit meetings that preceded Ford's Oct. 8 economic proposals. *(Ford proposals, p. 70)*

Seidman's suggestion, however, that the summit might not be immediately followed by any policy recommendations from Ford was overruled by the President's political advisers, reportedly including Hartmann.

Still, Seidman clearly is the man on the economic team to whom Ford listens most closely, a status topped outside the team only by Buchen and Hartmann.

Simon: Tiger From Wall Street

If every organization needs at least one hard-charger, Treasury Secretary Simon holds the undisputed title for the Ford economic team.

Simon's record in Republican Washington and his style of operating are much better known than Seidman's, since he has been around longer. His admirers say he is a man of action. Others say he borders on the frenetic.

"He's a little scary," says one former Simon staffer. "He'll call you on the carpet and do things that make you feel just terrible, and other times he'll make you feel terrific by calling you at home and saying, 'I just read this paper you did and it's absolutely splendid.' He gets mad almost instantly, and he also cools down if he discovers he's wrong. He chews people out regularly. But he is very exciting to be around because he's willing to run with any idea that sounds good. When you feel you've got him behind you, you can do anything."

William E. Simon

Another observer: "Whenever somebody on his staff comes up with an idea, he says, 'Good, you go work on that, go staff it out.' As a result he has an awful lot of people working terribly hard on a lot of things at once. Now, that's great except it doesn't exactly fit into the kind of administration Ford has, of people who want to think things through before they do anything. A person like Simon always generates another group of advisers somewhere else who always say, 'Hang on now, let's look at this idea a little more closely.' If that kind of group, who looked at the long-range implications of a policy, didn't exist, they would have to be created because of the activities of this man."

According to this source, Simon is "the kind of person who will say something like, 'We've got to stop running around putting out fires, we've got to do some long-range thinking,' and then he'll say, 'Now I want a good long-range plan, and let's have it by tomorrow afternoon. There's a certain frantic element about it."

Exploding With Energy

Simon's defenders note that he was asked by Nixon to start some action in the energy field after Nixon lost confidence in Gov. John Love of Colorado, then the latest in a series of White House energy policy advisers. Whether rumors in late 1973 that Love was indecisive and not a man of action were true, or whether the indecisiveness came from Nixon's end because of his own bedevilment over Watergate, is debatable. In any case, Simon left his post as under secretary of the Treasury, where he had been for a year since leaving his successful Wall Street securities firm, and hit the White House, exploding with energy.

One of Simon's first acts was to fire Vice Admiral Eli Reich, who had retired from the Navy to head the administration's energy allocations program. According to witnesses of the scene, Simon provoked a confrontation with Reich, whom Simon saw as having prima donna tendencies that were intimidating to civilians. Reich was angry because Simon had brought Reich and his 10 regional directors under Simon's direct control and had replaced most of Reich's choices of directors with Simon's own picks.

Reich began angrily lecturing Simon during a Sunday afternoon meeting in Simon's office for placing a conference call to the regional directors without first clearing it with Reich. Simon cut off the naval combat veteran, telling him the nation was in the midst of an energy crisis, that teamwork was called for, and that there was no room for a "pompous" prima donna. Reich agreed to resign.

Simon has had brushes with others in the White House bureaucracy, including OMB chief Ash. But most observers awarded him high marks for his intelligence and grasp of issues as well as for his aggressiveness.

"I think the main thing that qualifies him to the economic team is that he's willing to listen," says a friend. "He cuts through the crap and wants the answer. When he had the energy job we were in a critical time and he brought the nation together and he brought the whole energy group together. He took a really rough situation and he saw it like World War II, and he saw himself as one of Roosevelt's production czars. He gave a lot of spirit to everybody by getting something done."

If there is room for discontent in the Ford economic advisory structure, Simon's dislike of working with committees is a likely pocket. Simon's style favors short and pointed meetings with individuals, a preference he evidently will have to forgo as chairman of the policy board and its powerful executive committee.

Another difference between Simon's role in the economy and his role in the energy crisis is the breadth of his new assignment.

"It's harder to find the enemy in the economy than it was in the energy crisis," one administration official noted when asked whether Simon will be able to transfer his skills to the economic team. "It's harder to focus and to figure out which way to shoot the gun."

Although Simon agrees with Seidman and the rest of the team on the need for tight control of federal spending, observers note that Simon's basic approach of activism may cause chafing. Simon is a strong believer in allowing free market pressures to operate in the economy as much as possible, and indeed as energy chief he resisted gasoline rationing, fearing that the creation of a vast bureaucracy to enforce such a plan would cause more harm than good.

Controversy

However, according to two knowledgable sources, Simon advocated tougher measures than Ford's economic plan contain. The sources declined to specify what the measures Simon advocated were. But generally, they point out, those who argued for emphasizing volunteerism in reducing food and energy consumption carried the day.

"There was a surprising degree of unanimity in agreement on the program as stated," another member of the team told Congressional Quarterly. However, he added, "Naturally there are some disagreements, and sometimes people get a little huffy. And if the program as we have it doesn't work, you look to further steps."

According to those who have worked with and for Simon both on Wall Street and in Washington, the move to government hasn't changed Simon's habits much. In both places he was busy. Part of this activity is due to his insistence that he read everything that goes out of his office over his signature. Most cabinet secretaries allow aides to sign the bulk of their letters for them. But Simon is a fast reader and he takes time to find out what is going on in his agency. Signing all his own letters is one way.

However, that is not to say Simon insists on doing everything himself. "He trusts people to do a good job," says a former aide. "He's not like Philip of Spain, where everything holds up because it waits for him. Nothing holds up. He just keeps his in-box clean and his out-box full most of the time."

It was Simon's capacity for work and his knack for sizing up situations that made him one of Wall Street's most successful executives. In 1964, he moved from Weeden & Co., where he headed municipal bond trading operations, to a new position as a partner in Salomon Brothers, a securities firm. Salomon Brothers at the time was a medium-size concern. Since then it has become one of Wall Street's blue-bloods, with capital exceeding $130-million and taxable income at the end of the fiscal year of $37-

---

"We all have a stake in this economy. Everybody is hurt by inflation. If you really wanted to examine percentage-wise who was hurt most in their income, it was Wall Street brokers."

—Alan Greenspan, Sept. 19

---

million. Simon is given much of the credit for its expansion as head of the firm's department that works with bonds and other securities that are sold by the federal government. Simon's personal star rose on Wall Street in 1970 when he was picked to join the firm's seven-man management committee.

Wall Street observers put Simon's personal earnings at between $2-million and $3-million in 1971, the year before

Nixon nominated him to the $42,500-a-year number two job at the Treasury. Some Wall Street sources believed Simon's acceptance of the post was influenced by his perception that the securities industry was becoming less profitable than it had been. But a former associate told Congressional Quarterly, "My explanation is he's gone about as far as he could, he made $3-million in one year, and he wanted to try another stage. He's got all the money he needs. Now he wants to see if he can be a great success in something else."

Greenspan: Laissez-Faire Capitalist

The two remaining major figures of the President's economic team, Council of Economic Advisers Chairman

Alan Greenspan

Greenspan and Federal Reserve Board Chairman Burns, both served as advisers in former President Nixon's 1968 campaign. Burns, who had been John Bates Clark professor of economy at Columbia University since 1959, was part of a network of about a dozen economic advisers the Nixon inner campaign group consulted and the one upon whom the staff relied most heavily.

Greenspan, formerly a senior fellow at Stanford University's Hoover Institution on War, Revolution and Peace, and head of a New York consulting firm he helped found in 1963, served as part of the inner team as director of domestic research.

Both men are strong conservatives, and both have peerless reputations—Burns as an academic economist and Greenspan as a practitioner—among conservative and liberal economists alike. Walter Heller, who chaired the Council of Economic Advisers during the Kennedy administration, calls Greenspan the conservative he most likes to argue with. Another former Democratic official said, "Alan has never been one of those insufferable ideologues—he's always willing to argue his points quietly and reasonably."

Even so, his views are sometimes upsetting to liberals. During Greenspan's confirmation hearings in August 1974, Sen. William Proxmire (D Wis.) called attention to "the controversial nature of this nomination," in reference to Greenspan's devotion to the teachings of the controversial philosopher, Ayn Rand. *(Box, next page)*

In a letter to members of the Senate, after the hearings, Proxmire listed his doubts about Greenspan in numerical order: "(1) Mr. Greenspan made it emphatically clear in the hearings that he opposes vigorous enforcement of our anti-trust laws. (2) Mr. Greenspan has made it clear in public statements that he does not support consumer-protection legislation. (3) Mr. Greenspan has the almost incredible posture for an economic realist in these days—of opposing the progressive income tax. (4) In addition, Mr. Greenspan has been on retainer by 100 of the largest corporations in the country, including almost all of the 10 largest banks in the country and a number of manufacturing concerns which dominate their particular industry."

Greenspan was pleased that Proxmire mentioned the success of his firm, but he felt the citation of his views was unfair. During the hearings he acknowledged that, in the

The Rand Factor

"Alan is my disciple philosophically, but his career as an economic analyst is his own achievement," author-philosopher Ayn Rand told a reporter soon after former President Nixon nominated Alan Greenspan to be head of the Council of Economic Advisers. "He is an advocate of full *laissez-faire* capitalism—but neither he nor I expect it overnight."

Rand, who in recent years has avoided interviews because she believed her controversial views would be distorted in the press, advocates virtually complete withdrawal of the government from the economy and teaches what she calls "rational selfishness."

In each of her novels, *The Fountainhead* (1943) and *Atlas Shrugged* (1957), Rand told stories of one or two strong characters surrounded by weak or cowardly people who lacked the courage to act on their convictions. The weak characters eventually destroyed themselves, while the strong central figures stepped in to save the system from destruction.

Born in St. Petersburg, Russia (now Leningrad), Rand came to the United States in 1926. She now is the editor of *The Objectivist*.

Greenspan met Rand about 20 years ago, when he told *The New York Times*, "I was a free enterpriser in the Adam Smith sense—impressed with the theoretical structure and efficiency of markets. What she did—through long discussions and lots of arguments into the night—was to make me think why capitalism is not only efficient and practical but also moral."

Rand is doubtful Greenspan or anyone else can do much for the economy, though she saw his acceptance of the challenge as "heroic." She added: "The desperate state of the country is what may attract the best people to government."

true Ayn Rand tradition, he believed in *laissez-faire* capitalism to the point of opposing anti-trust laws and the progressive income tax. But he insisted these views would not affect his performance as the President's chief economic analyst.

"My view," Greenspan told reporters after his confirmation, "is the Council of Economic Advisers should be advisers on matters of research and basic economics. Now, what that will entail, as far as I am concerned, is to put before the President all of the various options and options stated by the profession. In other words, I consider it my job to make available to the President not only the views of the [Council], but also as best as I can, what others are saying...."

One of Greenspan's principal objectives is to "depoliticize" the council. He explains that he wants to avoid commenting on specific issues, such as wages and prices, and to refrain from making public statements about the latest economic figures.

One issue Greenspan has not been at all hesitant to speak out on, however, is fiscal restraint, which he believes is the single most important remedy for the economy. He repeatedly has stated his belief that lowering federal spending is a political problem.

"I am fairly well convinced at this stage," he has said, "that if we were to do one thing and one thing only, that is

cutting the growth in federal expenditures...we will finally get at the roots of the inflationary pressures."

He sees inflation "as essentially a political, not an economic problem."

Computer Politics

Greenspan brings considerable political experience to the team. Richard Whalen, another member of the 1968 Nixon campaign, describes Greenspan as "an expert in playing political war games on the computer." In his book, *Catch the Falling Flag: A Republican's Challenge to His Party*, Whalen recounted the following story:

Greenspan "shuttled between his downtown office near Wall Street and the Nixon headquarters bearing stacks of print-outs indicating the reaction of the electoral model to rightward and leftward maneuvering. The computer consistently awarded the game to the rightward moves. This displeased the conservative Greenspan not at all, but he maintained scholarly detachment as he sifted the evidence and stated his findings. 'It's my judgment that we can win five percentage points back from [presidential candidate George C.] Wallace, at a cost of one, or at the most two points moving from [Nixon] to [presidential candidate Hubert H.] Humphrey,' he wrote in late June."

After the campaign, Greenspan stayed in Washington temporarily to head the transition of the Bureau of the Budget in 1969. Nixon invited him to join the administration, but Greenspan preferred to return to his consulting firm.

Nixon offered Greenspan the chairmanship of the Council of Economic Advisers early in 1974 to replace Herbert Stein, who often was criticized in the press and by other economists for injecting politics into the council by commenting on issues and trying to put a good light on bad news. Greenspan credits Burns—his friend and former professor—as the person most instrumental in persuading him that he was needed in the job and that he would have some power in policy-making.

Nixon announced his nomination in July 1974, but resigned before Greenspan could be confirmed, and there were reports that Ford intended to withdraw the nomination. According to these reports Ford wanted to invite still another Nixon campaign adviser, Paul McCracken—who had been a member of the council under President Eisenhower and its chairman for the first two years of the Nixon administration—to fill the job. McCracken helped work on Ford's economic plan as an unofficial adviser, and rumors continued that Ford eventually intended to bring him into the administration in some capacity, perhaps eventually as chairman of the council.

Wall Street Brokers

Greenspan added to the charge that the Ford team lacked sensitivity by an embarrassing episode during one of the White House economic pre-summit meetings. Representatives of the poor, the aged, the sick and the handicapped Sept. 19 were arguing that reduced federal spending would mean higher unemployment and cuts in social welfare programs that would hit the poor the hardest.

Greenspan responded, "We all have a stake in this economy. Everybody is hurt by inflation. If you really wanted to examine percentage-wise who was hurt most in their income, it was Wall Street brokers."

Greenspan tried to continue his statement, but boos and catcalls drowned out the rest. One man in the hall shouted, "That's the whole trouble with this administration—Wall Street brokers!"

Burns: The Independent

Greenspan is not the only member of Ford's economic team who has taken to puncturing the President's more optimistic statements. At a news conference Oct. 9, Ford said, "I do not think the United States is in a recession." The next day Federal Reserve Board Chairman Burns, during testimony before the Joint Economic Committee, said the country is in a recession—although he called it "a most unusual recession—a recession for which there is no precedent in history."

Arthur F. Burns

Contradicting presidents is nothing new for Burns. In 1971 he disregarded the official Nixon euphemism for the state of the economy—"downturn"—and called 1970 a year of recession. At the same time, Burns bluntly rejected the administration's appeal for a faster expansion of money and credit, saying it was unnecessary and inflationary.

That was in February. As the year dragged on and the 1972 presidential election drew closer, Burns continued to disagree publicly with Nixon. He further infuriated White House officials by pressing his argument for a price and wage review board. In late July the administration leaked the news through the office of Herbert G. Klein, director of communications for the executive branch, that Nixon was being urged to double the size of the Fed's seven-man board

---

Vital Statistics

Seidman. L. William Seidman was born in Grand Rapids, Mich., April 29, 1921. He has degrees from Dartmouth (1943), Harvard (1948) and the University of Michigan graduate school of business administration (1949). He joined Ford's vice presidential staff Feb. 1, 1974, and was named assistant to the President for economic affairs Sept. 28, 1974.

Simon. William E. Simon was born in Paterson, N.J., in 1927 and was graduated by Lafayette College in 1952. He was nominated Treasury deputy secretary in December 1972. In December 1973 he became administrator of the Federal Energy Administration. He was named Treasury secretary in April 1974.

Greenspan. Alan Greenspan was born in New York City March 6, 1926. He received an undergraduate degree from New York University in 1948 and a master's degree there in 1950. He was nominated chairman of the Council of Economic Advisers in July 1974.

Burns. Arthur F. Burns was born in Stanislau, Austria, April 27, 1904. He was graduated by Columbia in 1925 and received a graduate degree there the same year. Columbia awarded him a Ph.D. in 1934. Among other government posts, he served as chairman of the Council of Economic Advisers in 1953-1956. He was appointed chairman of the Federal Reserve Board in January 1970.

---

of governors and thus weaken Burns' control. Burns refused to back down, and Nixon finally was obliged to publicly state his support for the Fed chairman.

Burns' independence stems from the fact that members of the board are appointed for 14-year terms, and chairmen for four years at a time. Nixon appointed Burns chairman in early 1970 and reappointed him in 1974.

At the time of his first appointment, it was widely assumed that Nixon had at last gained a control of monetary policy that had not been equaled in almost two decades. Ten years before, when Nixon, then vice president, opened his 1960 presidential campaign, Burns told him that unless the Eisenhower administration loosened controls on the economy, the nation would be plunged into a recession that could cost the Republicans the election. Nixon listened —but no one else did. The recession was hurting just as the voters went to the polls to elect John F. Kennedy.

Nixon never forgot Burns' advice on the impact of prosperity on politics, and that was one of his reasons for wanting him in his 1968 campaign. After the election Nixon gave him a title new to White House staffs—counselor. The new President put him in charge of pulling together Nixon's campaign statements, the Republican platform planks, 21 task force reports and other materials into specific policy recommendations for the administration. Burns delivered a report the day after the inauguration containing about 100 directives to department heads.

"That book was the well of ideas for the early Nixon administration, and they kept dipping into it well after Arthur left," said Martin Anderson, a Nixon campaign aide who stayed during the transition. "I think one of the things Nixon understood clearly when he named him to the Fed was that Arthur was independent and that he may not have liked it, but Arthur was so uniquely qualified for the job that there was really no alternative."

Intelligence and Integrity

Burns' qualifications include a towering reputation as an academic economist and a man of integrity. Aside from the fact that many economists disagree with his conservatism, perhaps the hardest criticism one hears is that he tends toward aloofness and arrogance. Anderson maintains that those critics are usually people "who have proposed ideas, debated with him, and were overwhelmed by his facts and logic and the imperfections of their own views. They just get very upset."

Burns' control of monetary policy has been fairly flexible. In mid-1971, Burns conceded that the rate of money supply growth had been too great and had to be cut back. This period followed a "money drought," with a resulting drying up of credit, in 1969-1970.

In September 1974, Burns told a pre-summit conference that there would be no "credit crunch in our country." Though a "policy of moderate monetary restraint remains appropriate," Burns said, "it would be undesirable to further intensify monetary restraint."

However, Burns consistently has refused to be cowed by threats from White House economists, political advisers or anyone else.

Burns already has suggested that the Federal Reserve system needs a complete overhaul and review since its complexity now "boggles the mind." The message to Burns' colleagues seems to be to treat the Fed chairman as they would treat a wise old lion—with respect and very carefully. At least, they may be sure that he is not likely to let politics interfere with his economic theory. ∎

IN SEARCH OF AN ECONOMIC PLAN OF ITS OWN

Especially on taxes, Congress seems unlikely to buy President Ford's economic program, particularly with recession rivaling inflation as the major congressional concern.

But while generally unimpressed by a presidential program built around a 5 per cent income tax surcharge, the Democratic-controlled 93rd Congress seemed unable to put together a comprehensive economic program of its own.

Congress long has left it to presidents to take the political risks inherent in economic troubles, a tendency that was especially glaring in 1974 as inflation and recession combined to make the economy the nation's most pressing post-Watergate worry. And since their party expanded its hold on both the House and Senate in the Nov. 5 elections, congressional Democratic leaders were not expected to press for action in 1974 on the surcharge and other measures that Ford requested Oct. 8. *(Ford proposals, p. 70)*

But with inflation eating at Americans' incomes—and with rising joblessness arousing fears of recession and even depression—Congress could not postpone action much longer to deal with the social and economic issues that the "stagflation" combination posed. For rising prices took more from some incomes than others, and the costs of curbing inflation were harsher for those who lost their jobs or their businesses.

"Inevitably, the solutions to inflation are going to involve some degree of sacrifice," commented Rep. Barber B. Conable Jr., an upstate New York Republican who supported Ford's anti-inflation strategy. "And there's always a suspicion in a democracy that the burdens of sacrifice fall unevenly."

Democrats in Congress particularly were suspicious of Ford's program, questioning both the fairness of the sacrifices it demanded and the administration's willingness to tolerate rising unemployment. While administration policy-makers made fighting inflation their top objective, congressional Democrats were worried more about recession.

Those suspicions were heightened by Ford's plan to put a surcharge on middle- as well as upper-income taxes to offset the cost of assistance to the housing industry and the unemployed and to lower taxes for business and lower-income families.

"It simply is not fair," complained Sen. Edward M. Kennedy (D Mass.), "to single out the ordinary man and woman to bear the heaviest burden in the war against inflation," especially since the surcharge would have little effect on upper-income individuals and corporations who paid little in taxes through a loophole-ridden tax system.

Alternatives

In economic policy alternatives submitted to Ford's Sept. 27-28 summit on inflation, House and Senate Democrats and the bipartisan Joint Economic Committee had proposed revenue-raising tax reforms to offset the costs of stronger federal action to provide jobs, discourage price

and wage increases and relieve tax burdens at low- and middle-income levels. But those were merely recommendations, and congressional leaders failed to mount concerted efforts to follow them up with legislation. *(Congressional alternatives, p. 70)*

"There's no reason why Congress should be so feckless on the economy as it has been this year," lamented Rep. Henry S. Reuss (D Wis.), a critic of Ford's program and author of an economic policy package endorsed by the House Democratic Caucus.

The Tax Issue

Ford's Oct. 8 surcharge proposal quickly became the focal point for economic policy debate, posing in specific terms the question of who should pay the costs of the nation's anti-inflation and counter-recession efforts.

The need to increase federal revenues to avoid a deeper deficit was not at issue, at least in the initial congressional reaction to the surcharge plan. What was disputed, however, was the equity of taxing hard-pressed wage-earners more while some favored incomes were lightly taxed to start with.

By proposing to add 5 per cent to the taxes that persons above certain levels already paid, Ford indirectly reminded many that the existing U.S. income tax system bore unevenly on people with different kinds of income.

"While demanding too much from the hard-pressed ordinary taxpayer" Kennedy contended, "the surcharge offers a free ride to wealthy individuals and corporations who use the loopholes to pay no tax at all, or to pay far less than they should."

Ford proposed the surcharge less than a month before the Nov. 5 election, a tactic he conceded was politically risky. Predictably, most Republican as well as Democratic candidates quickly disassociated their campaigns from what Ford termed "the acid test of our joint determination to whip inflation."

The political risks of raising taxes notwithstanding, some members of Congress found the surcharge distasteful on grounds of fairness and its possibly dampening effect on consumer demand during a recession they expected to continue well into 1975. "When you put a 5 per cent surcharge on incomes above $15,000," Reuss argued, "the major part falls upon people, who while not poor, spend about all of their income on consumption."

While reducing over-all demand would ease pressures on the prices of scarce materials, he added, by cutting the buying power of middle-income families the surcharge "would prevent them from buying all kinds of things that are not in short supply.

"When added to the other somber portents on the demand side—the fall-off in inventory accumulation, falling imports and the poor performance in consumer purchases generally," Reuss concluded, the surcharge's drain on real income would only feed recession.

Alternatives: Parties Split Over What to Attack First

Despite a common recognition that inflation must be licked, the Ford administration's strategy and congressional counter-proposals generally conformed to the traditional economic perspectives of the two political parties.

While acknowledging the dangers of recession, Ford and his advisers held firm to their view that inflation was the pre-eminent threat. Allowed to continue unchecked, they argued, inflation would undermine both social stability and prospects for future economic growth.

But congressional Democrats, while conceding the ravages of inflation, were at least equally worried about recession. Congressional policy proposals accordingly leaned toward stronger government measures to combat unemployment and ease the burden on those hit hardest by inflation.

Ford Proposals

Even with the embellishments he offered on Oct. 8, Ford's basic economic strategy remained a fundamentalist fiscal and monetary restraint on demand. Relying on a long-held view that federal budget deficits were the principal cause of inflation, the President made budget restraint the centerpiece of his program.

Accordingly, in urging special measures that would increase federal spending on housing and jobs while cutting taxes for lower-income persons and for business, Ford called for a 5 per cent surcharge on corporate and middle- and upper-income individuals to pay for those initiatives.

While trying to balance the budgetary impact of his new proposals, the President urged Congress to cut fiscal 1975 spending back to $300-billion. Fitting his new proposals into that budget framework, he offered measures that were limited and low-cost.

He called for more effective anti-trust enforcement and for review of restrictive regulatory policies, but he eschewed wage and price control powers.

Congressional Alternatives

In its 1974 economic policy statements, Congress did not challenge the necessity of reducing over-all economic demand to bring inflation under control. But while accepting, for the time being at least, fiscal and monetary policy restraint, congressional economic pronouncements called for stronger measures to spread out the uneven effects of inflation and to counter the hardships caused by stagnation.

Those viewpoints were expressed in several forums: separate policy statements by House and Senate Democrats, an interim report by the bipartisan Joint Economic Committee on its study of inflation, and personal prescriptions such as one offered at the September economic summit by Senate Majority Leader Mansfield.

The proposals all incorporated measures to replace the buying power that inflation and the economic slowdown were exacting from those most affected, including middle-income workers as well as the poor. Accepting the need for federal budget restraint, the policy proposals would raise federal revenues needed to offset the cost of relief measures by closing the tax loopholes.

In general, the congressional policy statements called for:

● A more extensive and more expensive public service jobs program than proposed by Ford.

● Deeper tax cuts for the poor and middle-income taxpayers than contemplated by the Ways and Means Committee bill.

● Prompt tax reforms that would raise enough revenue to pay for such initiatives.

● Federal spending cuts spread through the defense budget as well as domestic programs.

● Stronger government intervention against inflationary private actions, including, if necessary, limited use of wage and price controls in key industries.

Even the President's closest Republican supporters in Congress had doubts about adding 5 per cent to middle-income tax bills. "I have a feeling that $15,000 is a little low figure," Rep. Elford A. Cederberg (R Mich.) remarked after Ford's Oct. 8 address. "A family living on $15,000 a year now has about all it can handle."

In defense of the proposal Ford and his advisers stressed that the actual increased tax bite would be small on incomes just above the surcharge phase-in levels. And some members—including Al Ullman (D Ore.), the second-ranking Democrat on the Ways and Means Committee—suggested that the surcharge could be graduated or adjusted to shift its impact to higher income levels.

Even with a relatively small impact on middle-income levels, congressional tax-reform advocates found the surcharge objectionable so long as some taxpayers by using preferences paid less than others with comparable incomes.

"It's symbolically unfair," Humphrey said. "It does not relate at all to ability to pay."

"Even for a well-off person," Reuss concurred, to be compelled to pay more to a loophole-ridden tax system would be inequitable.

Tax Reform Alternative

To members such as Reuss and Humphrey, the obvious way to raise needed federal revenues would be to close revenue-losing loopholes built into the existing tax laws.

"There need to be added revenues," Reuss said, "but the way to attain them is to plug those loopholes that are sticky for economic reasons."

By "sticky" loopholes, he meant tax preferences that encouraged economic actions that ran counter to the best interest of the U.S. economy as a whole. He cited as an example the tax exemption for capital gains on assets passed on to survivors at death, which encouraged investors to keep securities rather than sell them on the lagging stock markets, and deferral of taxes on exporting income that gave firms an incentive to export scarce goods needed in the United States.

Taxes, Jobs and Spending

The expected Democratic landslide at the polls Nov. 5 made it even more likely that congressional leaders would postpone any substantive action on the economy until the 94th Congress convened in January 1975. The elections also increased the chance that the new Congress would turn to loophole-closing tax revision as its response to meeting federal revenue needs.

Taxes

The surcharge was unpopular on its own merits, and its chances were made even dimmer by the uncertain 1974 performance of the House Ways and Means Committee. Although the administration wanted a separate surcharge measure, Ullman had indicated that the committee should wrap the surcharge into its own tax revision bill.

In contrast to the unity the committee had shown on past tax bills it had sent to the House floor, it was badly divided over the 1974 measure. Conservatives were unhappy with provisions that would phase out the percentage depletion allowance on oil and gas income, and liberals objected just as much to provisions that would lighten taxes on capital gains and introduce other revenue-depleting tax incentives.

Even if the committee reported the bill, "there is strong sentiment in the House against its coming to the floor as an embarrassment to the Democratic Party," Reuss said.

And even if the House acted on the measure, Mansfield noted, "I doubt we can pass a tax bill this year" in the Senate. As for the Ways and Means measure, he added, "I don't even know what the hell is in it."

As Sen. Humphrey and Rep. Reuss acknowledged, it probably would take a much different Congress to enact the kind of tax reforms they want. In 1974, the Senate rejected tax reform floor amendments several times; the Ways and Means Committee in its deliberations proved more receptive to proposals that would open new tax benefits.

But the 94th will be a different Congress.

"If the election results come out as they are now anticipated," Humphrey predicted, "we're going to see a tremendous move for tax reform next year. Particularly in the House, we find that possibility." The elections did turn out as expected.

The House, as Humphrey noted, "has the predominant role in tax legislation." And the Ways and Means Committee, especially Chairman Wilbur D. Mills (D Ark.), for years had dictated the shape of House-passed tax legislation. By resisting Senate-passed amendments in conference, moreover, the Ways and Means Committee members could head off any major changes that the Senate wanted in the House-passed versions of tax measures.

If the new Congress includes more members who favor tax reform, Reuss suggested that "the first order of business should be to reform the Ways and Means Committee to make it more responsive to the majority."

Reuss had in mind a movement to enlarge the 25-member committee "and putting on it people whom the new Democratic caucus selects. If the Democratic caucus reflects the will of the voters on Nov. 5, there'll be some changes in the next Congress."

Public Jobs

As on taxes, there was general dissatisfaction in Congress with Ford's limited plan for public service jobs to fight unemployment.

House and Senate subcommittees held hearings on expansion of the existing program before the October election recess. Prospects for action in 1974 would be increased by a dramatic jump in the unemployment rate, which stood at 6 per cent at the end of October.

Federal Spending

With both the House and Senate on record in favor of cutting fiscal 1975 spending, Ford enjoyed general congressional support for his goal of reducing outlays for the ongoing fiscal year to $300-billion.

But the test of congressional determination would not come until Ford submitted his proposals for specific cuts of $5-billion or so that must be eliminated to keep spending at the $300-billion level. And, as Treasury Secretary William E. Simon told the Ways and Means Committee, "it's going to be a political nightmare when you see the list."

Under impoundment procedures that Congress enacted in July as part of comprehensive budget reform legislation, Ford had pledged to submit to Congress after the elections proposals for deferring outlays and for outright recision of unspent appropriated funds that would keep total spending at $300-billion or less. *(Budget reform, p. 75)*

"Unless major changes are effected at the beginning of the new Congress, Congress will further decline and lose power, and the nation will have trouble pulling through."

—Rep. Henry S. Reuss (D Wis.)

Under those procedures, either the House or the Senate could overrule the President on deferred spending by passing a resolution instructing him to spend the funds. In the case of recisions, positive action by both the House and Senate was required to approve reversal of earlier congressional actions appropriating the funds. And if Congress had not acted 45 days after the President proposed a recision, the executive branch would be forced to go ahead and spend the funds.

While endorsing spending cuts, congressional leaders insisted that they needed to see Ford's proposals before committing themselves on specific reductions to meet the $300-billion target. If Ford's package focused on domestic social programs without requesting defense spending cuts, there would be a fight.

"Any package that would get a majority vote would have to cut a little here and a little there," one House staff member observed.

"Across the board cuts are not the best way to cut spending," said House Appropriations Committee Chairman George Mahon (D Texas), "but politically sometimes it's the only thing you can do."

Long-Term Policy

Whatever action Congress took in response to Ford's anti-inflation proposals, members who were most informed on economic issues had doubts about the ability of Congress to perform a constructive role in economic policy-making.

"Congress is notoriously short-term in its approach to national problems," Conable observed, and congressional contributions to economic policy "will have to be based on more understanding of the principles of economics than most members have been willing to develop."

When its newly enacted budget reform procedures become fully operative in fiscal 1976, for instance, Congress

Johnson's Tax Surcharge: Ford Played A Role

In proposing a tax surcharge, President Ford took a page from a history in which he himself played an important part. President Johnson, faced with growing inflation in 1967, asked Congress to impose a 10 per cent surcharge on individual and corporate income liability. He did not get it until over a year later, and then only at the expense of some of his domestic spending priorities.

In the last years of his administration, Johnson faced inflation fueled by the cost of the Vietnam war and recently enacted "Great Society" programs. As a remedy, Johnson in January 1967 proposed a 6 per cent surtax to reduce soaring consumer demand and cut down U.S. spending abroad. The proposal received such unfavorable reception from Congress, the public and some economists that it languished in the White House until summer.

By then, however, administration economists were predicting a possible budget deficit of up to $29-billion and Johnson decided to wait no longer. On Aug. 3, he sent a strongly worded message to Congress calling for a 10 per cent surcharge effective Oct. 1 for individuals and retroactive to July 1 for corporations. The increase was designed to generate $6.3-billion in revenues.

The proposal touched off an immediate and prolonged controversy in Congress. Conservatives, alarmed by the costs of new domestic programs, saw it as an opportunity to force spending cuts on the administration. Liberals, in turn, were concerned for the safety of funds for their hard-won domestic programs.

The principal obstacle to the proposal in Congress was the House Ways and Means Committee, where tax legislation must originate. Chairman Wilbur D. Mills (D Ark.) and others on the committee said that no surtax would be approved without concessions from the ad-

ministration—specifically, spending cuts. That fall the committee voted 20-5 to shelve the bill for the year.

Johnson responded that Mills and Gerald Ford, who as minority leader had helped marshal opposition to the measure, would "rue the day" they decided to oppose it. He did offer a $4-billion spending cut later in the year, but the committee stood firm against the surtax. "I feel that we still have some distance to go," Mills said.

The committee did take up the surcharge matter again in 1968, holding hearings in the winter, but again it did not act. In floor debate over a routine excise tax extension in February, Mills said that new administration offerings on expenditure control were an improvement, but not sufficient.

The Senate, however, alarmed by devaluation of the British pound and an increasing outflow of gold from the United States, did not agree with Mills. When the tax extension bill got to the Senate, conservatives offered an amendment adding the surcharge and a $6-billion spending cut. The amendment was adopted, 53-35, and the bill passed the Senate.

On May 1, a month later, the House Appropriations Committee approved a resolution recommending a $22-billion package of budget reductions. It included a cut of not less than $10-billion in administration-proposed fiscal 1969 appropriations, a recision of not less than $8-billion in unspent prior-year appropriations and a reduction of not less than $4-billion in fiscal 1969 spending. Five days later the Ways and Means Committee reported a bill recommending the surtax and the same package of spending cuts approved by the Appropriations Committee. On May 8 conferees agreed on the 10 per cent surtax with a reduction of $6-billion in federal spending.

could at least have the machinery to discipline its actions on the federal budget to fit fiscal policy requirements. But whether members would be willing to accept that kind of discipline over pet programs and funds for their own districts still must be demonstrated.

Another case in point could be the congressional response to proposals to eliminate existing federal restrictions and programs that economists contend restrict competition, discourage price reductions and thus contribute to inflation. While both administration and congressional experts endorse review of such policies, their elimination would have to be approved by Congress, which enacted many of them to protect favored constituents' interests.

"It's difficult to work against all kinds of vested interests" who benefit from existing policies, Conable said, noting that congressional committees tend to be protective of programs within their jurisdictions. "You get congressional outrage added to constituent outrage."

To bypass the protective instincts of congressional committees, some economists have proposed an omnibus bill that would eliminate inflationary government policies at one time.

"Maybe the way to do it is by pulling a stable of these sacred cows together," Reuss concurred. "Nothing else will work, so it's worth trying."

But in Congress, as Conable cautioned, "the conventional wisdom is that if you step on a lot of toes in one bill, then it's easy to get a lot of votes against it."

Legislative Coordination

Since Congress as a legislative body must represent such diverse economic and social interests, formulation of a coordinated congressional economic policy would require more assertive leadership and discipline than demonstrated by the 93rd Congress.

While finding consultations among House and Senate Democratic leaders to devise a coordinated congressional economic program "a possibility," Mansfield was not optimistic about the chances of making such a program a reality.

"It's awfully hard to develop a program which will include 435 members" of the House, he said. "It's hard enough with 100 over here" in the Senate.

In Reuss' view, it might take wholesale changes in the membership and organization of Congress for the legislative branch to redirect the course of economic policy.

"Unless major changes are effected at the beginning of the new Congress," he warned, "Congress will further decline and lose power, and the nation will have trouble pulling through." ∎

CONGRESSIONAL BUDGET REFORM: WILL IT WORK?

Congress in 1974 has demonstrated that it at least knows what it should do to break its spending habits of the past. But rhetoric about reasserting congressional budgetary powers notwithstanding, neither Congress nor its critics are confident of its ability—much less its will—to really do its budget-making job.

Amid much self-congratulatory talk about reform, Congress in June cleared legislation (HR 7130—PL 93-344) that could give the legislative branch the final say on how much the federal government spends for what purposes. By passing that one piece of legislation, some members seemed to claim, Congress would put an end to years of presidential domination of federal budget decisions.

Yet, as one retired federal budget official pointed out, "the only question is, will it work?" And whether it works will depend on how serious Congress really is about ending inflation, and whether individual members and separate congressional committees are willing to sacrifice political and jurisdictional interests for the sake of more reasoned fiscal policy.

"To make it work," observed Samuel M. Cohn, a former assistant director of the Office of Management and Budget (OMB), "Congress and its individual members will have to act a hell of a lot differently than they do now."

Even assuming that Congress finds the resolve to change its ways, much work remains to be done, both in hiring a staff to analyze budget options and in educating members in the complexities of budget figures.

"We have a task that might be impossible," Sen. Walter F. Mondale (D Minn.) warned his colleagues on the newly formed Senate Budget Committee Aug. 22, "but if we don't try, we'll all be condemned."

An earlier effort to reform congressional budget procedures ended in failure. *(Box, next page)*

Budget Framework

On paper, at least, the budget reform measure established an institutional and procedural framework that would enable Congress to give more orderly and informed scrutiny to each fiscal year's federal budget.

"The idea is a great idea," Cohn said. "For the first time, if it works, we'll be able to see that Congress has to reconcile its action on the totals with its action on the pieces."

Under its existing procedures, Congress never really looks at budget totals—for spending and tax revenues—contenting itself instead with piece-by-piece action on the President's requests for authority to spend the government's money.

New Committees

As a remedy, the budget reform measure has created new House and Senate committees— aided by a staff of budget experts—to focus congressional attention on the totals, and how action on the pieces would affect the budget.

> *"To make it work, Congress and its individual members will have to act a hell of a lot differently than they do now."*
>
> —Samuel M. Cohn, former assistant director, Office of Management and Budget

When fully implemented, the new law will require Congress to examine the totals, setting itself target figures through a budget resolution, before acting on the pieces through authorization and appropriations bills. Once the customary appropriations process was completed, moreover, Congress would have to review both the target totals and the pieces, reconciling any discrepancies.

There are other provisions promising major changes in the way Congress does business. One will give the House and Senate Appropriations Committees a chance to review new backdoor spending programs (legislation that bypasses the regular appropriations process, such as veterans benefits) that create obligations that Congress later must meet by making the required appropriations.

Another major innovation would spell out procedures by which the President could impound funds merely to defer their expenditure but be required to ask Congress to rescind its earlier appropriations if he intended never to spend the money at all.

To fit the expanded budget-making procedures into the annual congressional sessions, the measure will shift the start of the fiscal year back to Oct. 1 from July 1—starting with fiscal 1977 on Oct. 1, 1976—and set forth a detailed timetable for completing congressional action on the necessary legislation before that date.

Using the Framework

As the principal authors of the budget reform measure readily agree, the new budgetary framework will work only if Congress wants to use it.

"To make this design work is going to be just as onerous, perhaps more onerous and more difficult, than coming up with the design," Rep. Richard Bolling (D Mo.), who helped devise the framework in the House Rules Committee and in conference, warned as the House adopted the conference report on HR 7130.

To put the design to effective use, Congress will have to overcome a lack of budgetary expertise, some committee jurisdictional jealousies, the temptation to waive budget-making deadlines and, occasionally at least, the personal political interests of 100 senators and 435 House members.

With such formidable forces likely to resist budget-making changes, Congress "will quickly find ways to warp and bend the reform rules laid down here...," predicted Rep. H.R. Gross (R Iowa), a long-time critic of congressional spending habits who was retiring from the House after 1974.

While less pessimistic, Sen. Edmund S. Muskie (D Maine), the recently designated chairman of the Senate Budget Committee, nonetheless acknowledged that "it may take two or three years before we get these procedures operating smoothly."

Timetable Waivers

To encourage orderly consideration of the budget, the budget reform measure set a rather detailed timetable for completing action on the target-setting budget resolutions, authorization measures, appropriations bills and the budget reconciliation process.

But although that timetable actually was printed out in the law, Congress took care to leave itself the flexibility to ignore the deadlines established by the legislation.

Muskie, who helped draw up the budget reform bill as a member of the Senate Government Operations Committee, said that the specific timetable was intended to supply the discipline that Congress needs to follow in making its budgetary decisions.

If First You Don't Succeed...

In reforming its budget procedures, Congress will be undertaking a task that it tried and abandoned nearly 25 years ago.

In three years of trying, the House and Senate never got together to fully implement a legislative budget created by the Legislative Reorganization Act of 1946 (PL 79-601). After unsuccessful attempts in 1947, 1948 and 1949, Congress abandoned the experiment as an unqualified failure.

Similar in some respects to the reform procedures adopted by Congress in 1974, the 1946 act required that Congress set by concurrent resolution a maximum amount to be appropriated for each fiscal year.

That appropriations ceiling was part of a legislative budget based on revenue and spending estimates prepared by a massive Joint Budget Committee composed of all members of the House and Senate Appropriations Committees and of the tax-writing House Ways and Means and Senate Finance Committees.

In 1947, conferees failed to agree on Senate amendments to the budget resolution providing for use of an expected federal surplus for tax reductions and debt retirement.

In 1948, Congress appropriated $6-billion more than its own legislative budget ceiling, and in 1949 the legislative budget never was produced as the process broke down completely.

After failure of the legislative budget, Congress in 1950 experimented with an omnibus appropriations bill wrapping all appropriations requests in a single measure. The project produced a $2.3-billion cut in the President's requests and speedier action on the budget, but it was abandoned in 1951.

"That discipline is in the statutory timetable," Muskie said, "but whether or not we'll operate within the timetable, we'll have to see."

In its final form, the budget reform bill provided specific waivers at several points along the budget process. Using those waivers, Congress could choose to ignore certain deadlines or to allow consideration of some spending bills before the time allowed.

As enacted, for instance, the bill required congressional committees to report authorizing legislation by May 15 of each year, more than four months before the start of the fiscal year on Oct. 1. That deadline could be waived, however, by majority votes in both houses.

Similarly, the bill forbids floor consideration of spending or tax measures before May 15, the deadline for final action on the budget resolution setting targets for appropriations, outlays and revenues. In the Senate, however, that prohibition could be waived by majority vote.

At the end of the budget-making process, the bill requires that all appropriations bills be cleared by the middle of September—no later than the seventh day after Labor Day—so that the budget reconciliation process can be completed before the fiscal year begins on Oct. 1. Again, that deadline for final action could be waived for any appropriation bill if its consideration had been delayed because Congress had not acted promptly on legislation needed to authorize programs.

Even without those waivers written into the bill, the House and the Senate through their normal operating procedures could decide to bypass the budget timetable's requirements. In the House, for example, the Rules Committee can recommend for any legislation waivers of points of order against floor action that would violate House rules.

And in the Senate, Muskie pointed out, "most of the time we operate under unanimous consent agreements that suspend the rules."

Even if the bill did not provide for waiving deadlines, Muskie noted, "the Senate still has that right at any time." While recognizing that possibility, he added, the authors of the bill thought it was "better to write in points of responsibility. Whether we've picked the right points only experience will tell us."

With the waiver provisions part of the statutory budget-making procedures, "if a committee applies for a waiver, the budget bill will still be operating," a Senate aide noted. If normal unanimous consent agreements were used to suspend those rules, on the other hand, the Senate in effect would be setting the budget bill's requirements aside.

As the most enthusiastic budget reform advocates admit, Congress probably will miss some deadlines, at least as it gets used to the budget reform bill's requirements.

"The deadlines are going to be awfully difficult to meet, especially the authorization reporting deadline," said Rep. Elford A. Cederberg (R Mich.), the top-ranking Republican on the House Appropriations Committee and a minority member of the House Budget Committee. "I think there's going to be some slippage."

Even if the earlier deadlines were missed, "the only really important date is the conclusion date," before the fiscal year begins, Bolling told Congressional Quarterly.

But in Muskie's view, whether the whole process works will depend on how closely individual members and separate committees are willing to discipline their actions to the budget timetable. "If they ask for an extension here and an extension there, we could end up with the whole timetable collapsing," he said.

Staff Requirements

In organizing themselves for the task ahead, the House and Senate Budget Committees assigned a high priority to hiring a staff of budget experts to help them devour the massive budget documents sent to Capitol Hill each year by the Office of Management and Budget (OMB).

While both committees by the August congressional recess had picked men to head their own separate staffs, the key appointment clearly would be a director to head the Congressional Budget Office, a joint staff created by the budget reform bill to give Congress the budget analysis capability it previously lacked.

No announcement had been made, but the Budget Committees and congressional leaders reportedly were looking for a well-known and experienced budget expert, such as Kermit Gordon or Charles L. Schultze, who both served as Bureau of the Budget director under President Johnson.

"There is some merit to having a well-known name," Muskie said. "He would bring some prestige to the office, as well as knowledge of the budget process."

While Muskie contended that the budget office director must be nonpartisan, whoever fills the post undoubtedly will need political skills if his staff is to perform its function effectively.

The congressional budget director "has got to deal with both Congress and the executive departments," one House staff member noted. "He can be a competent technician, but if he doesn't have political sense, he won't be very effective.

"The first guy will set the imprint of the office," he added. "There's the potential for him to be influential, but we'll have to see how the actual relationships shake out between him and the Budget Committees."

Without a strong director, the aide suggested, the Congressional Budget Office "could become a Library of Congress type of operation with mostly educational responsibilities, with the center of power in the two committees."

In Cohn's view, "if they get the right kind of people for that staff, and if the Budget Committee chairmen pay attention to them, then this thing just might work.

"They need people like Larry Woodworth," Cohn said. [Lawrence N. Woodworth, staff director of the Joint Committee on Internal Revenue Taxation, provides advice to the House Ways and Means and Senate Finance Committees on tax legislation.] "And they need chairmen who will pay attention to them the way [Ways and Means Committee Chairman] Wilbur Mills pays attention to Woodworth."

In an Aug. 26 organizational session devoted to staffing matters, members of the Senate Budget Committee made clear that they realized their need for expert help. "We've got to be educated, from the ground up," admitted Sen. Frank E. Moss (D Utah) as the committee discussed how to make its case for adequate staff assistance to the Senate Rules and Administration Committee.

During the committee's initial hearings on proposals to cut the fiscal 1975 federal budget, "to be very frank about it, I'm unprepared" to ask probing questions on budget issues, said Mondale.

Potential Rivalries

When the revamped budget procedures go into full effect, the House and Senate Budget Committees could find themselves stepping on the sensitive toes of some of the most powerful committees in Congress.

"There's a potential conflict between the Budget Committees and every committee on the hill," Cohn said. With each congressional committee and subcommittee looking out for federal programs within its jurisdiction, the Budget Committees will encounter resistance when they make recommendations for setting limits on federal budget totals.

For when the Budget Committees recommend how much the federal government should spend in each fiscal year, they inevitably must grapple with budget priorities, making judgments on which federal programs are essential and which should be cut back to fit the over-all budget parameters required by fiscal policy goals.

To be sure, the Budget Committees' main concern will be the budget totals. In reporting budget resolutions to the floor, they will recommend over-all targets for appropriations, spending, revenues and, public debt that Congress would aim for in subsequent legislation.

But the budget resolution also will include allocations of appropriations and outlays among the functional categories—defense, health, income security and so forth—followed by the President's budget document. And in their statement on the conference agreement of the initial budget resolution, the conferees representing the Budget Committees would break down the final target figures among congressional committees that would consider legislation providing the funds to be spent within the total and functional category targets.

At the reconciliation stage as well, the Budget Committees could recommend in reporting a second budget resolution that Congress overrule committees whose legislative actions had put total appropriations or spending above the target levels.

"The Budget Committee will actually be performing a function that isn't performed around the Senate now" by forcing senators to look at the totals as well as the separate spending legislation, Muskie insisted. "The Appropriations Committee within itself does that in drawing up separate appropriation bills," he noted, "but there's no public debate about priorities."

Committee Make-Up

In mapping out the Budget Committees' role, Muskie said, "Meticulous care was taken not to intrude on other committees. But there is overlapping, no question about that."

House

In the House, conflicts with other committees could be minimized by the composition of the Budget Committee itself. In creating the House Budget Committee, the budget reform measure allocated the committee's 23 seats to representatives of the majority and minority leadership and to members from each House committee.

Recognizing the budgetary significance of appropriations and revenue legislation, the bill required that five House Budget Committee members also serve on the Appropriations Committee and that five other members come from the tax-writing Ways and Means Committee.

While assuring that the House Budget Committee will include members well versed in appropriations and revenue legislation, that arrangement could serve to perpetuate the predominance of two largely conservative committees on budget-making decisions. As the new Budget Committee's chairman, House Democrats selected Rep. Al Ullman (D

Ore.), the Ways and Means Committee's second-ranking Democrat.

The bill also required that House Budget Committee membership be rotated, with no member allowed to serve on the committee for more than four years out of every 10. Although rotation will give more House members an opportunity to serve on the committee—and learn budget intricacies—it also could require members to leave the committee before they develop the expertise required for the job.

As a result, the House Budget Committee could be less of an independent force for budgetary restraint than its Senate counterpart, a different breed of committee.

Senate

As a regular Senate committee, the 15-member Muskie panel has a permanent membership, and after 1976 each of its members will be able to serve on only one other major Senate committee. Although Senate Democrats and Republicans both assigned Budget Committee seats to members of the Appropriations and tax-writing Finance Committees, the bill did not require such representation.

With the Senate Budget Committee potentially a major force in Senate budget decisions, "some senior members of the Senate Appropriations Committee are fearful that in time it might eclipse their committee," one House observer noted.

Recognizing that concern, Jacob K. Javits (R N.Y.) Aug. 26 told his Budget Committee colleagues that "under no circumstances should we be considered competitive with or duplicative of the Appropriations Committee. We should make that clear to them."

"The personal relationships between the chairman of the Budget Committee and the chairman of the Appropriations and Finance Committee will be very interesting," Muskie commented in an interview before his designation as chairman.

Political Interests

Yet perhaps the most fundamental obstacle to congressional budget control is the very nature of Congress as a legislative institution representing different areas, groups and needs. Whatever the overriding merits of responsible fiscal policy, Congress and its members also must respond to other imperatives, some selfish and political, others generous and humanitarian.

In jesting fashion, President Ford put his finger on one problem in his Aug. 12 address to a joint session of Congress. Ford, who represented a Grand Rapids, Mich., congressional district for 24 years, made a mock confession to House Speaker Carl Albert, an Oklahoma Democrat, conceding that he had "sometimes voted to spend more taxpayers' money for worthy federal projects in Grand Rapids while vigorously opposing wasteful federal boondoggles in Oklahoma."

Jesting aside, Ford went on to call for continued opposition to "unwarranted cuts in national defense" at the same time he termed federal budget reductions the best weapon against inflation.

"There are a lot of guys who voted for this thing (budget reform) who don't really believe in it," a House staff member observed. "They feel that the substantive programs that they are interested in—for instance on health programs, they act on the premise that the more

dollars they put in, the quicker they'll find a cure for cancer—that that's more important than the orderly management of fiscal affairs."

While contending that the pressure on a member to support federal funds for his district or state was "not really as great as it's made out to be," Cederberg nevertheless noted that "any member who doesn't try to do what he can for his district just doesn't stick around here very long."

Congress may be sincere about budget control, Cohn noted, "but I've worked with presidents and budget directors and secretaries of the Treasury who were sincere but couldn't do anything about it.

"There's always pressure to somehow shove in more money," he went on. "The politics are such that they'd rather be for things than against them."

Outlook

Although the budget control bill will not be fully in effect until fiscal 1977, the Budget Committees want to put the fiscal 1976 budget that President Ford will submit in January 1975 through a trial run of the revised procedures.

As outlined by Muskie in an Aug. 22 memorandum to his committee, the trial run would include an initial budget resolution and scorekeeping procedures to keep track of how subsequent congressional actions match up to the overall targets. In light of pressures to balance the fiscal 1976 budget, Muskie suggested that the committees might be called on to go through a budget reconciliation as well.

Cederberg sees some danger than in a 1975 trial run "we might get off on a foot where we stub our toes." The budget control effort might be discredited, Cederberg warned, "in that we could come up with an over-all budget total and then realize that the law doesn't mandate that we stick to the total."

When the new procedures go fully into effect, the first test of how serious Congress is about using them could come at the reconciliation stage in September 1976, just before the start of fiscal 1977.

At that point, Cohn suggested, the success of the experiment may depend on by how much the separate congressional spending measures have exceeded the budget resolution targets. "If the difference is small, I wouldn't say it wouldn't work," Cohn said, because "if the amounts are not too large, they could find a gadget or gimmick" to adjust the figures.

"But if they are large, God help us," he warned. In that case, Cohn said, the new procedures "will be forgotten."

The roles played by Muskie and Ullman could be crucial. They may have to fight on the floor against bills that would violate the ceiling targets and against attempts to raise the ceilings at the reconciliation stage.

To be successful, Cohn said, the experiment "needs a commitment on the part of at least the Budget Committee chairmen that they want to stick to it."

"In my experience," he went on, Congress "showed no inclination to carry out such a commitment.... But this is a different period of time; we never had double-digit inflation before."

When it comes down to reconciliation, Cederberg said, "there is only way that you can enforce a ceiling, and that is that Congress is willing to enforce it.

"If the votes are there, the ceiling will be enforced." ∎

INCOME TAXES: BREAKS TOTAL ALMOST $80-BILLION YEARLY

If Congress or the president suddenly decided to increase the federal government's budget by close to $80-billion a year—with the bulk of the increase devoted to large corporations and those in the highest income brackets—America's middle-income taxpayers probably would not stand for it.

For the middle-income taxpayers—those neither poor nor wealthy wage earners who have been bearing the brunt of inflation and tax increases for the past number of years—would have to fork up the bulk of that $80-billion to the federal government.

Of course, neither President Nixon nor the Democratic-controlled 93rd Congress is about to propose an $80-billion increase in federal spending. Yet, during the 1975 fiscal year, the federal government by one estimate in effect will spend at least $78-billion more than the official budget figure simply by not taxing certain forms of income.

And, with some exceptions, it will not be the middle-income taxpayers whose taxes are reduced as a result.

As Sen. Edmund S. Muskie (D Maine) pointed out while introducing tax reform legislation in 1973, "the revenues the federal government does not collect because of these special provisions are in reality 'tax expenditures' almost as if they were direct appropriations from the federal Treasury."

But unlike direct appropriations, that spending will not be proposed by the President or voted on by Congress. Except for some economists and federal officials, few will even know to what purposes the $78-billion has been put.

Tax expenditures generally are revenues that the government fails to collect because tax laws shield preferred forms of gains in wealth from normal application of the federal income tax. They take many forms—the oil depletion allowance, deduction for home mortgage interest and a lower tax rate on capital gains are just a few of the most obvious—and in most cases were introduced into the tax code as incentives for economic activities that the federal government has decided to encourage.

As roughly estimated by Tax Analysts and Advocates, a private tax research group, federal tax expenditures during fiscal 1975 will total about $78.3-billion. If added to President Nixon's budget prediction that the federal government would spend $304.4-billion in the fiscal year that will start July 1, those tax expenditures would bring the fiscal 1975 budget total to $382.7-billion.

If accurate, that $78.3-billion figure would account for about 20 per cent of the fiscal 1975 budget effort and offset about 44 per cent of the estimated $177-billion that the federal government expects to collect from individual and corporate income taxes in 1975.

"Yet buried as they are in the tax system, these tax subsidies are immune from scrutiny at a time when the regular budget is being carefully scrutinized for every possible saving," Stanley S. Surrey, a former assistant

secretary of the treasury, complained in a 1973 book analyzing the tax expenditure system.

To subject tax expenditures to more rigorous examination, Congress in revising its budget-making procedures is moving to take a closer look at how much the federal government loses through its various tax preferences.

With the tax burden growing heavier on middle-income Americans—in part, some say, because wealthier taxpayers receive special treatment—economists and

---

"(T)he tax expenditure system is the primary source of unfairness in our tax system."

—Tax Specialist Stanley S. Surrey

---

members of Congress also are calling for closer examination of how effectively tax expenditures work—and who gets most of the benefit.

"There can be tax expenditures that are perfectly noble ones," Rep. Henry S. Reuss (D Wis.) noted in an April 4 interview. But tax expenditures—especially those that clearly benefit only the wealthy—inevitably become targets for tax reform.

With Nixon's $467,000 back-tax bill promising in Reuss' words "a very quickening effect on the attention of the taxpayers" to the tax systems' deficiencies, Congress itself may be giving closer attention to the tax expenditure budget.

As Surrey contended, "whether one considers the effect on individuals at the same income level or the effect on individuals with different amounts of income, the tax expenditure system is the primary source of unfairness in our tax system."

Tax Expenditure Budget

Under existing congressional procedures, of course, there really is no tax expenditure budget, only a series of tax law provisions that Congress had adopted over the years with little thought or examination of their consequences.

Tax expenditures, Surrey maintained, "tumble into the law without supporting studies, being propelled instead by cliches, debating points and scraps of data and tables that are passed off as serious evidence."

In recommending some new form of tax subsidy, the House Ways and Means Committee—the tax-writing panel whose proposals most often end up in law—in effect both authorizes a new federal program goal and appropriates tax revenues toward that end. Once a provision is enacted, at no time does the committee or

Congress authorize continuation of the program or vote on its funding.

While escaping annual congressional review, tax expenditures in effect reorient the total federal effort. As the result of tax incentives for investment and business activities, "the annual federal effort is significantly more oriented toward business enterprise...than would appear" from the government's budget documents, Samuel Hastings-Black, a tax law attorney for Tax Analysts and Adovcates, said in Feb. 15 testimony before the Joint Economic Committee. According to the group's estimates, 38 per cent or about $28-billion of fiscal 1975 tax expenditures will be devoted to capital gains, investments, manufacturing and business, mining, timber and oil.

To give tax expenditures the study they deserve, Surrey and others have concluded, Congress must start treating them like it treats direct budget outlays. By drawing up a tax expenditure budget, they contend, the government could improve its ability to judge whether tax subsidies are working.

"The translation and consequent restatement of a tax expenditure program in direct expenditure terms generally show an upside-down result utterly at variance with usual expenditure policies," Surrey argued. "In fact, almost any of these tax expenditures is seen as woefully unfair or inefficient when cast as a direct expenditure program."

To improve its ability to analyze tax expenditures, Congress in reforming its structure and procedures is seeking more information about their effects.

Both the House and Senate versions of budget reform legislation (S 1541 and HR 7130) included provisions dealing with tax expenditures. The House-passed bill required the executive branch to list tax expenditures in its regular budget presentation, but the Senate-passed bill would go further.

Under the Senate measure, Congress in considering the President's appropriations and spending proposals would have to relate them to existing and proposed tax expenditures in each program area in order to improve its grasp of the total federal effort in each program area. *(Budget reform, p. 90)*

In the House, meanwhile, the Select Committee on Committees in recommending revision of the House committee structure proposed that each legislative committee be given general oversight responsiblity to review the impact of tax expenditures on federal policies within its jurisdiction.

Tax Expenditures and Tax Reform

While advocates offer the tax expenditure budget as a tool for better analysis of tax law provisions, discussions of tax expenditures almost inevitably become discussions of tax reform possibilities.

The clear presumption underlying the concept is the belief that many, if not most, special tax preferences waste potential federal revenues either by directing resources to unnecessary objectives or by inefficiently attacking problems that could be better solved by direct government subsidies.

Tax expenditures, critics point out, bear little relation to the basic purposes of the federal income tax system: to raise revenues to run the government while distributing the burden of taxation as equitably as possible according to ability to pay.

If anything, Surrey and others contend, tax expenditures inhibit—if not undermine—the fair operation of a progressive federal income tax system that was intended to tax most heavily those most able to pay.

In theory, the rate of the federal income tax rises to a maximum of 70 per cent (50 per cent on earned income) from a minimum of 14 per cent as the taxpayer's income increases. In practice, however, the average taxpayer pays less than 30 per cent of his total income in federal income taxes because exemptions, deductions and other forms of tax expenditures pare down the amount of his earnings subject to the tax.

Ideally, Surrey wrote, "an income tax seeks to tax fairly and equitably by placing the same income tax burden on those substantially in the same economic position.... The tax expenditure items represent departures from that standard, where the structure of the tax and tax equity are asked to yield ground to some non-tax objective."

The performance of an income tax system depends critically on how the system defines the income to be taxed. In general, under the federal system a taxpayer first determines his adjusted gross income—total income from all taxable sources less certain expenses made in earning that income—and then computes his taxable income by subtracting personal expenditures that are allowed as deductions and a $750 personal exemption for himself and each dependent.

By introducing exceptions into the definition of adjusted gross income, critics charge, special tax provisions erode the over-all income base on which the income tax is levied. While the effective rate of income taxation thus is lowered by tax expenditure preferences, the government must maintain high nominal tax rates in order to raise the revenues it needs.

Whatever the justification for separate tax preferences, a Brookings Institution study of the fiscal 1974 federal budget found that in combination they have three important effects on the tax system: reducing the revenue raised by the tax system, making the tax less progressive than intended and causing unequal treatment of persons in similar economic circumstances.

Revenue Loss

As Congress and the executive branch battled in recent years over the size and content of federal direct spending programs, tax expenditures largely escaped notice. Yet when lumped together, tax expenditures annually cost the government revenues equal to approximately one-fourth of each fiscal year's total budget outlays.

As House Ways and Means Committee Chairman Wilbur D. Mills (D Ark.) pointed out to the House as long ago as 1967, the granting of a tax preference "has precisely the same effect on the budget as an outright expenditure."

Since 1967, according to figures published by the Treasury and the congressional Joint Committee on Internal Revenue Taxation, tax expenditures have grown to nearly $60-billion a year from about $36.5-billion. According to the most recent report, filed on June 1,

1973, the federal government lost the following amounts of revenue through tax expenditures:

1967	$36,550,000,000
1968	$44,140,000,000
1969	$46,635,000,000
1970	$43,945,000,000
1971	$51,710,000,000
1972	$59,810,000,000

For fiscal 1975, the federal fiscal year starting on July 1 that was covered by the President's $305-billion budget submitted in February, Tax Analysts and Advocates estimated that tax expenditures would total $78.3-billion. The group's analysis included several tax provisions not considered tax expenditures in the Treasury's list.

The Treasury and Tax Analysts and Advocates figures were qualified totals, arrived at by adding together estimates of revenue lost by each tax expenditure provision included in their studies. As the Tax Analysts and Advocates study noted, the actual total revenue loss could be higher because changes in two or more tax law provisions frequently would produce more revenue than the sum of the amounts that would be raised by repealing each provision separately.

Using a different approach, a 1972 study by Joseph A. Pechman and Benjamin A. Okner of the Brookings Institution found that federal income tax collections at 1972 rates could be increased by $77-billion if adjusted gross income were redefined by elimination of most existing tax expenditures. If such a comprehensive income tax base were adopted, the study added, existing tax rates could be cut by 43 per cent without any loss of total federal revenue.

Horizontal Equity

For a democratic country, an income tax offers an attractive means of raising government revenue with each taxpayer contributing his share according to his share of total wealth. According to this ability-to-pay principle, taxpayers with roughly equal incomes should pay roughly equal taxes.

But as Pechman noted in a 1966 book on federal tax policy, "a personal income tax conforming strictly to the principle of horizontal equity is easily described, but difficult to implement." While continuing to make allowances for expenses incurred in making money and for the taxpayer's responsibilities to his dependents, Pechman maintained, such an ideal tax system "would include in the tax base all income from whatever source derived."

Departing from that ideal, the federal tax system provides special treatment for all kinds of income that many economists contend should be counted in assessing a person's tax liability.

One result: a taxpayer's total tax bill depends to a great extent on how he receives his total income as well as on how much money he takes in. Even if their total incomes were equal, one taxpayer who receives the bulk of his income from wages probably pays more federal income tax than another taxpayer who receives the bulk of his income from investments in economic activities that are granted special tax treatment to encourage their pursuit.

Individual Tax Preference Benefits

Percentage Distribution by Income Levels

Adjusted Gross Income	Aged, Blind, Disabled	Mortgage Interest Deductions	Charitable Contributions Deduction	All Provisions
Under $5,000	48	1	1	7
$5,000—$10,000	31	11	9	15
$10,000-$20,000	11	48	26	31
$20,000-$50,000	7	33	26	23
$50,000 and over	3	7	38	24

SOURCE: Benjamin A. Okner, based on *Estimates of Federal Tax Expenditures*, House Ways and Means Committee, June 1, 1973.

Another result: special tax treatment encourages investors to channel their resources into those activities, sometimes distorting the economic patterns dictated by a free market economy.

By giving preference to certain sources of income over others, the tax system "distorts the efficiency with which we use our resources by generating a lot of effort to earn income in lightly taxed forms," Warren L. Coats Jr., an assistant professor of economics at the University of Virginia, maintained in the January-February issue of *Challenge*. "The resulting inefficiencies mean that the economy enjoys fewer goods and services from given resources."

Vertical Progression

While tax expenditures usually are not explicitly aimed at higher-income taxpayers, their benefits accrue mostly to the wealthy. The result, critics charge, is distortion of the progressive rate system built into the income tax structure.

Tax preferences are most valuable to higher-income taxpayers in two ways. First, wealthier persons are more likely than those with less income to have the resources—as well as the knowledge or access to expert advice—to invest in activities enjoying tax advantages.

Secondly, because many preferences take the form of exclusions of certain kinds of income from taxable income (thus reducing the amount on which taxes are owed), their benefits are greatest to taxpayers who would pay higher rates on the excluded amounts.

For a lower-income taxpayer falling in a lower rate bracket, conversely, an exclusion from taxable income is worth relatively little. For a person too poor to pay taxes, an additional exclusion is worth nothing.

Unlike direct federal spending programs, the Brookings study on the fiscal 1974 budget contended, "tax expenditures are more beneficial to high- than to low-income taxpayers because of the ascending marginal tax rate structure. And tax expenditures provide no benefits at all to people too poor to pay income tax."

Taken separately, to be sure, some tax preferences are more useful to middle-income or poor taxpayers than to the rich. To take three examples, cited by Okner in his Joint Economic Committee testimony on Feb. 15, tax deductions for charitable contributions are most often claimed by wealthy taxpayers, the mortgage interest deduction is most useful to middle-income home-

Federal Income Tax Increases

Under Comprehensive Income Base

(millions of dollars)

Income Level	Taxes Owed 1972 Law	Taxes Owed Revised Law	Tax Increases Amount	Tax Increases Percentage	Distribution of Increases
Under $3,000	$ 36	$ 128	$ 92	255.6	0.1
$3,000-$5,000	475	1,489	1,014	213.5	1.3
$5,000-$10,000	7,655	14,238	6,583	86.0	8.5
$10,000-$15,000	18,843	30,263	11,420	60.6	14.8
$15,000-$20,000	19,354	31,737	12,383	64.0	16.0
$20,000-$25,000	13,301	22,866	9,565	71.9	12.4
$25,000-$50,000	20,707	38,099	17,392	84.0	22.5
$50,000-$100,000	9,672	17,121	7,449	77.0	9.6
$100,000-$500,000	9,241	17,076	7,835	84.8	10.1
$500,000-$1,000,000	1,324	2,638	1,314	99.2	1.7
$1,000,000 and over	2,279	4,489	2,210	97.0	2.9
All classes	**$102,888**	**$180,145**	**$77,257**	**75.1**	**100.0**

1 Totals may not add due to rounding.

SOURCE: Joseph A. Pechman and Benjamin A. Okner, *Individual Income Tax Erosion by Income Classes*, submitted to the Joint Economic Committee on May 8, 1972.

owners and tax benefits for the aged, blind and disabled are most beneficial to lower-income individuals.

Taking all tax preference provisions for individuals together, however, Okner maintained that "almost half of all tax preference benefits accrue to taxpayers with **adjusted gross incomes of $20,000 and over.**" *(Box p. 96)*

In constructing a comprehensive income base that could increase federal income tax revenues by $77-billion, Okner and Pechman found in their 1972 study that the elimination of preferences as contemplated by their analysis would hit hardest at the poorest and the wealthiest taxpayers.

"While about half of the total tax base increase would accrue to families with incomes of $10,000 to $25,000," Pechman and Okner concluded, "the largest percentage changes in taxable income occur at the bottom and very top of the income scale."

"Although increased collections would be substantial at all levels, the changes are striking for the very poor and the very rich," the authors added. "Those with incomes under $5,000 would find their tax liabilities increased three-fold, while all families with incomes of $500,000 and over would have tax increases of almost 100 per cent. *(Chart this page)*

While tax expenditures do help the poor as well as the wealthy, Surrey suggested, their benefits at low-income levels largely are concentrated on the elderly. If tax preferences to the aged were eliminated from the computations, Surrey went on, a different set of figures would emerge showing "that the tax expenditure system clearly affects the progressivity, and hence vertical equity, of the income tax.

On that basis, Surrey maintained, "the largest increases in tax that would come from elimination of tax expenditures would clearly fall on those over the $500,000 income level, and significantly so. The next largest would fall, still to an important extent, on the group above $100,000.

"Put the other way around," he added, "the presence of the tax expenditure system reduces taxes by 50 per cent for those above the $500,000 level and 43 per cent for those between $100,000 and $500,000."

The tax reductions are much less significant, however, for taxpayers with lesser incomes, Surrey's analysis found. For the three lowest brackets up to $10,000, preferences reduce taxes by about 14 per cent, he noted, and for the $10,000 to $20,000 group the reductions were about 20 per cent.

"It may be provable," Hastings-Black hinted in his Feb. 15 testimony, "that the incidence of many tax expenditures is such that the middle class is paying for the tax benefits of the upper class."

Indeed, he went on, a preliminary analysis had indicated that "there may be a redistribution from near the median income levels to the highest bracket, $100,000 and above, $50,000 and above, in the tax expenditure system.... The income seems to be redistributed from the $7,000 to $10,000 to $15,000 class to the $50,000 to $100,000 class and up."

That analysis, Hastings-Black told Congressional Quarterly April 1, was based on an incomplete study based on uncertain estimates of tax expenditure distributions.

Even with a nominally progressive federal income tax, Okner pointed out in his Feb. 15 testimony, federal, state and local taxes in the United States during the past 25 years "appear to have had little effect on the relative inequality in the distribution of income."

That fact, he went on, "means that there is little effective progression in the tax structure. And this coupled with the fact that existing tax preferences are extremely costly suggests that progressivity could be increased significantly if some preferences were eliminated.

"It would be strange," Okner concluded, "if it were not possible to find a sizeable portion of the $78-billion tax expenditure pie that could not be eliminated to increase over-all tax progressivity."

Income Distribution

That aspect of federal tax expenditures—their effects on the progressivity of the income tax—carries economic and political implications that economists and members of Congress are just now beginning to explore.

By reducing the tax burden on the wealthy, according to one line of thought, tax preferences increase the tax burden that must be borne by middle- and lower-income families—those less able to pay—if the federal tax system is to produce the revenues the government requires to support its growing spending programs.

With the President's tax troubles underscoring the tax code's multiple opportunities for a rich man to keep his tax bill down, Reuss told Congressional Quarterly, overburdened taxpayers "will realize that the reason **they have to pay so much is because others aren't paying** what fairness requires they pay."

Income Inequality

What concerns Reuss and other members of Congress is a shift since 1968 back toward relative inequality in the distribution of income in the United States, a trend that shows wealth being shifted away from middle-income Americans down to the very poor—and up to the very rich.

In Reuss' words, "that ironic situation is due to general tax reductions and loopholes at the top and at the bottom transfer payments" provided by the federal government for medical services, housing, food and other services.

With too much income to qualify for welfare assistance—but not enough to take good advantage of tax preferences—middle-income taxpayers "have been disadvantaged in recent years," Reuss said.

From 1947 to 1968, according to Census Bureau figures, the distribution of before-tax income gradually moved toward greater equality. Between 1968 and 1972, however, that trend reversed toward more inequality, with the poor- and moderate-income families losing ground and upper-income families gaining. *(Box this page)*

Even those figures, moreover, ignore the disproportionate inroads that inflation and Social Security payroll tax increases have made in middle and lower incomes since 1969.

As Reuss pointed out as he introduced a tax-cut bill (HR 13019) on Feb. 26, families with incomes of $15,000 or less are hardest hit by inflation. "They spend a higher proportion of their income on basic necessities," Reuss noted, "and the soaring costs of food, fuel and housing make sharp inroads on their real income."

"As a matter of equity," Reuss said while chairing the Feb. 15 joint committee hearing, "the $7,000-a-year family has a terribly tough time and really for humanitarian reasons deserves some attention right now."

Tax Cut Proposals

To give them that attention, Reuss and other members—including Sen. Walter F. Mondale (D Minn.) and Sen. Edward M. Kennedy (D Mass.)—have introduced tax-cut measures that would concentrate reductions on middle-income taxpayers.

While none of the proposals directly link tax reduction at middle-income levels to tax reform at upper-income levels, the sponsors of tax-cut measures usually note that the federal government could regain lost revenues by closing existing tax code loopholes.

Reuss, for instance, in HR 13019 proposed about $10-billion in tax relief to low- and middle-income taxpayers, to be accomplished by increasing the existing standard deduction and low-income allowance in the income tax code and by introducing personal exemptions and a low-income allowance to the payroll tax system.

Reuss told Congressional Quarterly that he "would recoup that $9- or $10-billion by plugging those loopholes which produce untoward economic effects." He cited the percentage depletion allowance for oil, deduction for hobby farm losses and exemption of capital gains from taxation at death as three tax law provisions that should be eliminated.

Reuss' tax reform proposals, which would eliminate other preferences as well, were embodied in separate legislation (HR 967) that he introduced in 1973.

Income Distribution Among American Families

1947-72

Year	Lowest 5th (Under $5,600)	Second 5th (Under $9,300)	Third 5th (Under $12,900)	Fourth 5th (Under $17,800)	Highest 5th ($17,800 and more)
1972	5.4	11.9	17.5	23.9	41.4
1971	5.5	12.0	17.6	23.8	41.1
1970	5.4	12.2	17.6	23.8	40.9
1969	5.6	12.4	17.7	23.7	40.6
1968	5.6	12.4	17.7	23.7	40.5
1966	5.6	12.4	17.8	23.8	40.5
1960	4.8	12.2	17.8	24.0	41.3
1950	4.5	11.9	17.4	23.6	42.7
1947	5.1	11.8	16.7	23.2	43.3

Totals may not add due to rounding.

SOURCE: Bureau of the Census, Money Income in 1972 of Families and Persons in the United States.

Reuss insisted that his tax proposals were not a package designed to transfer income from upper- to middle-income levels. "My proposal is in no way soak the rich as such," he said. "It rather is soak those who by dint of hiring clever lawyers can reduce their tax payments."

Reuss has linked his tax proposals to an effort to "build fairness into the tax structure" by easing the burden on lower-income workers and providing "an adequate minimum income for those unable to work."

Only by packaging welfare reform with relief for low- and middle-income taxpayers, Reuss suggested, can Congress hope to enact a minimum-income proposal such as President Nixon's family assistance plan (HR 1), which Congress killed in 1972. *(Welfare reform action, Congress and the Nation Vol. III, p. 622)*

"From the political standpoint," Reuss said Feb. 15, "you aren't going to get an HR 1 welfare proposal to rise from the ashes if you are going to tell the $7,000 and the $8,000 and the $9,000-a-year family that their case is being overlooked."

Nixon's HR 1 proposal and the negative income tax plan suggested by Sen. George McGovern (D S.D.) in his ill-fated 1972 presidential campaign "suffered from a fatal handicap: they helped only the poorest families... while doing nothing for low- and moderate-income workers," Reuss told the House Feb. 13.

"As a result, both HR 1 and McGovern were lost in the conflict between 'welfare righters' and the blue-collar workers from whose pockets part of the money would have had to come," Reuss continued.

With the poor and middle-income families "in the same boat, threatened by inflation, unemployment, the energy crisis," Reuss concluded, "today good economics and good politics coincide."

By ending some tax preferences, Reuss told Congressional Quarterly, the government "can then get the wherewithal to deal more fairly not just with the middle-income groups but with the lower too."

ECONOMY: JOINT COMMITTEE URGES QUICK ACTION

Urging "quick action to deal with a deteriorating economy," the Joint Economic Committee Sept. 21 offered its recommendations for a multi-faceted program for curbing inflation and restoring economic growth.

In a report aimed at President Ford's Sept. 27-28 economic summit conference, the committee concluded that the complicated combination of inflation and recession called for a variety of corrective and offsetting measures by the federal government.

The committee's prescription, based on interim findings by a staff study of economic problems due to be concluded by the end of 1974, would couple the Ford administration's fiscal and monetary policy restraint with efforts to distribute the burdens imposed by inflation and to remove obstacles to economic efficiency.

While endorsing Ford's intention to cut fiscal 1975 federal spending to $300-billion, the committee proposed a number of measures that were likely to draw opposition from the administration or from vested economic interests who would be most directly affected.

Among the most innovative proposals—most of them advanced earlier by economists and members of Congress—were a combination of tax cuts and tax reforms, wage and price guidelines, credit allocation, stepped up antitrust enforcement and omnibus legislation to eliminate existing federal policies that discourage competition.

Despite the controversial character of some of the recommendations, Sen. William Proxmire (D Wis.), the committee's vice chairman, contended in releasing the report that the program would "command broad support in the Congress and among the public."

As Proxmire noted, several committee members voiced reservations about specific proposals made by the report. Yet "taken as a whole the degree of unanimity is remarkable," he said.

Committee's Program

The committee's program was based on its assessment that the existing inflation was caused by a variety of forces, not simply the conventionally defined causes of excess economic demand or spiraling wages and costs. Accordingly, the committee incorporated measures to deal with the extraordinary effects of food, oil and other raw material price increases and with the inflationary consequences of government and private restraints on competition.

More than many conventional analyses of inflation, the report focused on structural distortions in the free enterprise system that help drive prices up and eliminate incentives that might bring them down. The committee attributed those distortions both to outmoded or ill-advised government policies and to concentration of economic power in key industries.

To encompass a broad range of policies, the report summed up the committee's recommendations under four categories: fiscal and monetary policy, prices and incomes

policy, assistance to groups hurt most by inflation, and restoration of an efficient market economy.

Fiscal Policy

Concurring in the President's fiscal policy goal, the committee supported reduction of fiscal 1975 spending to $300-billion. It added two qualifications, insisting that defense spending as well as civilian programs be studied for possible cuts and urging that existing programs be cut sufficiently to make room for an expanded public service jobs program costing perhaps $2-billion.

By demonstrating their determination to cut federal spending in fiscal 1975 and restrain growth of the budget in fiscal 1976, Congress and the administration could increase public confidence and allow some easing of monetary policy, the committee argued.

"At the same time, care must be exercised that federal spending is not slashed so drastically as to interrupt the efficient delivery of vital public services or to plunge the economy into recession."

In a series of footnotes to the report's text, two House Republican members of the joint committee—Clarence J.

As Proxmire noted, several committee members voiced reservations about specific proposals made by the report. Yet "taken as a whole, the degree of unanimity is remarkable," he said.

Brown of Ohio and Ben B. Blackburn of Georgia—challenged much of the committee's analysis and argued for more stress on budget reductions as a damper on inflation.

Monetary Policy

Recommending a course that many observers believed had already been adopted by the Federal Reserve Board, the committee advocated "a moderate shift toward less restrictive monetary policy" to accommodate a gradual expansion of investments in housing, agriculture and small business and by state and local governments.

To make sure that increased credit made available by monetary policy relaxation would go to desired uses, the committee urged that the Federal Reserve implement "a system for channeling credit" to productive investments away from speculative investments.

Price and Incomes Policy

In perhaps its most controversial recommendations, the committee proposed a government-monitored "social contract" to head off a wage-price spiral that could be set off by struggles among labor, business and consumers to protect their shares of the distribution of income.

New Pressure

Fresh from their 1974 election triumphs, a group representing elected Democratic officials from all levels of government Nov. 11 pressed their party's congressional leaders for prompt action on economic problems.

The group, known as the Democratic Advisory Council of Elected Officials, passed along to House Speaker Carl Albert (D Okla.) and Senate Majority Leader Mike Mansfield (D Mont.) a set of 11 specific policy proposals drawn up by economists, businessmen and labor leaders.

The package generally followed closely policies previously recommended by members of Congress. Going beyond what most members were willing to advocate, however, the council advised Congress to be prepared if necessary to resort to mandatory energy conservation, export controls and "an across-the-board system of economic controls, including prices, wages, executive compensation, profits and rents."

In letters to Mansfield and Albert, council Chairman Arthur B. Krim, a businessman, said that Congress "might find these suggestions useful in its consideration of ways to begin the long struggle back to economic well-being for the United States."

The economic study group, which was chaired by economists Walter W. Heller and Robert R. Nathan, criticized President Ford's ecnooomic proposals for failing to deal adequately with either inflation or recession.

The President "continues to act as though inflation were our only economic worry instead of facing up to the most serious economic slump since 1960-61," their statement said. "Most serious of all, President Ford is not even offering an effective anti-inflation program...."

Their policy statement called for a general easing of monetary policy accompanied by efforts to direct credit to housing, small business and other productive enterprises; tax relief financed by tax reforms; a permanent public service jobs program and more adequate unemployment compensation; and less stress on cutting federal spending, especially if the recession continued.

Other proposals included revival of the Reconstruction Finance Corporation to provide credit to hard-pressed businesses, retention of oil price ceilings, an export-monitoring system followed by controls if necessary, and a stand-by system for enforcing energy conservation.

A much-discussed concept among Democratic economists and members of Congress, the proposed social contract would ask organized labor to restrain wage demands in a trade-off for federal tax reductions to restore lost purchasing power for low- and middle-income workers. To prevent those reductions from increasing the federal deficit, the proposal would couple them with elimination of "unjustified tax subsidies," a tougher minimum income tax on high-income taxpayers and new taxes to encourage energy conservation, such as a tax on high-horsepower automobile engines.

The joint committee suggested that the newly established Council on Wage and Price Stability be assigned to monitor the social contract, using measures including guidelines for "appropriate non-inflationary behavior for prices, wages and executive compensation on a specific industry-by-industry basis."

If inflation continued at high rates—and if business or labor failed to cooperate—the committee suggested that Congress consider strengthening the council's powers to allow it to subpoena records, delay wage and price increases for 30 or 60 days, and to roll back unjustified increases in concentrated industries.

In his own footnote, Proxmire challenged "the practicality of this nebulous social contract." Organized labor was unlikely to reduce wage demands on the basis of promised tax cuts, Proxmire argued. Because revenue-raising tax reforms were unlikely to be adopted, he added, the result might be a growing federal deficit.

Inflation Relief

Since the social contract proposals would help only those who had jobs and paid taxes, the committee recommended additional measures for the unemployed and the poor:

● An expanded public service jobs program to create 150,000 jobs when unemployment reached 5.5 per cent—and 500,000 to 600,000 jobs should unemployment reach 6 per cent.

● Increases in the maximum weekly benefits and duration of benefits provided by the unemployment insurance system.

● Expansion of food stamp and supplemental security income benefits and eventual reform of the entire welfare system.

In footnotes, Proxmire warned that the three recommended steps could prove costly, requiring offsetting reductions in other programs, and Rep. Henry S. Reuss (D Wis.) called for immediate installation of a program providing 500,000 public service jobs.

Restoring Market Efficiency

While making specific recommendations for agriculture, oil and over-all productivity, the committee suggested that Congress and the President jointly appoint a commission to draw up comprehensive legislation to "eliminate both governmental and private barriers to an efficient market economy."

In making its legislative recommendations, the commission would be directed to consider such government policies as subsidies, production quotas and marketing orders, price supports, excess stockpiles, prevailing wage determinations, transportation and communication regulations, import quotas and voluntary import restraints, retail price maintenance "and other similar governmental impediments to economic efficiency."

In surveying private competition, the commission would be instructed to consider such actions as tougher antitrust laws, divestiture and reorganization in concentrated industries, and artificial barriers to employment based on age, sex, race or education.

As an advisory panel, the joint committee had no power to report legislation to implement its policies. But its interim proposals—and whatever additional steps were advocated in a follow-up report expected by the end of 1974—gave Congress some starting points for making an economic policy of its own.

FIGHTING INFLATION: 'TRUST BUSTING' MAY BE BACK

Antitrust laws—old economic weapons long left to corporate counsel and law professors—were being honed for use in the war against inflation late in 1974. The resources of those who wield them were being beefed up, the range of their application extended and the penalties for violating them toughened.

The laws, the nation's original consumer legislation, were "passed by Congress with the sole purpose of making sure that the consumer is the final arbiter on what goods he wants to buy, what price he wants to pay for them," explained Keith I. Clearwaters, deputy assistant attorney general for antitrust. "In the marketplace, the consumer is supposed to be king.... When groups of competitors get together to set prices or to avoid producing a particular product, the consumer is no longer king."

Mutterings from long lines at gas pumps and suspicions of conspiracy voiced in supermarket aisles have reached the federal officials responsible for enforcing antitrust laws. The list of business giants who were in 1974 the target of antitrust charges by either the Justice Department's antitrust division or the Federal Trade Commission and its bureau of competition was a long one. It included:

● The nation's eight major oil companies charged with monopolization—Exxon, Gulf, Texaco, Mobil, Standard Oil of California, Standard Oil (Indiana), Shell and Atlantic Richfield.
● Four major breakfast food manufacturers—Kellogg, General Foods, General Mills, Quaker Oats.
● International Business Machines—charged with monopolizing the computer market.
● Two giant tire manufacturers—Goodyear and Firestone.
● Three leading New York department stores—Saks Fifth Avenue, Bergdorf Goodman and Bonwit Teller.
● The National Broiler Marketing Cooperative—which sells half the nation's broiler chickens.
● Xerox, the copy machine giant.
● American Telephone & Telegraph Co.—charged with monopolizing telecommunications equipment and service.

The link between inflation and tougher enforcement of the antitrust laws was drawn repeatedly in late 1974. President Ford, the first chief executive in 20 years to take a firm public stand in favor of a strong antitrust policy, told Congress Oct. 8 that he was "determined to return to the vigorous enforcement of antitrust laws," and that his administration would "zero in on more effective enforcement of laws against price-fixing and bid-rigging."

"We are not merely concerned with punishing those who acted illegally," explained antitrust chief Thomas E. Kauper to a House Republican antitrust task force early in August 1974. "Our principal concern is the protection of the public, the American consumer who in the end pays the price for all the goods and services produced. We promote competition and prosecute those who seek to destroy it in the firm belief that only through vigorous free competition

can we develop and maintain the economic potential to produce the things we all need at prices we can all afford."

Violating the nation's antitrust laws "is pocketbook crime," Kauper explained. "It impacts directly on the buying power of each of us." The cost of anticompetitive practices and concentrated economic power is estimated at $80-billion a year—a cost which the American taxpayer and shopper ultimately pays.

To illustrate the impact which antitrust enforcement can have on prices, Justice Department officials point to the tetracycline cases. After government and private antitrust cases were filed against the producers of the widely used antibiotic, the price of 100 capsules dropped from $30.00 to $4.25. Such dramatic price results are unusual, but Kauper has noted that "the ultimate result of every case should be expressed in downward price pressure."

Price-Fixing Probe

And prices were the primary target of government antitrust activities in 1974. "As inflation has become more and more a continual threat," explained Assistant Attorney General Kauper, "price-fixing becomes even more dangerous, both economically and socially, than it has been in the past. We simply cannot now afford the economic waste.... An agreement to fix prices, or not to compete on the basis of price, strikes at the very heart of our free enterprise system, and, if widespread, renders it incapable of functioning properly. In part, the economic conditions we face today are the result of these and other kinds of interferences with the allocative mechanisms of our economy."

"Price fixers should go to prison!" declared Attorney General William B. Saxbe in October. "Those business firms and officials who fix prices and rig bids rob the public—or vast segments of it—as surely as those who rob at the point of a gun." Elaborating on the premeditated nature of these "white-collar crimes," Saxbe later said: "Antitrust violations are not casual crimes. Business tycoons are not seized by a fit of passion that compels them to rig bids. Corporate executives do not gather in the boardroom to fix prices because they are in the throes of a joint irresistible impulse. They violate the antitrust laws deliberately because they want to and because they feel it's

"Price fixers should go to prison!"

—Attorney General
William B. Saxbe

good for business. Well, it's not good for the public's business.... We are determined that this kind of law-breaking will be uncovered and prosecuted as vigorously as any other."

Three years earlier, consumer advocate Ralph Nader had outlined the consumer connection to antitrust enforcement in his introduction to a task force study of the subject: "What people are charged; what kinds of goods and services they are offered; what level of product hazards and pollution prevail...what important innovations are permitted...what amount of power is unaccountable; what chance is there for small business; what is the response of the professions; what is the choice for the consumer? These...are what antitrust policy and violations are all about."

"Antitrust enforcement—private and public—will make a comeback to show the modern relevance of this traditional wisdom first formulated into law by a conservative Congress in 1890," Nader predicted.

Charter for Competition

To preserve "free and unfettered competition as the rule of trade," in the face of the rapid aggregation of vast economic power by the "trusts" after the Civil War, Congress in 1890 enacted the nation's basic antitrust law, the Sherman Act.

This and subsequent antitrust laws were based upon the belief that competition was the only proper regulator of the free enterprise system and that it would result in lower costs, lower prices and better products than a controlled system.

As FTC Chairman Lewis A. Engman recently explained: "Competition policy...is founded on a deeply rooted conviction that private property and private ownership of the means of production, when governed by the natural forces of competition, free of artificial restraints and excesses of monopoly power, can produce the best goods for the least price, with the greatest opportunities for innovation and change."

Monopoly and restraint of trade were the two major obstacles to competition outlawed by the Sherman Act. Monopoly, control of a market, or the attempt to obtain a monopoly was declared a crime. In addition "every contract, combination...or conspiracy in restraint of trade" was declared illegal—a broad category since defined to include such practices as price-fixing, market division, non-competitive agreements and group boycotts.

The penalties for such illegal actions was up to $5,000 in fines or up to a year in prison; in 1955 the maximum fine was raised to $50,000. Violations of the Sherman Act usually are criminal offenses, although the government also has the right under the Sherman Act to bring civil proceedings asking a court, for example, to halt a merger or enjoin a certain practice or to order a company to divest itself of an acquired enterprise. The Justice Department is responsible for enforcing this law.

Despite the clear intent of the law, enforcement got off to a slow start. In 1894, the Supreme Court read the scope of the new law narrowly and held that it did not apply to the sugar trust. That same year the attorney general explained his failure to bring suits under the law against obvious violations by describing the law as "no good."

In 1911, however, the Supreme Court upheld rulings ordering that the Standard Oil trust built by John D.

"Our principal concern is the protection of the public, the American consumer...."

—Antitrust Chief
Thomas E. Kauper

Rockefeller and the American Tobacco Company consolidated by James B. Duke be broken up.

'Rule of Reason'

But the wording of Chief Justice Edward D. White's opinion in the oil case gave rise to the controversial "rule of reason" for judging concentrated economic power. White wrote that the trust should be divided because it was an unreasonable restraint of trade.

Drawn by implication from that reasoning, the rule held that some combinations in restraint of trade were unreasonable and therefore illegal—but that others were reasonable and thus escaped the force of the antitrust laws. This, noted essayist James F. Watts Jr., "permanently dulled the cutting edges of the Sherman Antitrust Act by bestowing upon the frequently conservative Supreme Court the subjective determination of the 'reasonableness' of corporations engaged in restraint of trade."

One example of the use of the rule came in the court's 1920 finding that the monopoly power of U.S. Steel was reasonable and legal, a decision which, Watts writes, "ushered in the age of kaleidoscopic corporate mergers which has continued on to very recent years when business is dominated by mammoth agglomerations."

The "rule of reason" led directly to enactment of new antitrust laws—the Clayton Act and the Federal Trade Commission Act in 1914. As Charles Warren explained it in his history of the U.S. Supreme Court: "When it appeared that unreasonable restraint and improper methods by which the restraint was attained or maintained were to be controlling features in determining the legality of the corporate combination, it became more and more the general belief that the national power over these interstate combinations should be exercised in regulation, rather than destruction, and that the economic evils—the evils of monopoly control and unjust and unfair business methods—must be remedied, without attacking the principle of mere combination."

And so the Clayton Act was directed at the behavior of companies rather than their structure or market share. The Clayton Act declared illegal certain types of practices when they tended to create a monopoly or substantially to lessen competition. As interpreted—and as amended in 1936 by the Robinson-Patman Act—the new law focused on price discrimination, exclusive dealing and tying contracts, acquisitions and mergers of competing companies and interlocking directorates.

The Justice Department and the FTC share primary responsibility for enforcing this law, although other independent regulatory commissions also have some authority for enforcing it in the industries they regulate.

ANTITRUST CASES, 1942-1974
Private and Government
(fiscal years)

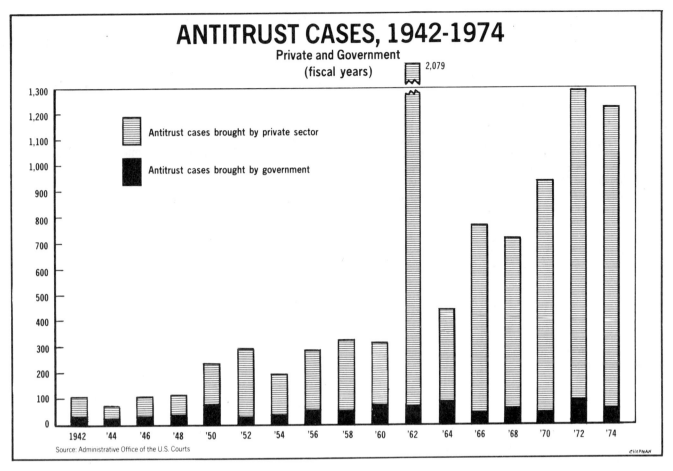

Source: Administrative Office of the U.S. Courts

Violations of the law are civil offenses, against which cease-and-desist orders may be issued, or which may result in divestiture orders, or in damage suits. The government can recover actual damages for injuries it suffers from violations of this law; private persons and state, local and foreign governments may recover triple damages—and the cost of bringing the suit.

Origin

The Federal Trade Commission Act created the FTC. The primary antitrust impact of the law came in its fifth section, which stated tersely: "Unfair methods of competition in commerce, and unfair or deceptive acts or practices in commerce, are hereby declared unlawful." Violations of this ban are dealt with through cease-and-desist orders. Noncompliance with those orders is punished by fines of up to $10,000 per day for each violation.

These basic antitrust laws have hardly been changed since their enactment. From time to time Congress has amended them to close loopholes and restrict conduct not envisioned in 1890 or 1914. On the other hand, Congress also has approved legislation exempting certain groups or industries from the antitrust laws, among them public utilities, agricultural cooperatives, insurance firms and professional sports.

Enforcement: The Velvet Glove

"A real antitrust, decentralization, procompetition economic policy has never been seriously pursued, and is not now being pursued, as far as I can tell," stated Sen. William Proxmire (D Wis.) Nov. 18, opening hearings by the Joint Economic Committee on the FTC's role in combatting inflation. "There has been a lot of lip service to the goal of competitive free enterprise...[but] there has been little performance as far as policy makers and higher government officials are concerned."

"Four generations of the velvet glove are enough," stated the Nader task force study—"The Closed Enterprise System"—criticizing the government's enforcement of the antitrust laws.

Illustrating the steady increase in concentration of economic power despite the antitrust laws, the study pointed out that in 1971 the nation's 200 largest corporations controlled as much of the nation's manufacturing assets as the 1,000 largest had in 1941.

Problems

Antitrust officials themselves agreed there clearly were problems—problems of politics, of approach, of resources and of remedies.

The revelations concerning White House efforts to influence the settlement of the government's antitrust case against the International Telephone and Telegraph Corp. gave dramatic illustration of the role of politics in relation to antitrust policy.

In other cases, behind-the-scenes political pressure played a role in decisions to bring, or not to bring, or to settle antitrust cases. The ultimate decision to file a suit or complaint lay with political appointees—the attorney general or the members of the Federal Trade Commission.

But politics was not a major problem, concluded the Nader task force in 1971; it came into play in only a minority of cases. "The real erosion of enforcement is...more subtle and pervasive," involving problems of resources, personnel and attitude.

Lack of Resources

The limited manpower allocated by Congress and the executive to enforcing the antitrust laws in large measure determined the way in which those laws were enforced. Arguing for an increase of almost $3-million—and 83 staff positions—for the antitrust division, Rep. H. John Heinz III (R Pa.) pointed out that in real dollar terms, the antitrust division in 1974 was operating with a smaller budget than it had in 1950. From 1942 to 1974 the number of antitrust suits filed by the government varied within a fairly narrow annual range while the number of privately initiated suits multiplied: by 1974 there were 20 private suits filed for every one brought by the government.

Comparison of the Justice Department's antitrust budget with some of the sums recently distributed in private antitrust settlements provided perspective for the problem. When IBM settled the antitrust case brought against it by Control Data Corp., it agreed to pay CDC $15-million to cover attorneys' fees and other expenses of the suit. At the time, that figure was larger than the entire annual budget of the antitrust division. And Kauper has pointed out that the damages awarded in the electrical equipment price-fixing cases of the early 1960s—some $450-million—was enough to run the division for more than 20 years.

Because of limited manpower to investigate potential abuses in any systematic way, investigations were usually sparked by complaints from the mailbag, or private citizens and businesses. This system resulted in an ad hoc approach to enforcement of the antitrust laws.

Also as a result of limited manpower, the antitrust division was prone to attack proposed mergers rather than existing monopoly power—to deal with behavior such as price-fixing, rather than structure such as concentration. Explaining the division's propensity to move on proposed or recent mergers rather than monopolies, Deputy Assistant Attorney General Bruce C. Wilson noted: "It's certainly a lot easier to keep the eggs from being broken into the pot than to unscramble them once they are in there."

Still another aspect of the impact of limited manpower was the reluctance to take cases to trial if they could be settled in any reasonable manner by a consent decree—an agreement between the government and the company, ratified by the court. Clearwaters pointed out that "the trial of an antitrust case...just gobbles up people. When you have several major trials in a particular section [of the division], that section is pretty well hamstrung as far as new investigations."

The slow pace of antitrust litigation is startling, even in days when crowded court dockets are an accepted fact of life. The IBM monopoly suit, filed on the last business day of the Johnson administration in January 1969, had not yet gone to trial in November 1974. The FTC complaint against the eight major oil companies for attempting to monopolize the oil business was filed in mid-1973 and it was estimated that it would not reach trial stage until at least 1978.

Part of the problem in preparing such suits for trial was the difficulty in obtaining information from the defendants. The delay also worked to the obvious advantage of the defendant. As Wilson pointed out: "If we're right [in charging a company with monopolization], and he's making monopoly profits, then he has every incentive to use every tactic to delay, delay, delay that case because as long as he delays it he continues to make the monopoly profits." Such long-term cases, he added, clearly require "an enormous commitment of the resources of your antitrust enforcement agencies."

One recurring problem for government antitrust officials is their inability to appeal the ruling of a federal district judge denying them an order that would direct a defendant to cease his challenged action until the suit is resolved.

Remedy Problems

The penalties imposed upon persons charged with antitrust violations and convicted, or admitting guilt in a pre-trial settlement, could hardly be called impressive sanctions. Partially because of the "white-collar" nature of the antitrust crime and the antitrust defendant, the maximum fine—$5,000 until 1955 and $50,000 since that time—was rarely if ever imposed, and the maximum prison sentence, one year, never imposed.

As Kauper has noted: "Too few have been treated sternly, and none has been treated harshly." The first jail sentence served by a person accused simply of violating the antitrust laws—without involving a labor question or the use of violence—came in 1959, 69 years after the penalty had been authorized by the Sherman Act. From 1890 until 1970 only 19 persons had been sent to jail for such violations. The total of their sentences was 28 months.

And the impact upon market structure and performance of such remedies was scarcely noticeable much of the time. As Sen. Philip A. Hart (D Mich.) described it: "Defendants are told to go and sin no more, but the underlying market structure which facilitated the offensive behavior is left untouched."

Signs of Change

Lack of a real constituency, of public or congressional attention to antitrust contributed to the problem of enforcement. And in that respect the ITT scandal may have contributed to the solution. At least, one observer noted, after ITT people knew there *was* such a unit as the antitrust division.

Furthermore, officials in the division were quick to note that the revelations, particularly from the White House tapes concerning the ITT matter, showed the determined resistance of then-Assistant Attorney General Richard McLaren to White House pressure.

Inflation and the post-Watergate atmosphere have fostered promising changes in antitrust enforcement. McLaren's successor as head of the division was Kauper, his young deputy (only 39 years old in 1974), who had come to the department in 1969 from the faculty of the University of Michigan law school. Moving quietly but surely, Kauper reorganized the division, won congressional support for increased resources and in late 1974 was on his way to filing a record number of antitrust suits.

Kauper's efforts were backed by Attorney General Saxbe, who in mid-1974 ended the decades-old practice of personally approving all complaints to be filed by the antitrust division, a practice not followed with suits brought by other divisions.

Another change, designed to reduce the amount of behind-the-scenes pressure brought to bear on antitrust decisions, was awaiting the approval of Congress in

November 1974. A pending antitrust bill would require the Justice Department to make public—before a consent decree became final—more information about the settlement proposed, and would require defendants in antitrust cases to disclose publicly all contacts with government officials by them or on their behalf concerning the case.

Resources and Reorganization

Both the antitrust division and the FTC bureau of competition in 1973-1974 allocated more of their manpower to systematic economic analysis. Moving away from dependence upon the mailbag for complaints, the economic suit at the antitrust division was focusing on price analysis and studies of particular concentrated industries—in which most of the market or the economic power was controlled by a handful of companies.

At the FTC the first industry-wide investigation was focused on the food industry. "We simply do not have the resources to investigate fully every possible violation," said James T. Halverson, director of the bureau of competition. "We try to select cases which will result in a maximum benefit to consumers...in relation to the enforcement dollar invested." The new analytic capability of both units could provide antitrust officials with their own data to use in selecting areas of the economy to probe for possible antitrust violations.

The FTC in fiscal 1975 was to inaugurate another program to gather heretofore unavailable information—the line-of-business reports requiring 500 large manufacturing firms to tell the FTC their cost, sales and profit figures for approximately 200 product categories. Such information often had been buried in total figures reporting costs, sales and profits for a conglomerate enterprise.

To separate out profit information for the leading producers of items like carpets, refrigerators and electric lamps—most minority components of conglomerate firms—was "like playing pickup sticks wearing boxing gloves," said FTC Chairman Engman.

The antitrust division in 1974 won a 20 per cent increase in its budget—from $14-million to $16.9-million. But it took a floor fight in the House to win the funds and the amendment adding them was approved by a relatively close vote of 216-185. Rep. John B. Anderson (R Ill.) argued for giving additional help to the division which, he said, was "trying to enforce the antitrust laws in an economy that has doubled since 1950 with a staff that has not grown at all.... [W]ith a staff of 327 lawyers, [it] is trying to police the largest and most complex industrial economy the world has ever known.... [A]dding 83 staff members to the antitrust division—of whom 40 would be lawyers and seven would be professional economists—is an investment in the fight against inflation that just cannot miss."

Even before winning the increase in manpower, the division in April 1974 created an energy unit, putting six attorneys and two economists fulltime on an investigation of possible criminal antitrust violations by the nation's oil and other energy-producing companies. (The FTC complaint against the oil companies charged them with civil violations of the antitrust laws, leaving open the criminal field for the Justice Department to investigate.)

The additional positions provided by Congress for fiscal 1974 would enable the division to open an eighth field office—in Texas. And further supplementing the efforts of the men and women in the division, Attorney General Saxbe moved to enlist FBI agents and the U.S. attorneys across the nation in investigating and prosecuting antitrust violators.

The FTC also requested increased funds for its antitrust activities in fiscal 1975, but as of late November, the fate of that request was unclear. The budget asked for nearly a 20 per cent increase—from $8.3-million to $9.9-million, which included funds for the investigation and preparation of the case against the oil companies. With this increase in funds, the bureau would have almost 400 positions, a little more than half of whom would be attorneys.

Congress had granted this request in an appropriations bill which was vetoed by President Nixon. The second version of the bill, which the House approved in October, reduced FTC funds.

New Remedies

To equip the prosecutors—and the judges—with potential sanctions which more nearly fit the crime of antitrust violations, Congress responded quickly in late 1974 to President Ford's request that the fine which could be imposed on corporations who violated the antitrust laws be increased to $1-million from the existing $50,000.

"Crime ought not to pay!" Kauper declared, urging the increase in penalties. "The illegal gains from many antitrust violations frequently run into the millions.... A $50,-000 fine is simply not going to be looked upon by those who willfully violate the law as anything more than a relatively cheap license fee."

The House Nov. 19 approved such a bill, which included language concerning the new requirements of disclosure regarding consent procedures, and which also gave the government the right it had lacked to appeal lower court rulings denying injunctions to halt practices challenged as anticompetitive. The bill also raised the maximum fine for an individual to $100,000 and increased the possible prison term to three years from one year, making the offense a felony rather than a misdemeanor.

The principal function of a criminal sentence in the view of the antitrust division is its deterrent impact. Kauper explained: "Our hope is that these increased penalties will have a broader effect than merely additional punishment for...those who are caught.... Our main objective is to emphasize the seriousness of the offense and thus cause those who might become involved to consider more carefully the consequences of their action."

Criminal charges, carrying with them the threat of prison for the individuals involved, are more effective as a deterrent than civil charges. And Kauper promised in August that the trend toward an increase in criminal suits brought by the government—and an increase in individuals charged—would continue. Five criminal cases were filed in 1970; 34 were brought in 1974. Eighty-four individuals were indicted in 1974, more than triple the number named in 1972.

As of late 1974, 22 individuals had gone to jail since 1970 for "pure" antitrust violations, three more than in the entire history of antitrust enforcement up to that time.

Outlook

Bolstered by new resources and by the attentions it was receiving from Congress, the President and the public in general, government antitrust policy appeared late in 1974 to be on the verge of a new era. After years of preparation and hesitation, the Justice Department Nov. 20 filed a suit against American Telephone and Telegraph Corp., charging "Ma Bell" with monopolizing telecommunications

Antitrust and the Attorney's Fee

Do lawyers violate the antitrust laws when they adopt and adhere to minimum fee schedules, which set the minimum that an attorney can "ethically" charge a client for certain services?

"Yes," reply Lewis and Ruth Goldfarb, who brought to the Supreme Court in 1974 a case challenging the minimum fee schedule as price-fixing, a violation of the Sherman Antitrust Act resulting in overcharging clients. Irritated at the high and unvarying cost of hiring an attorney to perform the required title examination of a home they were buying in Reston, Va., the Goldfarbs brought their suit in early 1972.

A few months earlier, when purchasing their new house, they had checked with a number of attorneys to see what the title examination would cost them. The answer was always the same—$522.50, the minimum prescribed by the county bar association schedule for the house they were buying. This suggested fee schedule, promulgated by the county bar association, was given force by formal opinions from the Virginia State Bar, stating that it was both unethical and punishable for an attorney habitually to charge less than the recommended minimum amount.

"No," reply attorneys for the county bar association, who argue that the antitrust laws do not apply to the law, which is a "learned profession" in which price competition would reduce the quality of the product.

The first judge hearing the case ruled for the Goldfarbs. The fee schedule was clearly price-fixing, he held, and the county bar association was liable for damages to compensate the Goldfarbs and others who had been similarly overcharged for legal services as a result of the fee setting.

The judge dismissed the bar association's argument: "It seems that there is a basic inconsistency between the lofty position that professional services, not commodities, are here involved and the position that a minimum fee schedule is proper.... Certainly fee-setting is the least 'learned' part of the profession."

The bar association appealed to the court of appeals, 4th circuit, where a three-judge panel divided 2-1 and reversed the lower court ruling. They held that the "learned professions" exception did protect the attorneys from such a suit.

The government's challenge to such fees moved more slowly; not until May 1974 did the Justice Department file a suit against fee schedules. Then it charged the Oregon State Bar with imposing unreasonable restraints on trade by such schedules, fixing the price of legal services at artificial levels and stifling competition.

The slow process of moving the government to such a challenge was outlined by Bruce C. Wilson, deputy assistant attorney general: "In 1970 Dick McLaren [then assistant attorney general for antitrust] says it's probably illegal. In 1972 I got clearance to say it is illegal. In 1973 Kauper [now assistant attorney general for antitrust] says indeed it is illegal; and in 1974 we file suit and the President says it is illegal!"

equipment and service. Claiming they were "astonished" by the government charges, AT&T executives said they would settle for no out-of-court agreement, but would "fight to the end."

The traditional thrusts of antitrust policy were clearly continuing—with greater apparent force than in decades. The suit against IBM, the AT&T suit and the FTC complaint against the oil companies were all potential landmarks in the law of monopoly.

Price-fixing, as Kauper and Saxbe pointed out, was receiving priority attention from the antitrust division. And those cases were expected—as Wilson pointed out—to have greater immediate impact than the more monumental monopolization cases. With price-fixing, he noted, "you can put people in the slammer—individuals, businessmen, corporate presidents—you're going to take them and put them in jail! But if we win a major monopolization case, I wouldn't expect to roll out of bed the next morning and see someone else whom I regard as a monopolist...saying 'I'm going to break myself up today.' ...You don't get that deterrent effect with monopolization cases."

New Areas

But antitrust was pushing into new areas as well:

• Exemptions—intensifying the push for narrow judicial interpretation of the exemptions which Congress has allowed for certain businesses from the force of the antitrust laws. The case against the broiler chicken cooperative was one example.

• Concentrated industries—turning the tools of economic analysis upon markets controlled by a few firms, known as shared monopoly or oligopoly. On Capitol Hill, Sen. Hart was completing the second year of hearings on his Industrial Reorganization Act, which would set up a commission and a special court to dismantle such concentrated power. Hearings were to continue in the 94th Congress; the areas upon which they were targeted included chemicals and drugs, electrical machinery and equipment, computers and communication, energy, iron and steel, motor vehicles and nonferrous metals. The Justice Department had expressed no position on Hart's proposal, but antitrust officials indicated approval of the attention Hart was focusing on the question.

• Service industries—"Services," Kauper pointed out to the Joint Economic Committee in September 1974, "represent 40 per cent of our gross national product," and should be given particular scrutiny by antitrust officials. Unreasonable prices in the service industry has an immediate impact on the consumer's pocketbook, he added. As of late 1974, the antitrust division had under investigation or already had charged with possible antitrust violations linen suppliers, real estate brokers, architects, accountants—and even lawyers. *(Box, this page)*

• Regulated industries—the strongest new thrust, challenged the anticompetitive regulation by independent government agencies of sectors of the national economy—including transportation and communication—accounting for 10 per cent of the gross national product. Kauper has called repeatedly for review and elimination of such regulations, a call taken up by President Ford, who asked in October for a commission to perform that task.

The Justice Department participated through the antitrust division in proceedings before all these regulatory agencies—with a notable lack of success in arguing for competition in many cases.

INFLATION FUELS DEBATE OVER REGULATION

Hidden from view in Washington's alphabet soup of bureaucratic agencies and departments are 48 men and women who exert an immeasurable impact upon the cost and quality of the goods and services available to the American consumer. They are the members of seven independent regulatory agencies, physically housed in the executive branch and vested by Congress with the authority to oversee in the public interest major segments of the American economy—amounting to more than ten per cent of the gross national product.

Their decisions impinge upon everyday life in a multiplicity of ways—from the cost of a long-distance telephone call to the type of television programming available, from the price of airline fares to the bill for heating and lighting one's home or office.

Spiraling inflation focused new attention on regulatory agencies in 1974. Led by President Ford, officials and consumers alike were beginning to ask whether or not this sort of regulation was costing the consumer more than it was worth. On Oct. 8, Ford asked Congress to create a commission on regulatory reform—to select out and recommend elimination of government regulations which increased the consumer's cost without sufficient reason.

"Much of today's regulatory machinery does little more than shelter producers from the normal competitive conse-

Lewis A. Engman

quences of lassitude and inefficiency," said Lewis A. Engman the day before Ford made his request. Engman, chairman of the Federal Trade Commission, urged that "each and every regulation...that contributes to inflation should be re-examined to make sure that the trade-off between costs and benefits which presumably brought about its institution is still valid. We may find that some of the more costly ones look a lot less attractive in a world of 12 per cent inflation than they did in a world of 3 per cent inflation."

There were many varieties of government regulation in the 1970s—safety regulation, health regulation, welfare regulation and economic regulation among them. Economic regulation was the target of Engman's complaint and Ford's expressed concern. The agencies upon which this reexamination was expected to turn were:

● The Interstate Commerce Commission (ICC), grandfather of the regulatory agencies, created in 1887 to oversee interstate railroad traffic—in the public interest. The ICC mandate was expanded with the growth of interstate transportation to include, among other things, the interstate trucking industry.

● The Federal Trade Commission (FTC), set up in 1914 to foster competition by preventing and punishing deceptive trade practices and unfair methods of competition.

● The Federal Maritime Commission (FMC), organized in 1961 as successor to the Federal Maritime Board, which was set up in 1916 to regulate U.S. shipping in the public interest.

● The Federal Power Commission (FPC), created in 1920 to regulate interstate aspects of the electric power and natural gas industries.

● The Civil Aeronautics Board (CAB), established in 1938 to regulate and promote the civil air transport industry.

● The Securities and Exchange Commission (SEC), created in 1934 to protect the investor against malpractices in the securities and financial markets.

Two other such commissions—the Consumer Product Safety Commission and the Atomic Energy Commission (AEC)—were expected to remain on the outskirts of the scrutiny urged by Ford and Engman: the consumer commission because of its youth (created in 1972) and the AEC because it was undergoing division in 1974 into two new agencies, one to foster research and development and the other to regulate the atomic energy industry.

Rationale for Regulation

Competition is the basic regulatory mechanism of the free market. But beginning in the late 19th century, certain sectors of the national economy were removed from the competitive system and placed under the regulatory eye of independent commissions. Decisions regarding the basic operations of those regulated industries no longer were made by businessmen alone; questions involving matters such as new routes or higher rates required participation by the regulator.

In exchange, the industry was shielded from many of the pressures of the free enterprise system: the regulator controlled new entries into the field through licensing or certification, for example. And often the supervision of the regulator immunized the actions of the industry from challenge under the antitrust laws.

Several justifications were given for substituting regulation for competition in communications, transportation and the other regulated industries. They included:

● The natural monopoly argument—that a certain service must be provided on a large scale in order to be efficient. Telephone lines must be strung and water mains laid, for example, to serve one house on a street or all the houses. The unit cost of these services would decline and efficiency increase as the number of homes served increased.

● The injury of failure—the concern that failure of certain segments of the economy, like the banks, would so damage the public interest that it should be avoided, even at the cost of reduced competition.

● The space limitation rationale—that only so many radio stations could be fitted into the available frequencies or that only so many airplanes could fly certain routes at one time.

● The destructive competition argument—that price competition contributed to deterioration in quality of the product or the services.

● The need for uniform adequate service—to provide such service to all areas and persons. As A. Daniel O'Neal, a member of the ICC, has explained it: "Congress in deciding to establish regulatory policies had in mind certain goals, such as making transportation service generally available to all comers, without discrimination between shippers, cities, ports, states or regions.... This necessarily meant that some protection from competitors would be necessary so that the regulated carrier could afford to provide some services that from a strictly profit motive viewpoint might not be justifiable."

Costs and Criticism

Criticism of the regulatory system was nothing new. Studies of the problem were numerous. Justice Department Antitrust Chief Thomas A. Kauper pointed out in November to a committee hearing testimony on the Ford commission proposal that the regulatory system had been studied in 1937, 1949, 1955, 1960, 1968 and 1971.

The conclusions had not been particularly favorable. In 1968 a task force report found "the bias of [regulatory] policy and its enforcement...overwhelmingly against competition." Four years later economist Walter Adams of Michigan State University was equally frank: "What starts as regulation ends up as protection—not of the public but [of] the industry that is supposedly regulated."

Engman agrees: "Most regulated industries have become federal protectorates living in the cozy world of 'cost plus,' safely protected from the ugly specters of competition, efficiency and innovation."

Another observer summarized his view: "What the regulatory commissions are trying to do is difficult to discover; what effect these commissions actually have is to a large extent unknown; when it can be discovered, it is often absurd."

More recently, critics claimed that the effect of regulation was harmful to the consumer. Ralph Nader wrote in 1973 that often "the intended beneficiary of the elaborate regulatory structure—the consumer—becomes its first victim. The consumer ultimately pays for the increased prices, encouraged waste and retarded technology that economic regulation fosters."

As Nader associate Mark J. Green wrote in his essay "Uncle Sam, the Monopoly Man": "Excessive air rates mean that many middle-income consumers are overcharged while many poor citizens never get the opportunity to travel by air. Excessive truck and railroad rates for shippers are ultimately passed on to consumers in the form of higher prices for the finished product. Telephones cost more and telephone calls cost more because public telephone utilities inadequately monitor rates and rate bases. The complexity of the subject matter should not obscure the intimate consumer harm due to the public policy of favoring monopoly over competition." Green cited estimates of the annual economic waste from regulation, totalling between $16-billion and $24-billion.

So why do the decisions of these independent regulators, called by some the original consumer agencies, cost the consumer so much money? One answer is that there are ongoing "love affairs" between most of the regulated industries and their regulators. These close ties result, this explanation says, in decisions being made in favor of the industry—rather than in the public interest.

Congress has given many of these agencies contradictory responsibilities, according to the 1971 report of the Ash Council (President's Advisory Council on Executive Organization). "To hold a regulatory agency responsible for the development of the industry it regulates," it said, "distorts its responsibility to both the industry and the public."

Turning Point

Historians of the regulatory system view 1920 as a turning point, moving the regulators away from the initial consumer- and competition-oriented policy of the laws setting up the ICC, the FTC and the antitrust structure toward an anti-competition, pro-industry policy. The ICC is used as an example: the 1887 law gave the agency the power of overseeing *maximum* rates charged by railroads to prevent overcharging; the 1920 Transportation Act gave the ICC the power of setting *minimum* rates.

The thrust of these charges, Roger G. Noll of the Brookings Institution has written, was "to make regulatory agencies a form of legal cartel for the regulated firms. Activities [such as setting minimum rates, a form of price-fixing] that would be clear violations of antitrust statutes if practiced by trade associations or informal meetings of industry executives were permitted and even condoned if overseen by regulators."

There were other reasons too that the regulators might find themselves in accord more with the regulated industries than with the average consumer. Noll explained one: "Most regulatory issues are of deep interest to regulated industries, with a very substantial amount of income...riding on the decision. The stake of the general public may...be even higher, but it is diffused among a large number of unorganized individuals.... The motivation of a single firm to fight an unfavorable regulatory decision is very high, while a regulatory decision unfavorable to the general public is unlikely to generate enough interest to cause a general public issue to be raised."

Revolving Door

And, many members of the regulatory commissions come to their posts with ties to the agencies they are to oversee. If they don't come with such ties, they often leave at the end of their terms to take positions with industry. James Needham resigned his seat on the SEC in 1972 to become chairman of the New York Stock Exchange, for example.

Despite the fact that the Senate must confirm all nominees to these commissions, there traditionally has been little scrutiny of the qualifications or the ties of these individuals, a number of whom came from the ranks of Congress or members of congressional staffs. As Sen. Philip A. Hart (D Mich.) explained the confirmation process: "We have generally taken the position that if the man is intelligent and not on probation, if that's the man the president feels is required...the president is entitled to him...."

But in 1973, for the first time in more than 20 years, the Senate did reject a nomination to one of the major regulatory commissions, that of Robert H. Morris to a seat on the FPC. Opposition to him was based primarily on the fact that for 15 years he had served at attorney for Stan-

Case Study: Congress, the President and the CAB

In late 1974, as the issue of whether regulatory agencies were serving the interests of the public or the industries they were supposed to regulate was being debated, the Civil Aeronautics Board (CAB) found itself embroiled in a squabble that was to become a case study on the question.

By the time the dispute had fully developed, nearly everyone was involved: the CAB, the President, the Justice Department, Congress and the airlines.

On Sept. 18, the White House announced that President Ford had decided against giving financially ailing Pan American Airlines a $10-million government subsidy it had requested. But he did favor a plan that would allow scheduled airlines to raise their fares on international flights and, at the same time, would force fare increases on unscheduled lines for charter groups. In effect, Pan Am and Trans World Airlines, the nation's two major international carriers, would be able to charge more for their international flights, yet suffer less from competition by the charter carriers.

CAB Ruling

On Oct. 21, the CAB did just that. It approved an average 10 per cent increase in trans-Atlantic air fares for scheduled airlines while establishing a unique set of guidelines that would compel the trans-Atlantic charter lines to raise their minimum rates by as much as 35 per cent. It was the fourth time the CAB had approved fare increases for scheduled North Atlantic flights within a year; both the industry and the agency insisted the fare hikes were necessary because of the soaring price of aviation fuel.

Ten days later, the CAB approved another fare increase, this time a 4 per cent boost for all mainland U.S. flights. But the board members were narrowly split 3-2, and the two dissenters—G. Joseph Minetti and Lee R. West—were angry.

They claimed the airlines already had been compensated for higher fuel costs, that they were taking in record profits and that the fare increases were "clearly contrary to the national interest." West and Minetti also said they felt obliged "to take into account the seemingly out-of-control inflation gripping the nation's economy and the appeal of President Ford for every citizen and every government agency to join in the fight against inflation."

The reaction to the CAB's actions by some members of Congress was strongly negative. And the White House appeared to have been caught advocating contradictory policies, pushing for fare increases for scheduled and charter lines on the one hand, and calling for the elimination of inflationary government interference on the other.

Policy Switch

On Nov. 7, the administration indicated it had changed its policy on the trans-Atlantic fare hike. Keith I. Clearwaters, deputy assistant attorney general in the Justice Department's antitrust division, told a Senate Judiciary subcommittee that the government opposed the CAB ruling on international charter flights, that the Justice Department was considering suing the CAB to reverse the decision and that he personally felt the board's action was illegal.

(A week earlier, on Nov. 1, the Justice Department had charged before a U.S. appeals court that the CAB improperly approved anti-competitive agreements between United, American and Trans World Airlines designed to increase their profits. The agreement had involved a reduction in the number of daily flights in major market areas. The CAB had approved the reductions on grounds that they would prevent service cutbacks because of the Arab oil embargo.)

Clearwaters, who said he was speaking for the administration, charged that the CAB's decision "tends to set the prices of the cheapest form of air travel available to air travelers on North Atlantic routes above a competitively determined level." He added that the airlines' "incentive to innovate and cut costs would be seriously diluted" by the board's action.

Sen. Edward M. Kennedy (D Mass.), chairman of the subcommittee, expressed amazement with the board's ruling, referring to it as "a government subsidy for inefficiency."

Defending the ruling, Assistant Secretary of Transportation Robert H. Binder pointed out that charter air fares still could be lowered below the minimum, but that the airline would have to prove it could do so and still keep operating.

"In other words," Kennedy shot back, "the airline would have the burden of proving it could do the job more cheaply. The rationale behind that baffles me."

dard Oil of California, one of the major companies in the industry regulated by the FPC. *(1973 Almanac p. 652)*

Regulation of Transportation

All of the regulatory agencies receive a share of the current criticism, but most prominent among those charged with anti-competitive and inflationary activities were those with jurisdiction over part of the transportation field—the ICC, the CAB and the FMC.

Engman pointed out that as a result of CAB control of entry to the airline market, of the distribution of routes, and CAB power to disapprove any rate changes, "in the area of rates and routes, for all intents and purposes, there is no

competition at all. Competition...is concentrated on the one unregulated aspect of airline activity, customer service. That is why the average airline commercial looks like an ad for a combination bawdy house and dinner theater. This may lead to some pleasing amenities, but it puts the customer in the position of captive buyer. Nobody asks him if he would rather have the money than the movie.... He is just asked to pay up...."

"Many products purchased by business and consumers bear a higher price tag because price-fixing and other forms of shelter from competition sanctioned by our regulatory agencies protect the least efficient carriers and permit rates far over cost," John W. Barnum, deputy secretary of transportation, told a Senate committee Nov. 19 in supporting the creation of a commission to review the regulatory situation. "The present regulatory structure is...outdated, inequitable, inefficient, uneconomical and frequently irrational. It often misplaces incentive and disincentive, distorts competitive advantage, protects inefficient carriers from effective competition, over-restricts market entry, artificially inflates rates and misallocates our nation's resources."

And when prominent economists suggested in 1974 a list of various "sacred cows"—government regulations whose elimination would make the economy more responsive to anti-inflation measures—transportation regulations were high on the list.

Recommendations and Remedies

Inflation provided the context in which recommendations from economists, and complaints from antitrust advocates, made their way to the President's ear, and perhaps on to the American people.

The Justice Department's antitrust division, which Kauper heads, already was moving to inject more competition into the regulated industries. As he explained in October, antitrust attorneys participated in proceedings before virtually every one of the regulatory commissions, challenging media cross-ownership before the FCC, working with the AEC to ascertain the competitive impact of issuing licenses for nuclear power plants, questioning merger proposal and rate bureau actions before the ICC and the FMC, and opposing minimum fare schedules for charter airlines before the CAB. *(CAB case study, box p. 109)*

"Deregulation" was the somewhat misleading label pinned quickly on the move to review and revise the regulatory system. But the alternatives available to those who advocated reform were more varied than the either/or situation which "deregulation" implied.

Structural change was one alternative. The Ash report in 1971 recommended replacing the commissioners with a single administrator for each regulatory body, consolidation of all transportation regulation and creation of an administrative court to hear appeals from rulings of the administrator. But, Kauper argued in November to a Senate committee, the structural approach does not deal with the central problem of regulation which "results more from agency inflexibility and protectionism toward established firms in the regulated industries than from administrative slowness" due to structure.

Partial deregulation was another option. Green suggested that "where there would be a viably competitive market but for economic regulation, that industry should be freed from regulatory restraint."

"Direct economic regulation of industries other than those few which are natural monopolies could simply be ended," Kauper suggested in September. Later, speaking in support of a one-year commission study of the subject, he also urged Congress to approve legislation confining regulation to areas "where it can be demonstrated clearly that the benefits of competition—competitive prices, technological innovation and optimal allocation of resources—are outweighed by the injury to the public interest which competition would permit."

A third alternative, Kauper noted, was the adjustment of the regulatory scheme to allow room for the workings of competitive forces. One example of this sort of increased flexibility within the structure would be the creation of a "zone of reasonableness" within which railroads and truckers and airlines could set their rates and fares and put them into effect without obtaining ICC or CAB approval in advance of the specific change.

An "historical hobgoblin," but still an alternative to the existing regulatory structure, Green noted, was nationalization of certain industries. The collapse of Penn Central, the creation of Amtrak and the massive financial support the government had provided to the aerospace industry in the early 1970s made nationalization of those industries a live possibility, he said.

Referring to the emergency aid provided in 1971 by the federal government to Lockheed Aircraft Corporation, he commented: "If Lockheed's losses can be socialized, one may well wonder why its profits must be untouchable."

Outlook: Cloudy

But would any changes really be made in the regulatory system as a result of this renewed talk? Late in 1974 the answer was unclear.

Ford's proposal for a one-year commission study had been generally supported by witnesses from the regulatory agencies and the government, although some argued on one hand that the subject would require more time to study, and on the other hand that there had been enough studies already, that this was the time to act.

"About the only people who would be content with letting things be are the members of the various regulatory commissions, and the industries they protect through their friendly regulation," said Reuben B. Robertson III of Public Citizen, a public interest lobby group, in November.

The degree of opposition which these officials and the regulated industries would generate was unclear. Kauper pointed out that opposition to change from the industries simply would prove the need for reform: "When those who are regulated scream with outrage at the possibility of deregulation instead of at the actuality of restrictions on their ability to freely compete, the regulatory cycle has run its course."

The biggest question mark in the future of regulatory reform, however, was the degree of public support which could be mobilized behind this effort. "I am certain," said Kauper's deputy, Keith I. Clearwaters, "that if the individual man in the street knew what was going on here in Washington almost every day in the halls of the regulatory agencies to stop new entry into the market, to encourage price-fixing cartels of carriers which drive up rates, to slow down or completely impede new technology developed by one carrier so that others more sluggish...remain comfortable, that man in the street would be demanding legislative change now!"

But would inflation and recognition of the role of regulation in such pressures galvanize such a constituency? The changed atmosphere toward regulation and competition in 1974, said Kauper, did not reflect a difference in government attitudes: "The difference is in how many are listening and who they are. Just maybe, that will be a real difference."

Engman expressed similar optimism in mid-November: "I sense a new receptivity to the suggestion that at least some aspects of the regulatory system may need overhauling rather than tinkering or fine tuning.... It accords with the sentiments of a public now, more than ever, sensitized to costs, a public that is beginning to view the price of government with the same jaundiced eye with which it views prices in the marketplace."

THE BUDGET: FORD PROPOSES CUTS OF $4.6-BILLION

Challenging Congress to make good on its budget-cutting pledges, President Ford Nov. 26 proposed a series of actions to trim fiscal 1975 federal spending by nearly $4.6-billion.

With all but $979-million of those reductions requiring consideration by a Congress that was increasingly concerned about recession, the administration strategy for curbing federal spending to fight inflation was likely to encounter resistence. *(Congress and inflation, p. 86; Ford administration, p. 76)*

Ford posed some uncomfortable choices for Congress, asking a combination of legislative actions to pare fiscal 1975 outlays by $3.6-billion, with the bulk coming from social spending programs at a time when many Americans already were being pressed financially by double digit inflation and rising unemployment.

And Office of Management and Budget Director Roy L. Ash conceded that the administration's proposed spending cuts could cost between 40,000 and 50,000 workers their jobs. Although federal employment would be reduced by about 3,000 workers, the bulk of the layoffs would come in industries that lost business from federal spending cutbacks.

But Congress nevertheless "has no excuse not to act" on the President's proposals, Ash maintained in briefing reporters. "It's all up to them."

Ford in fact acknowledged the recession's impact on federal budgetary decisions by abandoning his self-proclaimed goal of cutting fiscal 1975 outlays back to $300-billion. Even if Congress went along with all $4.6-billion in proposed reductions, total spending for the year was expected to reach $302.2-billion, leaving the budget with a $9.2-billion deficit.

In his message to Congress, Ford insisted that his proposals were aimed at eliminating less essential outlays while avoiding "actions that would unduly add to unemployment or adversely affect those hurt most by inflation." The $300-billion target could have been met, he noted, except that rising unemployment and stepped up federal programs to help the jobless had increased total spending projections by $2.7-billion.

"It would be unwise," Ford concluded, "to add additional dollar reductions for each dollar of increased aid to the unemployed."

But especially with unemployment standing at 6 per cent at the end of October, Congress could be expected to question budget-cutting priorities that would take the bulk of the reductions from federal health, veterans and income security programs.

Budget Overhaul

In what amounted to a substantial overhaul of the original fiscal 1975 budget submitted by former President Nixon in February, Ford recommended a combination of actions, including changes in federal program requirements as well as reductions in congressional appropriations.

In all, the President asked Congress to approve savings that would amount to $3.6-billion in fiscal 1975, with nearly $2.7-billion to be accomplished by rewriting the laws that authorize various federal programs and set regulations that determine their costs. The remaining $928-million in proposed spending reductions subject to congressional approval required reductions in the fiscal 1975 appropriations making the money available for use.

To that end, Ford revised administration requests for programs covered by three appropriations bills still pending in Congress, asked recision of funds already appropriated for fiscal 1975 and said he would defer the use of other previously appropriated funds as well.

Coupled with administrative changes allowed by existing law that would save $979-million, those measures would bring projected fiscal 1975 outlays down to $302.2-billion from the $306.8-billion total contemplated by revised budget estimates.

Of that $4.6-billion curtailment, about $3.1-billion would come from reductions in fiscal 1975 spending on federal health, income security and veterans programs. Only $600-million would come from reductions in defense outlays.

But, as Ash repeatedly stressed in outlining the budget proposals to reporters, economic developments and congressional action on earlier legislation had increased projected spending on income security and veterans benefits by substantial amounts above original budget calculations.

Expected defense outlays, on the other hand, were about $2.2-billion below budget projections because

Ford's Proposal for Actions

	Effect on Federal Spending (in millions of dollars)	
	1975	**1976**
Enact new legislation transmitted with this message (12 actions)	−1,783	−3,250
Enact legislation previously transmitted and pending before the Congress (8 actions)	−896	−1,798
Modify appropriation bills now pending before the Congress (32 actons)	−337	−281
Consider revised appropriations' requests transmitted with this message (3 actions)	−50	−30
Rescind (withdraw) funds previously provided (39 rescissions)	−224	−227
Defer use of funds previously provided (41 deferrals)	−317	+18
TOTAL actions for consideration by the Congress (135)	−3,607	−5,568
Executive Actions Under Current Law (11 actions)	−979	−1,110
TOTAL PROPOSED REDUCTIONS (146)	**−4,586**	**−6,678**

Congress cut fiscal 1975 Defense Department appropriations by nearly $5-billion. *(Defense Department appropriations, 1973 Almanac p. 167)*

Deficit

Even if Congress went along with all proposed reductions, the expected $9.2-billion deficit in fiscal 1975 would be only a slight improvement over the $9.4-billion deficit projected by Nixon's February budget document.

It would be significantly lower, however, than the $13.8-billion deficit that OMB projected on the basis of lagging revenues and additional spending dictated since February by congressional action and changing economic conditions.

Without efforts to cut spending, OMB projected fiscal 1975 outlays of $306.8-billion. In its mid-session review of the budget in June, OMB had estimated outlays at $305.4-billion.

OMB attributed the increased outlay total to congressional action on legislation mandating extra spending

---

Defense vs. Social Spending

In recommending fiscal 1975 spending cuts of $4.6-billion to fight inflation, the Ford administration not unexpectedly assigned most of the burden to social spending programs.

While President Ford in Dec. 2 news conference contended that the administration "tried...to spread the reductions across the board," he insisted that previous reductions voted by Congress limited the cuts that could be made in the Defense Department budget.

"If you look at what the Congress did in the first place and what we have proposed in the second, it is a fairly well balanced program," Ford said.

What Congress had done, Ford noted, was to cut fiscal 1975 defense outlays by $2.6-billion through reductions in fiscal 1975 appropriations. With the additional $400-million to $500-million in cuts proposed by the administration, total reductions in defense spending would reach roughly $3-billion.

"Since the Defense Department had already [suffered] a sizeable reduction by the Congress," Ford said, "I felt we had to go across the rest of the spectrum of the federal government to find additional reductions."

Before the fiscal 1975 reductions were proposed, Office of Management and Budget (OMB) Director Roy L. Ash had outlined a case for cutting social program spending in briefing reporters on budget deliberations.

Discounting the effects of inflation, Ash said, total federal spending had not increased since 1968. Yet during those six years real spending had doubled for income distribution programs such as Social Security, health care and food stamps.

Those increases had been financed, Ash maintained, by parallel reductions in actual spending with inflation discounted on all other governmental functions, including defense.

By 1975, Ash went on, continued cuts in real outlays for defense and other operational expenses were "no longer possible or even desirable."

---

and to additional spending on unemployment compensation programs.

While Congress had cut spending by about $2.6-billion through reductions in requested appropriations, it had increased expected spending through legislation that required spending of an additional $2.8-billion, chiefly for veterans benefits and for a federal pay raise that Congress refused to defer. Another $800-million was added by congressional inaction on savings proposed by the administration.

Other increases in fiscal 1975 outlays resulted from higher than expected unemployment and a $1.5-billion increase in interest on the national debt.

Revised Projections

At the same time, OMB revised federal revenue projections downward to $293-billion to reflect an expected $2.9-billion loss in individual income tax collections. That adjustment was offset in part by increases in projected corporate and payroll taxes, leaving expected revenues about $1-billion below the $294-billion projected in June.

That revenue forecast was based on an unemployment rate averaging from 6.1 per cent to 6.2 per cent during fiscal 1975, the year that started July 1, Ash said. Since unemployment had risen to 6 per cent only in October, that projection contemplated unemployment as high as 6.5 to 6.7 per cent by the end of the year in June 1975.

The $293-billion projection included the extra revenue that would be raised by Ford's proposed 5 per cent surcharge during 1975 on corporate and individual income taxes. With part of that increase offset by the President's proposal to increase the business investment credit, the net effect of Ford's tax program would increase fiscal 1975 revenues by about $800-million, Ash said.

Spending Reductions

In all, Ford proposed to reduce fiscal 1975 spending by $4.6-billion (and fiscal 1976 spending by $6.7-billion):

● Through new legislative proposals that would save $1.8-billion in fiscal 1975 and $3.2-billion in fiscal 1976 by changing federal program requirements.

● Through adoption of previously proposed legislation before Congress that would save $896-million in fiscal 1975 and $1.8-billion in fiscal 1976 through similar changes.

● Through changes in three appropriations bills still pending in Congress that would save $337-million in fiscal 1975 and $281-million in fiscal 1976.

● Through additional revised requests that would save $50-million in fiscal 1975 and $30-million in fiscal 1976.

● Through recision of previously appropriated funds that would save $224-million in fiscal 1975 and $227-million in fiscal 1976.

● Through deferral of the use of previously appropriated funds that would save $317-million in fiscal 1975 but add $18-million to fiscal 1976 spending.

● Through administrative actions under existing law that would save $979-million in fiscal 1975 and $1.1-billion in fiscal 1976.

Substantive Legislation

The revised budget package that the administration sent to Congress included six draft bills to hold down costs for Social Security, health and welfare programs, curtail federal education impact aid, reduce personnel levels in the armed forces reserves and impose user taxes for inland waterways and airports.

It also included the administration's proposals for replacing a veterans education bill that Ford had vetoed Nov. 26.

Including pending bills, the requests for congressional action on legislation would:

● Revise Medicare cost-sharing requirements to cut federal contributions for inpatient hospital services by $465-million in fiscal 1975 and $1.3-billion in fiscal 1976.

● Revise the formula for determining federal matching funds for Medicaid, saving $295-million in fiscal 1975 and $636-million in fiscal 1976.

● Eliminate the option of taking retroactive Social Security benefits for one year prior to actual retirement if that would result in retirement before age 65, saving $170-million in fiscal 1975 and $430-million in fiscal 1976.

● Curtail veterans education benefits provided by the vetoed bill, saving $502-million in fiscal 1975 and $187-million in fiscal 1976.

● Repeal a 1974 law (PL 93-337) that extended to 10 years from eight years the period in which veterans receiving education benefits must complete their program, saving $300-million in fiscal 1975 and $618-million in fiscal 1976.

● Eliminate federal impact aid payments to school districts whose entitlements under the program amounted to less than 5 per cent of their operating budgets, saving $65-million in fiscal 1975 and $30-million in fiscal 1976.

● Impose user charges on barge companies carrying goods on inland waterways, offsetting federal maintenance costs by $25-million in fiscal 1975 and by $100-million by fiscal 1976.

● Impose general aviation airport landing fees at airports with control towers operated by the Federal Aviation Administration, offsetting federal outlays of $25-million in fiscal 1975 and $95-million in fiscal 1976.

● Authorize production and sale of oil from the Navy petroleum reserve at Elk Hills, Calif., bringing in offsetting receipts of $125-million in fiscal 1975 and $148-million in fiscal 1976.

Revised Appropriations

Ford asked for amendments that would curb outlays of funds provided by three appropriations bills that were still pending in Congress. Changes were requested in fiscal 1975 appropriations for labor and health, education and welfare (HR 15580), for agriculture-environmental and consumer

1975 Outlays By Agency

(in billions of dollars)

	1974 Actual	1974 June estimate	Revisions	Current base estimate	Proposed reductions	Revised total	Effect on 1976
Department of Defense, including military assistance	78.4	85.8	—2.2	83.6	—0.4	83.2	—0.3
Agriculture	9.8	8.9	—0.1	8.8	—0.6	8.2	—0.7
Commerce	1.5	1.7	—0.1	1.7	*	1.6	*
Corps of Engineers	1.7	1.7	0.1	1.8	*	1.8	——
Health, Education, and Welfare	93.7	111.0	—0.8	110.2	—1.7	108.5	—3.5
Social security trust funds	(67.2)	(79.3)	(—0.6)	(78.7)	(—0.7)	(77.9)	(—2.1)
Housing and Urban Development	4.8	6.1	—0.4	5.7	—0.1	5.6	—0.1
Interior	1.9	2.5	—0.1	2.4	—0.1	2.4	*
Justice	1.8	2.1	—0.1	2.0	*	2.0	——
Labor	9.0	11.6	3.7	15.3	——	15.3	——
Unemployment trust fund	(6.1)	(8.0)	(2.0)	(10.0)	(——)	(10.0)	(——)
State	0.7	0.8	*	0.8	*	0.8	——
Transportation	8.1	9.3	—0.2	9.1	—0.1	8.9	—0.3
Treasury	36.0	38.7	1.4	40.1	*	40.1	—0.1
Interest on the debt	(29.3)	(31.5)	(1.5)	(33.0)	(——)	(33.0)	(——)
General revenue sharing	(6.1)	(6.2)	(——)	(6.2)	(——)	(6.2)	(——)
Atomic Energy Commission	2.3	3.0	*	3.1	—0.1	3.0	——
Environmental Protection Agency	2.0	4.1	—1.1	2.9	*	2.9	——
General Services Administration	—0.3	—0.8	0.1	—0.8	—0.2	—0.9	—0.5
National Aeronautics and Space Administration	3.3	3.3	*	3.3	—0.1	3.2	——
Veterans Administration	13.3	14.2	1.5	15.6	—1.1	14.5	—1.3
All other agencies	17.1	19.6	0.3	19.9	*	19.8	——
Allowances	——	0.9	—0.1	0.8	——	0.8	——
Undistributed offsetting receipts[1]	—16.6	—18.9	—0.6	—19.5	——	—19.5	——
Total	268.4	305.4	1.3	306.8	—4.6	302.2	—6.7

[1] Includes offshore oil land receipts.

*$50 million or less.

Outlays By Function

(fiscal years; in billions of dollars)

	1974 Actual	1975			
		June estimate	Revisions	Proposed reductions	Revised estimate
National defense	79.4	87.9	—2.1	—0.6	85.1
International affairs and finance	3.5	4.4	—0.1	—0.3	4.1
Space research and technology	3.3	3.3	—*	—0.1	3.2
Agriculture and rural development	5.2	2.1	—0.1	—*	1.9
Natural resources and environment	5.7	8.5	—0.6	—0.1	7.7
Commerce and transportation	12.6	13.8	—0.2	—0.2	13.4
Community development and housing	5.2	6.2	—0.3	—0.1	5.8
Education and manpower	10.6	11.6	+0.6	—0.2	12.0
Health	21.5	26.3	—0.3	—1.1	25.0
Income security	84.1	102.1	+2.3	—0.9	103.6
Veterans benefits and services	13.4	14.2	+1.5	—1.1	14.5
Interest	28.1	30.1	+1.5	——	31.7
General government	6.5	7.0	—0.1	—0.1	6.8
General Revenue Sharing	6.1	6.2	*	——	6.2
Allowances	——	0.9	—0.1	——	0.8
Undistributed offsetting receipts[1]	—16.6	—18.9	—0.6	——	—19.5
Total	268.4	305.4	+1.3	—4.6	302.2

[1] Includes offshore oil land receipts.

*$50 million or less.

protection (HR 16901) and the first fiscal 1975 supplemental bill (HR 16900). He also submitted additional amendments to fiscal 1975 requests for health, education and welfare.

In asking Congress to reconsider those measures, Ford accepted some congressional increases and all congressional decreases and reduced several previous requests. Among major changes proposed by Ford were:

● Reductions of $112-million in appropriations for the National Institutes of Health.

● An $11-million reduction in appropriations for vocational education grants to states.

● Reductions that in effect would discontinue the agriculture conservation program, water bank program and forestry incentives program.

● Reductions of $45-million in appropriations for health services grants to state health agencies and $9.9-million in appropriations for health manpower projects.

Recisions and Deferrals

Ford's budget cutting message made only limited use of impoundment procedures provided by the budget reform act that Congress enacted in June.

Under those procedures, Ford asked Congress to rescind appropriations of $864.1-billion—reducing outlays by $224-million in fiscal 1975 and $227-million in fiscal 1976—and said he would defer the spending of $317-million in previously appropriated funds in fiscal 1975.

To give Congress more time to study those cutbacks, Ford made them effective Dec. 16. After they go into effect, either the House or the Senate at any time could direct that deferred funds be spent immediately. And if Congress had not approved the recision legislation within 45 days while it was in session, those funds also would have to be spent.

The proposed recisions involved several agencies, but the bulk would come from the defense budget. The requested recisions would cut defense outlays by $136-million in fiscal 1975 and $169-million in fiscal 1976.

Those spending reductions in large part would result from proposed recision of $13.5-million appropriated in fiscal 1975 for procurement of Army helicopters and $248-million in fiscal 1975 appropriations for buying 36 fighters that had not been requested by the Air Force.

Deferrals also were spread among several agencies, with the highest totals coming from funds for the Atomic Energy Commission, National Aeronautics and Space Administration, Department of the Interior and the Corps of Engineers.

Administrative Actions

Using authority given the executive branch under existing law, Ford directed five departments to adopt cost control measures of various kinds. They included:

● A $450-million limit on Commodity Credit Corporation special export credit sales of farm products.

● An increase in the purchase price of food stamps to 30 per cent of monthly household income, the limit allowed by law, effective in March 1975.

● Stepped-up implementation of Medicare and Medicaid cost control regulations.

● Tighter regulations for public assistance programs.

● An increase in the interest rate on mortgages purchased under a special federal program started by President Nixon in May.

● Transfer of $300-million in existing fiscal 1975 obligational authority for urban mass transit assistance to a new program created by legislation recently enacted by Congress. ∎

APPENDIX

CQ

FORD'S MESSAGE ON BUDGET REDUCTIONS

Following is the text of President Ford's Nov. 26 message, as made available by the White House, to Congress. (Story, p. 111)

TO THE CONGRESS OF THE UNITED STATES:

Last month I sent a 31-point economic program to the Congress. That program was a balanced one, both dealing with the forces of inflation and anticipating the possibility of recessionary pressures. It was, and remains, my particular concern to help those hardest hit by inflation and by the slack that has developed in some sectors of the economy.

Responsible restraint of government spending is an integral part of my economic program. The Congress has publicly proclaimed its support of restraint. In June the Senate voted 74-12 in favor of legislation to hold Federal spending to $295 billion. In September the Joint Economic Committee unanimously recommended holding spending to $300 billion. Last month the House voted 329-20 for a budget target of the same level.

Soon after I took office I asked the heads of Federal agencies to undertake a thorough review of 1975 expenditures. In my October 8 Message to the Congress, I pledged to forward a package of proposed actions to reduce the 1975 budget. Today I am reporting on the results of this review and presenting my specific recommendations for reducing Federal outlays.

First, it is important to understand what has been happening to the budget. When the current fiscal year began last July 1, budget outlays for the year were estimated at $305.4 billion.

in some programs have been more than offset by actions it has taken to increase spending in others. Particularly disappointing was the Congressional unwillingness to join with me in deferring for three months a Federal pay raise. This cost the taxpayers $700 million. Equally discouraging was the passage by Congress over my veto of the Railroad Retirement bill costing $285 million this year and $7 billion over the next 25 years.

There have been some reductions in expected spending levels. The Environmental Protection Agency will spend less than planned because anticipated schedules for sewage treatment construction have not been met.

However, the most significant change is the increased aid to the jobless—including the National Employment Assistance Act I proposed last month—that added $2.7 billion to the budget. This increase is necessary to ease the burden on those who are most affected by current economic stress.

Taking these developments into account, my present recommendations for $4.6 billion of budget reductions will result in a budget total of $299.5 billion before considering $2.7 billion increased spending for aid to the unemployed. These recommendations represent a major effort at budgetary restraint. It would be unwise, in my view, to add additional dollar reductions for each dollar of increased aid to the unemployed.

The fiscal year 1975 budget actions by the Executive and the Congress since July 1, including those I now propose, are summarized and compared to last year's actual expenditures as follows:

CHANGES IN BUDGET SPENDING
(Fiscal years; dollar amounts in billions)

	Defense[1]	Interest on the Public Debt	Payments for Individuals[2]	Other	Total
Actual 1974 expenditures	$78.4	$29.3	$110.1	$50.5	$268.4
1975 Budget (July 1 estimates)	85.8	31.5	130.5	57.6	305.4
Changes (including those proposed)	−2.6	+1.5	+1.0	−3.2	−3.3
Presently proposed levels for 1975	83.2	33.0	131.5	54.4	302.2
1975: Percent change since July 1	− 3.0%	+ 4.8%	+ .7%	−5.5%	− 1.1%
1975: Percent change over 1974	+6.1%	+12.6%	+19.4%	+7.8%	+12.6%

[1] *Department of Defense, Military and Military Assistance.*
[3] *Nondefense*

Interest costs for Federal borrowing are now expected to be $1.5 billion more than the estimate last June.

The Congress has also added to 1975 budget pressures. Congressional reductions

The 1975 outlay estimates can be affected significantly by variations in income from oil lease sales on the Outer Continental Shelf. This income is treated in the budget as an offset to spending. If the

current schedule of lease sales is not met, for environmental or other reasons, or if the bids are significantly less than anticipated, outlays could further increase—possibly by $3 billion or more.

The reductions I propose to the Congress will require a number of changes in basic legislation and in pending appropriations. I am also transmitting proposed rescissions and deferrals, as required by the Congressional Budget and Impoundment Control Act, to reduce programs for which funds have already been appropriated. The rescissions would result in decreased outlays of over $200 million in 1975. Deferrals would reduce 1975 outlays by over $300 million.

Normally, funds are already being withheld when reports on rescissions and deferrals are transmitted to the Congress. Recognizing that these rescissions and deferrals are an integral part of a more far reaching and comprehensive proposal, I will not begin to withhold funds for the affected programs until December 16 although the law permits me to do so immediately.

The reductions I propose focus on programs that have grown rapidly in recent years or that have been increased substantially over budget proposals. In most cases, the level of 1975 outlays will be materially above actual spending last year. Even after the proposed cutbacks, Federal benefit payments to individuals are estimated to be $131.5 billion. This is $1.0 billion above the July estimate, and $21.4 billion, or 19%, above actual spending last year.

While I am recommending further cuts in defense spending, I have taken into account the substantial reductions already made by the Congress. My current expectation for defense spending is $83.2 billion, $2.6 billion below the June estimate. I believe that further cuts in defense spending would be exceedingly unwise, particularly at this time.

In determining which budget programs should be reduced, I have tried to eliminate the less essential and to overcome inequities. I have tried to avoid actions that would unduly add to unemployment or adversely affect those hurt most by inflation.

The $4.6 billion budget outlay reduction I now propose is not large when compared with total Federal spending. Nevertheless, the Congress may find it difficult to agree with all my proposals. I strongly urge the Congress to accept them and join with me in this belt tightening. The reductions are essential to demonstrate to the American people that the Federal Government is working seriously to restrain its spending. They are also a start toward the imperative of gaining control over budgets in the future.

GERALD R. FORD

THE WHITE HOUSE,
November 26, 1974.

FORD'S SPEECH TO CONGRESS ON ECONOMIC POLICY

Following are excerpts from the text of President Ford's nationally televised speech on economic policy, as made available by the White House, before a joint session of Congress Oct. 8. (Story, p. 76)

...I have reviewed the past and the present efforts of our Federal Government to help the economy. They are simply not good enough, nor sufficiently broad, nor do they pack the punch that will turn America's economy on.

A stable American economy cannot be sustained if the world's economy is in chaos. International cooperation is absolutely essential and vital, but while we seek agreements with other nations, let us put our own economic house in order.

Today, I have identified ten areas for our joint action, the Executive and Legislative Branches of our Government.

Food

America is the world's champion producer of food. Food prices and petroleum prices in the United States are primary inflationary factors.

America today partially depends on foreign sources for petroleum, but we can grow more than enough food for ourselves.

To halt higher food prices, we must produce more food, and I call upon every farmer to produce the full capacity. And I say to you and to the farmers, they have done a magnificent job in the past, and we should be eternally grateful.

This Government, however, will do all in its power to assure him, the farmer, he can sell his entire yield at reasonable prices. Accordingly, I ask Congress to remove all remaining acreage limitations on rice, peanuts, and cotton.

I also assure America's farmer here and now that I will allocate all the fuel and ask authority to allocate all the fertilizer they need to do this essential job.

Agricultural marketing orders and other Federal regulations are being reviewed to eliminate or modify those responsible for inflated prices.

I have directed our new Council on Wage and Price Stability to find and to expose all restrictive practices, public or private, which raise food prices. The Administration will also monitor food production, margins, pricing, and exports.

We can and we shall have an adequate supply at home, and through cooperation, meet the needs of our trading partners abroad.

Over this past weekend we initiated a voluntary program to monitor grain exports. The Economic Policy Board will be responsible for determining the policy under this program.

In addition, in order to better allocate our supplies for export, I ask that a provision be added to Public Law 480 under which we ship food to the needy and friendly countries. The President needs authority to waive certain of the restrictions on shipments based on national interest or humanitarian grounds.

Energy

America's future depends heavily on oil, gas, coal, electricity, and other resources called energy. Make no mistake, we do have a real energy problem.

One-third of our oil—17 percent of America's total energy—now comes from foreign sources that we cannot control, at high cartel prices costing you and me $16 billion—$16 billion more than just a year ago.

A primary solution has to be at home. If you have forgotten the shortages of last winter, most Americans have not.

I have ordered today the reorganization of our national energy effort in the creation of a National Energy Board. It will be chaired with developing, or I should say charged with developing a single national energy policy and program. And I think most of you will be glad to know that our former colleague, Rog Morton, our Secretary of the Interior, will be the overall boss of our national energy program.

Rog Morton's marching orders are to reduce imports of foreign oil by one million barrels per day by the end of 1975, whether by savings here at home, or by increasing our own sources.

Secretary Morton, along with his other responsibility, is also charged with increasing our domestic energy supply by promptly utilizing our coal resources and expanding recovery of domestic oil still in the grounds in old wells.

New legislation will be sought after your recess to require use of cleaner coal processes and nuclear fuel in new electric plants and the quick conversion of existing oil plants.

I propose that we, together, set a target date of 1980 for eliminating oil-fired plants from the Nation's base-loaded electrical capacity.

I will use the Defense Production Act to allocate scarce materials for energy development, and I will ask you, the House and the Senate, for whatever amendments prove necessary.

I will meet with top management of the automobile industry to assure, either by agreement or by law, a firm program aimed at achieving a 40 percent increase in gasoline mileage within a four-year development deadline.

Priority legislation—action, I should say—to increase energy supply here at home requires the following:

- One, long-sought deregulation of natural gas supplies.
- Number two, responsible use of our Naval petroleum reserves in California and Alaska.
- Number three, amendments to the Clean Air Act, and
- Four, passage of surface mining legislation to insure an adequate supply with common-sense environmental protection.

Now, if all of these steps fail to meet our current energy saving goals, I will not hesitate to ask for tougher measures. For the long range, we must work harder on coal gasification. We must push with renewed vigor and talent research in the use of nonfossil fuels. The power of the atom, the heat of the sun and the steam stored deep in the earth, the force of the winds and water, must be main sources of energy for our grandchildren, and we can do it.

Restrictive Practices

To increase productivity and contain prices, we must end restrictive and costly practices, whether instituted by Government, industry, labor or others. And I am determined to return to the vigorous enforcement of antitrust laws.

The Administration will zero in on more effective enforcement laws against price fixing and bid rigging. For instance, non-competitive professional fee schedules and real estate settlement fees must be eliminated. Such violations will be prosecuted by the Department of Justice to the full extent of the law.

Now I ask Congress for prompt authority to increase maximum penalties for antitrust violations from $50,000 to $1 million for corporations, and from $50,000 to $100,000 for individual violators.

At the Conference on Inflation, we found, I would say, very broad agreement that the Federal Government imposes too many hidded and too many inflationary costs on our economy. As a result, I propose a four-point program aimed at a substantial purging process.

- Number one, I have ordered the Council on Wage and Price Stability to be the watchdog over inflationary costs of all Governmental actions.
- Two, I ask the Congress to establish a National Commission of Regulatory Reform to undertake a long overdue total re-examination of the independent regulatory agencies. It will be a joint effort by the Congress, the Executive Branch and the private sector to identify and eliminate existing Federal rules and regulations that increase costs to the consumer without any good reason in today's economic climate.
- Three, hereafter, I will require that all major legislative proposals, regulations and rules emanating from the Executive Branch of the Government will include an Inflation Impact Statement that certifies we have carefully weighed the effect on the Nation. I respectfully request that the Congress require a similar advance Inflation Impact Statement for its own legislative initiatives.

• Finally, I urge State and local units of government to undertake similar programs to reduce inflationary effects of their regulatory activities.

At this point I thank the Congress for recently revitalizing the National Commission on Productivity and Work Quality. It will initially concentrate on problems of productivity in Government—Federal, State and local.

Outside of Government, it will develop meaningful blueprints for labor-management cooperation at the plant level. It should look particularly at the construction and the health service industries.

The Council on Wage and Price Stability will, of course, monitor wage and price increases in the private sector. Monitoring will include public hearings to justify either price or wage increases. I emphasize, in fact re-emphasize, that this is not a compulsory wage and price control agency.

Now, I know many Americans see Federal controls as the answer, but I believe from past experience controls show us that they never really stop inflation, not the last time, not even during and immediately after World War II, when, as I recall, prices rose despite severe and enforceable wartime rationing.

Now, peacetime controls actually, we know from recent experience, create shortages, hamper production, stifle growth and limit jobs. I do not ask for such powers, however politically tempting, as such a program could cause the fixer and the black marketeer to flourish, while decent citizens face empty shelves and stand in long waiting lines.

We Need More Capital

We cannot "eat up our seed corn." Our free enterprise system depends on orderly capital markets through which the savings of our people become productively used. Today, our capital markets are in total disarray. We must restore their vitality. Prudent monetary restraint is essential.

You and the American people should know, however, that I have personally been assured by the Chairman of the Independent Federal Reserve Board, that the supply of money and credit will expand sufficiently to meet the needs of our economy and that in no event will a credit crunch occur.

The prime lending rate is going down. To help industry to buy more machines and create more jobs, I am recommending a liberalized 10 percent investment tax credit. This credit should be especially helpful to capital-intensive industries, such as primary metals, public utilities, where capacity shortages have developed.

I am asking Congress to enact tax legislation to provide that all dividends on preferred stocks issued for cash be fully deductible by the issuing company. This should bring in more capital, especially for energy-producing utilities. It will also help other industries shift from debt to equity, providing a sounder capital structure.

Capital gains tax legislation must be liberalized as proposed by the tax reform bill currently before the Committee on Ways and Means. I endorse this approach and hope that it will pass promptly.

Helping the Casualties

And this is a very important part of the overall speech. The Conference on Inflation made everybody even more aware of who is suffering most from inflation. Foremost are those who are jobless through no fault of their own.

Three weeks ago, I released funds which, with earlier actions, provide public service employment for some 170,000 who need work. I now propose to the Congress a two-step program to augment this action.

First, 13 weeks of special unemployment insurance benefits would be provided to those who have exhausted their regular and extended unemployment insurance benefits, and 26 weeks of special unemployment insurance benefits to those who qualify but are not now covered by regular unemployment insurance programs.

Funding in this case would come from the general treasury, not from taxes on employers, as in the case with the established unemployment program.

Second, I ask the Congress to create a brand new Community Improvement Corps to provide work for the unemployed through short-term useful work projects to improve, beautify and enhance the environment of our cities, our towns and our countryside.

This standby program would come alive whenever unemployment exceeds 6 percent nationally. It would be stopped when unemployment drops below 6 percent. Local labor markets would each qualify for grants whenever their unemployment rate exceeds 6.5 per cent.

State and local government contractors would supervise these projects and could hire only those who had exhausted their unemployment insurance benefits. The goal of this new program is to provide more constructive work for all Americans, young or old, who cannot find a job.

The purpose really follows this formula. Short-term problems require short-term remedies. I therefore request that these programs be for a one-year period.

Now, I know that low- and middle-income Americans have been hardest hit by inflation. Their budgets are most vulnerable because a larger part of their income goes for the highly inflated costs of food, fuel and medical care.

The tax reform bill now in the House Committee on Ways and Means, which I favor, already provides approximately $1.6 billion of tax relief to these groups. Compensating new revenues are provided in this prospective legislation by a windfall tax, profits tax on oil producers and by closing other loopholes.

If enacted, this will be a major contribution by the Congress in our common effort to make our tax system fairer to all.

Stimulating Housing

Without question, credit is the lifeblood of housing. The United States, unfortunately, is suffering the longest and the most severe housing recession since the end of World War II. Unemployment in the construction trades is twice the national average.

One of my first acts as President was to sign the Housing and Community Development Act of 1974. I have since concluded that still more help is needed, help that can be delivered very quickly and with minimum inflationary impact.

I urge the Congress to enact before recess additional legislation to make most home mortgages eligible for purchase by an agency of the Federal Government. As the law stands now, only FHA or VA home mortgages, one fifth of the total, are covered.

I am very glad that the Senate, thanks to the leadership of Senator Brooke and Senator Cranston, has already made substantial progress on this legislation. As soon as it comes to me, I will make at least $3 billion immediately available for mortgage purchases, enough to finance about 100,000 more American homes.

Thrift Institutions

Savings and loan and similar institutions are hard hit by inflation and high interest rates. They no longer attract, unfortunately, adequate deposits. The Executive Branch, in my judgment, must join with the Congress in giving critically-needed attention to the structure and operation of our thrift institutions which now find themselves for the third time in eight years in another period of serious mortgage credit scarcity.

Passage of the pending financial institution bill will help. but no single measure has yet appeared, as I see it, to solve feast or famine in mortgage credit. However, I promise to work with you individually and collectively to develop additional specific programs in this area in the future.

International Independency

The United States has a responsibility not only to maintain a healthy economy at home, but also to seek policies which compliment rather than disrupt the constructive efforts of others.

Essential to U.S. initiatives is the early passage of an acceptable trade reform bill. My special representation for trade negotiations departed earlier this afternoon to Canada, Europe, Japan, to brief foreign friends on my proposal.

We live in an interdependent world and therefore must work together to resolve common economic problems.

Federal Taxes and Spending

To support programs, to increase production and share inflation-produced hardships. we need additional tax revenues. I am aware that any proposal for new taxes just four weeks before a national election is, to put it mildly, considered politically unwise. And I am frank to say that I have been earnestly advised to wait and talk about taxes anytime after November 5.

But I do say in sincerity that I will not play politics with America's future.

Our present inflation, to a considerable degree, comes from many years of enacting expensive programs without raising enough revenues to pay for them.

The truth is that 19 out of the 25 years I had the honor and the privilege to serve in this Chamber, the Federal Government ended up with Federal deficits. That is not a very good batting average.

By now, almost everybody—almost everybody else, I should say—has stated my position on Federal gasoline taxes. This time I will do it myself. I am not—emphasizing not—asking you for any increase in gas taxes.

Temporary Surtax

I am—I am asking you to approve a one-year temporary tax surcharge of 5 percent on corporate and upper-level individual incomes.

This would generally exclude from the surcharge those families with gross incomes below $15,000 a year. The estimated $5 billion in extra revenue to be raised by this inflation-fighting tax should pay for the new programs I have recommended in this message.

I think, and I suspect each of you know, this is the acid test of our joint determination to whip inflation in America. I would not ask this if major loopholes were not now being closed by the Committee on Ways and Means' tax reform bill.

I urge you to join me before your recess, in addition to what I have said before, to join me by voting to set a target spending limit—let me emphasize it—a target spending limit of $300 billion for the Federal fiscal budget of 1975.

When Congress agrees to this spending target, I will submit a package of budget deferrals and recissions to meet this goal. I will do the tough job of designating for Congressional action on your return to those areas which I believe can and must be reduced.

These will be hard choices and everyone of you in this Chamber know it as well as I.

They will be hard choices, but no Federal agency, including the Defense Department, will be untouchable.

It is my judgment that fiscal discipline is a necessary weapon on any fight against inflation. While this spending target is a small step. it is a step in the right direction, and we need to get on that course without further delay.

I do not think that any of us in this Chamber today can ask the American people to tighten their belts if Uncle Sam is unwilling to tighten his belt first.

Now, if I might, I would like to say a few words directly to your constituents and, incidentally, mine.

Ways to Help

My fellow Americans, ten days ago I asked you to get things started by making a list of ten ways to fight inflation and save energy, to exchange your list with your neighbors, and to send me a copy.

I have personally read scores of the thousands of letters received at the White House, and incidentally, I have made my economic experts read some of them, too. We all benefitted, at least I did, and I thank each and every one of you for this cooperation.

Some of the good ideas from your home to mine have been cranked into the recommendations I have just made to the Congress and the steps I am taking as President to whip inflation right now. There were also firm warnings on what Government must not do, and I appreciated those, too.

Your best suggestions for voluntary restraint and self-discipline showed me that a great degree of patriotic determination and unanimity already exist in this great land.

I have asked Congress for urgent specific actions it alone can take. I advised Congress of the initial steps that I am taking as President. Here is what only you can do: Unless every able American pitches in, Congress and I cannot do the job.

Winning our fight against inflation and waste involves total mobilization of America's greatest resources, the brains, the skills and the will power of the American people.

Here is what we must do, what each and every one of you can do. To help increase food and lower prices, grow more and waste less. To help save scarce fuel in the energy crisis, drive less, heat less. Every housewife knows almost exactly how much she spent for food last week. If you cannot spare a penny from your food budget—and I know there are many—surely you can cut the food that you waste by 5 percent.

Every American motorist knows exactly how many miles he or she drives to work or to school every day and about how much mileage she or he runs up each year. If we all drive at least 5 percent fewer miles, we can save almost unbelievably 250,000 barrels of foreign oil per day by the end of 1975.

Most of us can do better than 5 percent by car pooling, taking the bus, riding bikes or just plain walking. We can save enough gas by self-discipline to meet our one million barrels per day goal.

I think there is one final thing that all Americans do, rich or poor, and that is share with others. We can share burdens as we can share blessings. Sharing is not easy, not easy to measure like mileage and family budgets, but I am sure that 5 percent more is not nearly enough to ask, so I ask you to share everything you can and a little bit more. And it will strengthen our spirits as well as our economy.

Today I will not take more time of this busy Congress, for I vividly remember the rush before every recess, and the clock is already running on my specific and urgent request for legislative action. I also remember how much Congress can get done when it puts its shoulder to the wheel.

Further Plans

One week from tonight I have a longstanding invitation in Kansas City to address the Future Farmers of America, a fine organization of wonderful young people whose help, with millions of others, is vital in this battle. I will elaborate then how volunteer inflation fighters and energy savers can further mobilize their total efforts.

Since asking Miss Sylvia Porter, the well-known financial writer, to help me organize an all-out, nationwide volunteer mobilization, I have named a White House coordinator and have enlisted the enthusiastic support and services of some 17 other distinguished Americans to help plan for citizen and private group participation.

There will be no big Federal bureaucracy set up for this crash program. Through the courtesy of such volunteers from the communication and media fields, a very simple enlistment form will appear in many of tomorrow's newspapers, along with a symbol of this new mobilization, which I am wearing on my lapel.

It bears the single word WIN. I think that tells it all. I will call upon every American to join in this massive mobilization and stick with it until we do win as a Nation and as a people.

Mr. Speaker and Mr. President, I stand on a spot hallowed by history. Many Presidents have come here many times to solicit, to scold, to flatter, to exhort the Congress to support them in their leadership.

Once in a great while Presidents have stood here and truly inspired the most skeptical and the most unsophisticated audience of their co-equal partners in Government.

Perhaps once or twice in a generation is there such a Joint Session. I don't expect this one to be. Only two of my predecessors have come in person to call upon Congress for a declaration of war, and I shall not do that.

But I say to you, with all sincerity, that our inflation, our public enemy number one, will, unless whipped, destroy our country, our homes, our liberties, our property, and finally our national pride, as surely as any well-armed wartime enemy.

I concede there will be no sudden Pearl Harbor to shock us into unity and into sacrifice, but I think we have had enough early warnings. The time to intercept is right now. The time to intercept is almost gone.

My friends and former colleagues, will you enlist now? My friends and fellow Americans, will you enlist now? Together with discipline and determination, we will win.

I thank you very much.

MATERIALS ON INFLATION AND UNEMPLOYMENT

Books and Reports

Bach, George L., *The New Inflation: Causes, Effects, Cures*, Providence, Rhode Island, Brown University Press, 1973.

Bach, George L., *Making Monetary and Fiscal Policy*, Washington, D.C., Brookings Institution, 1971.

Blechman, Barry M., *Setting National Priorities: The 1975 Budget*, "The Budget and the Economy," p. 43, Washington, D.C., Brookings Institution, 1974.

Brown, Arthur J., *Great Inflation, 1939-1951*, New York, Oxford University Press, 1955.

Cagan, Phillip, "A New Look at Inflation," American Enterprise Institute for Public Policy Research, 1150 17th Street, N.W., Washington, D.C. 20036, 1973.

Clague, Evan, "Unemployment: Past, Present and Future," American Enterprise Institute for Public Policy Research, Washington, D.C. 20036, 1969.

Estey, Marten, "Wages, Wage Policy and Inflation, 1962-1971," American Enterprise Institute for Public Policy Research, 1150 17th Street, N.W., Washington, D.C. 20036, 1971.

Friedman, Irving S., *Inflation: A World Wide Disaster*, Boston, Massachusetts, Houghton-Mifflin, 1973.

Galbraith, John K., *The Affluent Society*, "Inflation," p. 181, Boston, Massachusetts, Houghton-Mifflin, 1969.

Galbraith, John K., *Economics and Public Purpose*, Boston, Massachusetts, Houghton-Mifflin, 1973.

Gartner, Alan, *Public Service Employment: An Analysis of Its History, Problems and Prospects*, New York, Praeger, 1973.

"High Employment without Inflation: A Positive Program for Economic Stabilization," Committee for Economic Development, 477 Madison Avenue, New York, 10022, 1972.

Keynes, John M., *The General Theory of Employment, Interest and Money*, New York, Harcourt, 1964.

Lekachman, Robert, *Inflation: The Permanent Problem of Boom and Bust*, New York, Vintage Press, 1973.

McLure, Charles E., "Fiscal Failure: Lessons of the Sixties," American Enterprise Institute for Public Policy Research, 1150 17th Street, N.W., Washington, D.C. 20036, 1972.

Moore, Geoffrey H., "How Full is Full Employment?" American Enterprise Institute for Public Policy Research, 1150 17th Street, N.W., Washington, D.C. 20036, 1973.

Morrison, Rodney J., *Expectations and Inflation: Nixon, Politics, and Economics*, Lexington, Massachusetts, D.C. Heath & Company, 1974.

North, Douglas C., *The Economics of Public Issues*, New York, Harper & Row, 1973.

Okun, Arthur M., *The Battle Against Unemployment*, New York, Norton, 1972.

Palmer, John L., *Inflation, Unemployment, and Poverty*, Lexington, Massachusetts, D.C. Heath, 1974.

Perlo, Victor, *The Unstable Economy: Booms and Recessions in the U.S. Since 1945*, New York, International Publishers, 1973.

Reuss, Henry S. *The Critical Decade: An Economic Policy for America and the Free World*, New York, McGraw-Hill, 1964.

Shultz, George P., *Guidelines, Informal Controls, and the Market Place: Policy Choices in a Full Employment Economy*, Chicago, Illinois, University of Chicago Press, 1966.

Silk, Leonard, ed., *Capitalism: The Moving Target*, Chicago, Illinois, Quadrangle Books, 1974.

Silk, Leonard, *Nixonomics: How the Dismal Science of Free Enterprise Became the Black Art of Controls*, New York, Praeger, 1972.

Theobald, Robert, *The Economics of Abundance: A Non-Inflationary Future*, New York, Pitman, 1970.

Tobin, James, *The New Economics: One Decade Older*, New Jersey, Princeton University Press, 1974.

Weber, Arnold R., *In Pursuit of Price Stability: The Wage-Price Freeze of 1971*, Washington, D.C., Brookings Institution, 1973.

Weidenbaum, Murray L., "New Initiatives in National Wage and Price Policy," American Enterprise Institute for Public Policy Research, 1150 17th Street, N.W., Washington, D.C. 20036, 1973.

Worcester, Dean A., *Beyond Welfare and Full Employment: The Economics of Optional Employment Without Inflation*, Lexington, Massachusetts, D.C. Heath & Company, 1972.

Articles

Alfaro, Jan, "Consumers and Inflation," *Antitrust Law & Economic Review*, Number 3, 1973, p. 19.

Bach, George L., "Inflation: Who Gains and Who Loses?" *Challenge*, July/August 1974, p. 48.

Beman, Lewis, "Inflation: Winners are Hard to Find," *Fortune*, November 1974, p. 143.

Boarman, P.M., "Internationalization of Inflation: Stable Rates vs. Flexible Rates," *Vital Speeches of the Day*, September 15, 1974, p. 722.

Brown, George H., "New Insights on Inflation," *Conference Board Record*, July 1974, p. 7.

Congdon, Timothy G., "Why Has Inflation Accelerated?" *National Westminister Bank Quarterly Review*, February 1973, p. 6.

Debs, Richard A., "Inflation and the Economic Outlook," *Federal Reserve New York*, April 1974, p. 56.

"Facing Inflation," Interview with Milton Friedman, *Challenge*, November/December 1973, p. 29.

Fellner, William J., "Accelerating Inflation: A Late-Hour Reminder," *Conference Board Record*, April 1974, p. 10.

Fortune, Peter, "An Evaluation of Anti-Inflation Policies in the United States," *New England Economic Review*, January/February 1974, p. 3.

Friedman, Milton, "A Cure for Inflation? Is Indexation the Answer?" *Current*, October 1974, p. 3.

Giersch, Herbert, "Some Neglected Aspects of Inflation in the World Economy," *Public Finance*, Number 2, 1973, p. 105.

Ginsburg, Helen, "Needed: A National Commitment to Full Employment," *Current History*, August 1973, p. 71.

Grayson, C. Jackson, "Beating Inflation Without Controls," *Nation's Business*, October 1974, p. 24.

Greenspan, Alan, "The Politics of Inflation," *Wall Street Journal*, March 19, 1974, p. 24.

Harriss, C. Lowell, "Inflation and Tax Reform," *Tax Review*, May 1974, p. 19.

"Hidden Unemployment," *Monthly Labor Review*, March 1973, p. 8.

"The High Cost of Inflation: What's Ahead for the Economy in the Near Future?" *Nation's Business*, October 1974, p. 20.

"How to Stop Inflation," Interview with C. Jackson Grayson, *U.S. News and World Report*, May 6, 1974, p. 23.

"Inflation," *Skeptic*, Special Issue Number 3, 1974.

"Is Jawboning the Answer?" Interview with Senator William Proxmire, *Duns*, October 1974, p. 66.

Kruse, Thomas, "Inflation: Does the Cure in 1974 Lie with Monetary or Fiscal Policy?" *National Public Accountant*, June 1974, p. 8.

Malabre, Alfred L., "America First: U.S. Inflation Rate Now Exceeds Increases in Many Other Lands," *Wall Street Journal*, March 13, 1974, p. 1.

Mueller, Willard F., "Monopoly and the Inflation-Unemployment Dilemma: Trustbusting or Administrative Controls?" *Antitrust Law & Economic Review*, Summer 1972, p. 15.

"The $100-Billion Oil Bill: How Oil and Inflation are Upsetting Monetary Stability," *Business Week*, July 6, 1974, p. 70.

"The New Questions About the U.S. Economy," *Fortune*, January 1974, p. 69.

"Plan for Subduing Inflation," Interview with A.H. Meltzer, *Fortune*, September 1974, p. 112.

"Recent Labor Market Developments," *Federal Reserve Bulletin*, July 1974, p. 475.

Samuelson, Paul A., "Worldwide Stagflation," *Morgan Guaranty Survey*, June 1974, p. 3.

Sorrentino, Constance, "Unemployment in the United States and Eight Foreign Countries," *Monthly Labor Review*, January 1974, p. 47.

Ulmer, Melville, "How to Fight Inflation," *Atlantic*, October 1974, p. 39.

"The United States Economy in 1985: An Overview of BLS Projections," *Monthly Labor Review*, December 1973.

"A Way to Halt Inflation: The Treasury Secretary's Blueprint," *U.S. News & World Report*, June 17, 1974, p. 32.

Wetze, James R., "Measuring Unemployment in States and Local Areas," *Monthly Labor Review*, June 17, 1974, p. 40.

"Why Inflation is Hard to Cure," *Business Week*, June 1, 1974, p. 80.

Documents

"Economic Adjustment Assistance Program: The President's Message to the Congress," February 19, 1974, *Weekly Compilation of Presidential Documents*, February 25, 1974, p. 224.

"Inflation: The President's Address to the Nation," July 25, 1974, *Weekly Compilation of Presidential Documents*, July 29, 1974, p. 830.

"The President's Remarks to the White House Conference on Domestic and Economic Affairs," November 1, 1974, *Weekly Compilation of Presidential Documents*, November 11, 1974, p. 1411.

U.S. Congress, House Committee on Appropriations, *The Federal Budget for 1975.* Hearings February 19-21, 1974, U.S. Government Printing Office, Washington, D.C. 20402, 1974.

U.S. Congress, House Committee on Banking and Currency, *Anti-Inflation Act of 1974*, Report August 19, 1974, U.S. Government Printing Office, Washington, D.C. 20402, 1974.

U.S. Congress, House Committee on Banking and Currency, *Economic Stabilization, 1974, Hearings March 6-8, 1974*, U.S. Government Printing Office, Washington, D.C. 20402, 1974.

U.S. Congress, House Committee on Education and Labor, *Emergency Employment Amendments of 1973, Report July 26, 1973*, U.S.Government Printing Office, Washington, D.C. 20402, 1973.

U.S. Congress, House Committee on Ways and Means, *Suspension of Import Barriers to Restrain Inflation, Communication from the President, April 2, 1973*, U.S. Government Printing Office, Washington, D.C. 20402, 1973.

U.S. Congress, Joint Economic Committee, *Action Programs to Reduce Inflation and Restore Economic Growth, Report September 21, 1974*, U.S. Government Printing Office, Washington, D.C. 20402, 1974.

U.S. Congress, Joint Economic Committee, *Cost of Living, Hearings March 21, April 4, May 8, 22, 23, 1973*, U.S. Government Printing Office, Washington, D.C. 20402, 1974.

U.S. Congress, Joint Economic Committee, *Economic Impact of Petroleum Shortages, Hearings December 11-13, 1973*, U.S. Government Printing Office, Washington, D.C. 20402, 1974.

U.S. Congress, Joint Economic Committee, *Economic Indicators 1974*, U.S. Government Printing Office, Washington, D.C. 20402, 1974.

U.S. Congress, Joint Economic Committee, *The 1974 Economic Report of the President, Hearings February 7, 8, 18, 1974*, U.S. Government Printing Office, Washington, D.C. 20402, 1974.

U.S. Congress, Joint Economic Committee, *The 1974 Economic Report of the President, Hearings February 19-22, 1974*, U.S. Government Printing Office, Washington, D.C. 20402, 1974.

U.S. Congress, Joint Economic Committee, *Joint Economic Report, March 25, 1974*, U.S. Government Printing Office, Washington, D.C. 20402, 1974.

U.S. Congress, Joint Economic Committee, *Reducing Unemployment to 2 Percent, Hearings October 17, 18, 26, 1972*, U.S. Government Printing Office, Washington, D.C. 20402, 1973.

U.S. Congress, Senate Committee on Banking, Housing and Urban Affairs, *Economic Stabilization Act 1974, Hearings February 19, 20, March 6, 1974*, U.S. Government Printing Office, Washington, D.C. 20402, 1974.

U.S. Congress, Senate Committee on Banking, Housing, and Urban Affairs, *Economic Stabilization Legislation 1973, Hearings January 29-31, February 1, 5-7, 1973*, U.S. Government Printing Office, Washington, D.C. 20402, 1973.

U.S. Congress, Senate Committee on Banking, Housing and Urban Affairs, *Oversight on Economic Stabilization, Hearings January 30, 31, February 1, 6, 1974*, U.S. Government Printing Office, Washington, D.C. 20402, 1974.

U.S. Congress, Senate Committee on Finance, *Compensation for Unemployment Related to the Energy Crisis, Hearings April 2, 1974*, U.S. Government Printing Office, Washington, D.C., 1974.

U.S. Congress, Senate Committee on Finance, *Fiscal Policy and the Energy Crisis, Report November 20, 1973*, U.S. Government Printing Office, Washington, D.C. 20402, 1973.

U.S. Congress, Senate Committee on Government Operations, *Materials Shortages, Resources and Shortages: An Economic Interpretation, Report September 1974*, U.S. Government Printing Office, Washington, D.C. 20402, 1974.

U.S. Department of the Treasury, *The Financial Conference on Inflation, September 20, 1974*, Washington, D.C. 20220, 1974. ∎

(Retirement Security continued from p. 34)

Social Security as an insurance system] a necessity?" asked an analyst of income maintenance programs for the aged.

Imminent changes of this nature are not expected. The labor movement and the increasingly influential senior citizens' societies are adamantly opposed to such a change and it is not likely that the American worker is as yet willing to embrace the idea that his retirement pay will be in the form of a gratuity rather than an earned right. Change is more likely to come by grafting on more welfare features—such as the existing ones of weighting benefits to provide a floor for the poorest recipient and injecting some general funding to provide social services.

What may change the entire picture is that a new breed of retiree is coming to dominate the scene—a person who is less work-worn, better educated, more sophisticated in the ways of government, better cushioned financially and with a better background of nutrition and medical care than his predecessor of even 10 or 20 years ago. All studies indicate that poverty among the older population tends to concentrate among the very oldest.

The Social Security Administration has begun a 10-year study of these new retirees. Through this Retirement History Study, a sample of persons aged 58-63 are followed as they enter into and continue in the retirement period. SSA hopes to find out why some retire early and some retire late, and to "learn in detail the connections between work life characteristics, retirement timing and the determinants of style, quality and conduct of retirement." From this study may come a new window on the actual conditions of retirement in the United States and what corrections of existing systems need to be made. ∎

INDEX